The publisher gratefully acknowledges the generous support of the Robert and Meryl Selig Endowment Fund in Film Studies of the University of California Press Foundation, established in memory of Robert W. Selig.

Hollywood 1938

Hollywood 1938

Motion Pictures' Greatest Year

Catherine Jurca

UNIVERSITY OF CALIFORNIA PRESS
Berkeley · Los Angeles · London

Portions of this book appeared as "What the Public Wanted: Hollywood, 1937–1942," *Cinema Journal* 47, no. 2 (2008): 3–25; and "Motion Pictures' Greatest Year (1938): Public Relations and the American Film Industry," *Film History* 20, no. 3 (2008): 344–56.

University of California Press, one of the most distinguished university presses in the United States, enriches lives around the world by advancing scholarship in the humanities, social sciences, and natural sciences. Its activities are supported by the UC Press Foundation and by philanthropic contributions from individuals and institutions. For more information, visit www.ucpress.edu.

University of California Press
Berkeley and Los Angeles, California

University of California Press, Ltd.
London, England

Library of Congress Cataloging-in-Publication Data

Jurca, Catherine, 1964–.
    Hollywood 1938 : motion pictures' greatest year / Catherine Jurca.
        p.   cm.
    Includes bibliographical references and index.
    ISBN 978-0-520-23370-6 (cloth : alk. paper)
    ISBN 978-0-520-27180-7 (pbk. : alk. paper)
    1. Motion pictures—California—Los Angeles—History—20th century.   2. Motion picture audiences—United States—History.   3. Motion picture industry—Economic aspects—California—Los Angeles—History—20th century.   4. Hollywood (Los Angeles, Calif.)—History—20th century.   I. Title.
    PN1993.5.U65J87   2012
    384'.809794940904—dc23   2011040729

Manufactured in the United States of America

20 19 18 17 16 15 14 13 12
10 9 8 7 6 5 4 3 2 1

Contents

Illustrations

Acknowledgments

I am grateful to many people for their contributions to this book. I first studied film with Jerry Christensen at Johns Hopkins, and his influence on my thinking about classical Hollywood is evident throughout. More recently, the manuscript has benefited from conversations with good friends and colleagues: Carolyn Gray Anderson, Mark Garrett Cooper, Tom Doherty, Mary Esteve, Kathy Fuller-Seeley, Deb Garfield, Julie Kerekes, Deak Nabers, Robert Rosenstone, Eric Smoodin, Cindy Weinstein, and Paul Young. I am fortunate to have enjoyed the good will and generosity of two film historians before I ever met them. Richard Maltby provided me with Motion Pictures' Greatest Year materials at the earliest stage of the project and served, near the end of it, as a reader. The book has benefited enormously from his comments and scholarly example. John Sedgwick answered every question I had about classical Hollywood economics, did calculations on my behalf, and read and improved the portions of the manuscript where I felt most out of my depth. Discussing our research over dinners was a highlight of my sabbatical in London.

Several institutions and individuals assisted me with the project. For their kindness and expertise I would like to thank archivists and librarians Jonathon Auxier and Sandra Joy Lee, Warner Bros. Archives, USC; Kevin Cawley, University of Notre Dame Archives; Ned Comstock, Cinematic Arts Library, USC; Barbara Hall, Margaret Herrick Library, Academy of Motion Picture Arts and Sciences; Joan Miller,

Cinema Archives, Wesleyan University; and Mark Quigley, UCLA Film and Television Archive. At Caltech John Wade and Leslie Maxfield provided invaluable (and invaluably cheerful) help with the images. John and Shady Peyvan tracked down the most obscure of my interlibrary loan requests. Susan Davis, Laurel Auchampaugh, and Sini Elvington made my job much easier. At the University of California Press Mary Francis and Eric Schmidt were a pleasure to work with. Eddie Brandt's Saturday Matinee enabled me to see most of the films associated with Motion Pictures' Greatest Year and is one of the reasons I love LA.

My family—Joe, Sonja, Chris and Morris, Jenn and Mike, Heather and Tim—supported and diverted me in various necessary ways. As did Ben, Tori, Justin, Zachary, Lily, Oscar, and Acacia. I'm a lucky aunt, indeed. Jo and Nate filled the last year with surprises.

Scott Fraser arrived late to this book, but he made all the difference.

Introduction

Hollywood Looks at Its Audience

Hollywood 1938 is a book about movies; the industry that produced, distributed, and exhibited them; and the relation of both to the public during what might well be considered, to that point, motion pictures' worst year. The American film industry faced a bewildering array of problems in 1938, most of which were only resolved or, more accurately, postponed by the box-office miracle known as World War II. An unanticipated decline in attendance and revenues began in the fall of 1937, with the recession that brought more than a year of economic recovery to a halt. There were labor troubles; television loomed; politicians were already sniffing around for Communists; legislators again sought to ban certain trade practices; and in July 1938 the U.S. Justice Department filed an antitrust lawsuit against the eight major film companies. The industry was in crisis. But then it was always in crisis, seemed almost to thrive on it. What distinguished 1938, what gave this year of crisis its unique texture, its particular hysterical edge, was not so much the concern that the antitrust suit would finally force changes to the film industry's basic economic structure. Rather, there were fears that the moviegoing public was itself irrevocably changing. Industry executives and commentators in the trade press periodically invoked the recession to account for the distressing drop in business, but by midyear other reasons for the disappearing audience had begun to emerge. The cry of 1938 was not that poverty and unemployment—the familiar villains of Depression-era box offices—were to blame. Rather, the industry had lost touch with the public. The attitude toward "the movies" had, within a short time, gone from "apathetic" to "definitely adverse." An "irate," "disgusted" public was staying away from theaters. In July, at the apex of the catastrophe, Oscar Doob, head of advertising at Loew's, identified a new "nationwide . . . pessimism about the movies; the dark, gloomy feeling that the movies are on the downgrade; that it is a great risk to buy a movie ticket with all the chances against getting your money's worth; that Hollywood is nuts; that the stars are poison; that show-business is racing to hell!" This was not crisis as usual.[1]

There is nothing like this language earlier in the 1930s, even in the midst of the box-office abyss or the controversies over movie morals. How the industry came to this pass, or imagined it had anyway, is part of the subject of this book, as is, more centrally, the solution it proposed. Amid industry quarrels about what might have made the public so mad—bank nights, double features, B pictures, prestige pictures, bad publicity, and so on ad infinitum—and uncertainty about what might pacify it, executives from all branches decided to launch the Motion Pictures' Greatest Year campaign (hereafter MPGY), an unprecedented four-month public relations offensive designed to sell the public on the movies again. Hatched over the summer and inaugurated during the September opening of the 1938–39 movie year, MPGY brought together producers, distributors, and exhibitors across North America to win back audiences by establishing the centrality of movies and moviegoing to peoples' lives and communities. A budget of almost $1 million was raised from the major companies, as well as from independent exhibitors large and small; an institutional advertising campaign ran in virtually every daily newspaper in the United States and Canada; proclamations by governors, mayors, and other officials urged public support for the campaign; theaters organized local events and tie-ins and promoted a $250,000 movie quiz contest organized around ninety-four films, "the finest array of productions ever released," or so the ads claimed.

Hollywood 1938 offers a comprehensive look at a single year of filmmaking and moviegoing during Hollywood's Golden Age, a year remarkable not for the artistic superiority of its productions, as in 1939, nor for its commercial triumphs, like those of 1946, but for widespread confusion and numerous mistakes. An analysis of the public relations campaign, including the events that inspired it and the messy aftermath, reveals how a terrible crisis of confidence changed the way the industry thought about and promoted itself and its films. *Hollywood 1938* contributes to a fuller understanding of the relationship between classical Hollywood and the public and of how the changing perception of that relationship shaped the making, marketing, and meaning of movies in this era. If the film industry's most basic question, as historians of audience research have noted, is "What does the public want?" and its most basic frustration the impossibility of a definitive answer, the campaign renders utterly conspicuous a moment when both question and frustration were especially all-consuming. A critical episode in the industry's history, MPGY brings into focus efforts to understand, communicate with, and influence the public and to enlist motion pictures in that cause, which may change the way we think about Hollywood and its films during a pivotal moment in its fortunes.[2]

MPGY was not a minor or obscure event but an enormous undertaking. An army of volunteers across the country supplemented the work of campaign staff in New York and Hollywood. Some seven thousand theaters joined, and MPGY was heralded on marquees across the country (see figure 1). Articles about it ran constantly in the trade press from mid-July through the end of September and frequently through October. Many newspapers provided substantial coverage in their entertainment and editorial pages. Publicity was so widespread that it would have been difficult for the vast majority of even casual moviegoers not to have known about it. Even now, promotions for the $250,000 contest linger on prints and videos of some of the campaign films. Yet MPGY has scarcely been mentioned in histories of the film industry, even those that focus on the 1930s. This is in part because our sense of the industry's public relations in this era has been affected so profoundly by the work of Will Hays and the trade organization he headed, the Motion Picture Producers and Distributors of America (MPPDA), and by debates over censorship and self-regulation. Thus, much of the research on the relationship between the film industry and the public has studied the efforts and effects of reformers, which is to say, the people, organizations, and processes that attempted to mediate that relationship, often with indifference or hostility to what the public was actually thought to want. A great deal of attention has been paid to the attempts of disgruntled groups and individuals to monitor and control film content, as well as audiences, and to the resultant Production Code of 1930, the industry's own guidelines by which movies were systematically self-regulated, especially after 1934 by the Production Code Administration (PCA) under Joe Breen. This scholarship has clarified how Hollywood films were variously imagined to influence the public and

FIGURE 1. Theaters across the country, including Grauman's Chinese in Hollywood, celebrated Motion Pictures' Greatest Year. WPA Collection, Los Angeles Public Library.

how films themselves were changed to eliminate, or strategically obscure, prurient and otherwise offensive images, language, and ideas that might have a deleterious effect on it.[3]

The "audience" for the Production Code, however, was not primarily moviegoers; as Richard Maltby has shown, the Code's most important function was to appease powerful critics of the industry: organized religious, women's, and other groups that constantly threatened to agitate for government intervention in its business. These groups did not represent the public so much as appoint themselves spokespersons for it, and observers at the time distinguished between this "vocal," "vociferous minority" and the "silent" majority it claimed to speak for. Hays himself knew well the difference, as he once put it, between "the classes that write, talk, and legislate" and the "mass public" that attended films, even if the interests of the industry demanded he routinely conflate them. The difference was also manifest in the "Better Films" movement in the mid-1930s, a collaboration of "public groups" and the industry that tried to raise the general level of taste, thereby to increase "public demand for finer pictures" while also potentially attracting new

audiences. The ideal product of this collaboration was not only different films but a different public, one made to want not what it wanted
but something else.[4]

The strategies for managing crisis earlier in the 1930s were irrelevant
to the new challenges. In 1938 the film industry perceived a real public
relations crisis, one involving *its* public, the millions of actual moviegoers, rather than the leaders of organized groups and their supporters.
Put another way, Doob's comment that the public thought "show-
business" was on the way to "hell" had nothing whatever to do with
concerns about morals. The laments about "pessimism" and "disgust"
expressed something much worse: the fear that many people no longer
found movies sufficiently interesting or pleasurable to merit a trip to
the theater. With the slogan "Motion Pictures Are Your Best Entertainment" blaring across North America at the start of the new season,
MPGY's confident rhetoric scarcely masked an underlying confession
of failure. Motion pictures themselves no longer made an adequate case
for their entertainment value to audiences. Hence the impulsive, desperate attempt to rekindle the public's loyalty and affection, to prove that
movies still mattered.

Hollywood 1938 raises an issue that the emphasis on censorship and
the Code has tended to overshadow: how the public itself—a sui gene-
ris collective, distinct from organized pressure groups and unmolested
by busy mediators—was imagined to influence films as eager, recalcitrant, and even irate consumers of them. There is a resemblance here
to work in reception studies, which has discredited the stereotype of
the passive mass audience that is simply, and uniformly, acted upon
by films, in part by focusing on what actual audiences do with them
in the exhibition context. Where possible, this book attempts to re-
cover what audience members thought of the films and of the campaign,
by considering the comments of exhibitors and later by analyzing the
handful of extant entries to the movie quiz contest. But my work also
emphasizes what the public, even a public that took shape largely in
the industry's imagination, was thought to do to films, in this case to
a specific package of films across budgets, genres, and studios, at the
moment of their production. Susan Ohmer has analyzed the extraordinary contributions of the famed public-opinion expert George Gallup
to filmmaking in Hollywood, where he conducted thousands of surveys
for studios and independent producers in the 1940s, testing, among
other things, the public's response to stories, stars, and titles before
filming had begun. Gallup's interventions marked a new, literal, and

more quantitative approach to the everlasting problem of giving the public what it wanted. From my perspective, however, they also represent a culmination of sorts to the struggles to reconceptualize the public and the industry's relation to it from the late 1930s until the industry settled into new patterns of wartime production.[5]

To achieve its goals with the public, MPGY addressed itself to two particular groups as well, sometime antagonists and allies of Hollywood, and their role in the campaign will also be considered. The first is independent exhibitors, who were called on to help finance and promote the campaign. The film industry and the public met face-to-face in theaters; the major companies owned the most opulent and profitable houses, but independent exhibitors operated some fourteen thousand others, the vast majority, and a truly national campaign required their cooperation. But their participation also mattered for political reasons. MPGY's most impressive aspect was its ability to mobilize different companies and individuals quickly into something that could be touted as "the first really cooperative venture in cinema history." The language of unity, about a divided industry, was no accident. Most independent exhibitors were at a significant disadvantage compared to theaters owned or affiliated with the major companies. Independents were subject to practices such as block booking and blind selling, which forced them to take as much as a studio's entire annual output, the bad with the good, sight unseen, in order to get any films at all, and their protests helped to fuel the antitrust lawsuit. In addition to addressing problems with a disenchanted public, then, MPGY might point to a cohesive industry and belie the charges of coercion by a handful of companies. For this reason Monogram and Republic, the most successful of the "poverty row" studios, were also invited to join, although only Monogram did. If the participation of disgruntled industry outliers was supposed to show widespread cooperation among parties with competing interests, independent exhibitors proved less tractable than hoped. MPGY offered them a forum to push back against the major companies and revealed much about the dynamics of their relationship. In the end the strategy to help counter the lawsuit would provide excellent evidence for why it was necessary.[6]

Persuading the public that the industry deserved its good will also meant persuading the press. Relations with newspapers were at a low point in the months leading up to MPGY. Executives and exhibitors protested the scrutiny and criticism of hundreds of self-proclaimed experts—gossip columnists, reviewers, editors—something no other business had to tolerate. From the substantial appropriation for institutional advertising in daily newspapers, to the industry representatives who met with editors and publishers across the country, MPGY marked a new commitment to building good press relations as a necessary step to developing better public relations. To help measure its success, I sampled forty-nine daily newspapers, one from each state and Washington, D.C., to get a sense of the frequency and kind of coverage of MPGY, as well as to determine how widely news about some of the industry's problems earlier in the year had really circulated (see appendix 1). Theater newspaper ads also indicate how exhibitors promoted the campaign and the contest and so suggest how these may have played out at the local level. The industry was right to worry about an antagonistic press but succeeded, at least temporarily, in enlisting support from a business with problems of its own in the late 1930s, as the press made use of MPGY to establish its ongoing relevance in a media landscape increasingly dominated by radio.

Much has rightly been made of the film industry's organizational sophistication in the 1930s, when "Hollywood" became "a modern business enterprise," according to the subtitle of Tino Balio's *Grand Design*. Headquartered in New York, the five largest companies—Loew's, Paramount, Twentieth Century–Fox, RKO, and Warner Bros.—were vertically integrated corporations, with studios that produced almost a movie a week, international distribution systems, and theater chains. The oligopoly was rounded out by Columbia, Universal, and United Artists, which enjoyed privileged access to those theaters, as well as other advantages limited to the elite companies. The "Big Eight" employed numerous measures to control risk, from the star system and the "scientific business management" of theaters to distribution practices such as block booking, which not only guaranteed a market for less attractive films but also limited the screen time available to independent productions. In a recent article describing the "'portfolio' of film projects," from the very expensive to the low budget, that studios assembled to manage the inherent risks of production, economists Michael Pokorny and John Sedgwick insist, *pace* William Goldman's famed remark that "nobody knows anything" in the movie business: "somebody . . . must know something."[7]

A lot of people surely knew a lot. The U.S. government certainly thought so. The shrewd businessmen who ran these companies counter the image of a Hollywood "dominated by maniacs, operated under the laws of lunacy, and populated by an assortment of illiterates," as the social scientist Leo Rosten framed the stereotypes in 1941. Rosten's study of Hollywood set out to refute such unrealistic but entrenched ideas about "a two-billion-dollar enterprise," while also doing much to reinforce them. It is worth keeping in mind, so many years later, that the image of Hollywood as "inhabited by a collection of dopes and nitwits" was, in fact, a popular conception. Hollywood had a reputation not only for extravagance but for a certain inspired madness, for producers who operated on "hunches," "instincts," and "intuitions," as befitted a business where every product was treated as an extraordinary gamble. As late as 1950 the anthropologist Hortense Powdermaker attributed a kind of "magical thinking" to filmmakers, whom she compared to the Melanesians of the Southwest Pacific and the Karen of Burma. The industry cultivated this peculiar reputation, with its publicity machinery always in overdrive, promoting "Goldwynisms," endless parades of Scarletts, and the unpredictable antics of stars. Newspapers ran with these stories. In and out of the gossip columns, the press entertained its readers with material that played up "the inconsequential and the freakish" and tweaked the industry as "the creation and the field of endeavor of zanies."[8]

In 1938 all of this brilliant lunacy was backfiring. It was one thing to seem to rely on instinct and hunches when they paid off and quite another when they badly missed the mark. A new, more dignified image was in order. MPGY sought to present the film industry as a "big and serious business," run by thoughtful and industrious executives who employed talented, hardworking artists and skilled technicians. The industry wanted "the movies" to be not only loved but respected as an enterprise essential to the well-being of the nation, as well as to moviegoers. At the same time, it did not want to appear remote or impersonal—Big Business—especially on the brink of the antitrust suit, which was announced just two days after the first mention of the public relations campaign in the trade press. Thus the campaign sought to establish how closely Hollywood was connected to the public, how well it met and understood its needs. The institutional ads presented film-making as an essentially democratic practice, in which the consumers of entertainment were the actual producers of it. The industry did not impose its own values or ideas; rather, its products let the public speak for itself. Over and over MPGY films purported to depict ordinary people and families, who were offered up as evidence that movies listened to and served the public. What the public wanted, demanded above all, the industry decided, was countless iterations of itself. Meanwhile, and somewhat paradoxically, for the first time the industry forcefully insisted on important differences among moviegoers. It abandoned the concept of the "mass audience" by which it had long justified the constraints of the Code and the repudiation of the arty, intellectual, and controversial in favor of the commercially popular. Ubiquitous films about ordinary, average people aimed to attract as broad an audience as possible. At a time of perceived dissatisfaction with the movies, however, the industry's rhetoric made clear that all films could not be expected to appeal to everyone, that Hollywood catered to a diverse range of tastes. Only later did it have to reckon with what these claims might mean for the limits it imposed on the subjects movies could treat.[9]

Despite the industry's mobilization of so many companies and individuals and the press, despite its concerted appeals for public understanding and favor, in the end the campaign was widely considered a failure, a less than stellar endeavor from this modern business enterprise. What ultimately became the Production Code had been formulated and reformulated over a number of years; MPGY was organized and launched in about six weeks. The reasons for the haste, as well as the specific grounds of the failure, become clear in what follows. Suffice it to say here that as much as the industry knew about the fine points, or the broad strokes, of publicity, of selling individual stars and films, it had a lot to learn about public relations. *Fortune* called 1938 the year that public relations "struck home to the hearts of a whole generation of businessmen"; every business had a "story" that desperately needed telling. The work of public relations is to promote abstractions like good will and understanding. It appears, in other words, to sell nothing at all, making public relations a product even less tangible than film, which is composed of "talent," rather than "oil or wood or steel," and can neither be standardized in a factory nor bought and held by consumers. Film was associated with a basic and often disconcerting immateriality, but the film industry had a substance many other businesses lacked. The urgency of public relations and its stories in this era was to humanize faceless corporations, to give them, in Roland Marchand's language, a "soul." An important difference between the products of classical Hollywood and those of General Motors or U.S. Steel is that films are hardly faceless. Close-ups and the force of strong and well-known personalities, of a Goldwyn as much as a Gable, brought the public into relation with many of the individuals behind the industry.

And Hollywood movies were themselves complex communications to the consumer. Whatever else they did, they always told stories, and their stories tell us something about the industry that made them.[10]

Films illuminate the industry's aspirations; they might help to build good will, or they might defeat that goal. And so in addition to providing a history of the campaign and situating it within a larger account of the movies' culture and commerce in the late 1930s, this book looks closely at campaign films, along with others from that era, considering them within a public relations framework. My aim is not to provide a catalog of the films released as part of MPGY, which included every production from the majors released over a three-month period and four films from Monogram, but to concentrate on those that shed particular light on the industry's struggles and attempts to cope with them (see appendix 2). Several campaign films worked at cross-purposes to the public relations agenda, sending messages that could not have been less suitable to MPGY's purported aims, while others furthered its mission, effectively dramatizing Hollywood's overriding allegiance to the public. I analyze some of the most celebrated films of the campaign, from superspecials *You Can't Take It with You* and *Marie Antoinette* and modest films that hit big, *Boys Town* and *Four Daughters,* to stinkers like *Time Out for Murder* and *Sons of the Legion,* which did no credit whatever to the industry; a minor film cycle on the wane (the "racket" picture) and what is now perhaps the most acclaimed cycle of the decade (screwball comedy); the films of established stars such as Spencer Tracy, James Cagney, Norma Shearer, Fred Astaire, and Ginger Rogers, as well as those that showcased newer talents Priscilla Lane, John Garfield, and Andrea Leeds. The films were in the works before the campaign was announced and not made specifically for it. MPGY was hurriedly organized around them, but they spoke to problems long in the making and that would take more than a public relations campaign to resolve.[11]

Among the unusual features of the campaign was the industry's decision to advertise, in advance of their release and in many cases well before their completion, ninety-four films as evidence that it was motion pictures' greatest year. They were not Hollywood's greatest films, not by a long shot, but films don't need to be great to teach us something important about the industry that made them, the exhibitors that screened them, and the public that consumed them. Hollywood's failures can be as instructive as its successes. *Hollywood 1938* responds to calls for work in cinema studies that provides a "social history of a cultural institution," but it rejects the idea that the practice of writing such histories of moviegoing is or should be distinct from the practice of interpreting films. This book operates on the assumption that examining a rich archive of the trade and mainstream press, production records, theater ads, letters from exhibitors and memos from executives, contest essays, fan magazines, and more enriches our understanding of the films and vice versa. There is still little work in the classical Hollywood period that integrates substantive archival research—film history—and close analysis of texts: film criticism. Given the importance of the topics of censorship and self-regulation to film studies, and the dominance of psychoanalytic and feminist theory within it, it is unsurprising that the important exception has been the use of PCA records and related material. The records provide valuable evidence for readings of films that foreground coded evasions of the industry's own prohibitions against overt representations of sexual and criminal behaviors. But the habit of looking for what is obscured or repressed has tended to neglect other forms of cinematic address. Whatever specific lessons it teaches about how the film industry spoke to and about the public, Motion Pictures' Greatest Year reminds us that in an era when film was still legally defined as commercial speech, the imperatives of self-promotion are as salient as self-censoring evasions and obscurities to making sense of the communicative acts that are Hollywood films.[12]

PART ONE

The Campaign

CHAPTER I

Annus Horribilis

GOLDWYN'S FOLLY

Let's enter the campaign by way of *The Goldwyn Follies* (1938). No film better represents the problems the industry faced in 1938 or the way that films might be imagined as vehicles for addressing them. Released six months before MPGY began, *The Goldwyn Follies* takes as its subject the difficulties of making movies for a recalcitrant public, on the eve of the industry's singular preoccupation with them, and exemplifies those difficulties through its own troubled reception. The film deals with the challenge of pleasing the public by creating a surrogate for it, to whom it assigns the task of demonstrating that the *Follies* cares deeply about what it wants and that what it wants is the *Follies*. In effect, the film functions as a two-hour exercise in public relations, in which dramatizing an allegiance to the public is as important as entertaining it. But the film does not finally offer the public what it was soon thought to want above all else, what its surrogate was already demanding: the sort of human characters and real stories that became the hallmark of MPGY. Samuel Goldwyn was one of the industry's most outspoken critics, and in the wake of the *Follies'* failure, the man, like his movie, illustrated and possibly even exacerbated many of the problems with "the movies" as such.

Goldwyn's Technicolor extravaganza starred Adolphe Menjou as Oliver Merlin, a Hollywood producer whose magic has suddenly abandoned him. A theater manager informs him at the disastrous opening of his latest film: "There's something missing—the human touch." While making a new picture on location, Oliver overhears Hazel Dawes (Andrea Leeds) criticize the dialogue and actors for their lack of reality, simplicity, and humanity. He follows this very simple and human young woman to the local soda shop, where she strikes him as the perfect spokesperson for the public, in part because of her vocal disdain for movies (see figure 2). Oliver invites her to come to Hollywood and become his "Miss Humanity," the voice of "common sense" that will restore the common touch to his films. Hazel goes and advises him on what is real, what is human, and what she likes. Along the way there are musical numbers and comedy sketches by those who are cast in Oliver's new film or hope to be. Performers include Edgar Bergen and Charlie McCarthy, the Ritz Brothers, and the tenor Kenny Baker. In addition, ballerina Vera Zorina and Metropolitan Opera singer Charles Kullman made their American screen debuts, while the *Follies* provided Kullman's colleague Helen Jepson with her first and only film role. Their decidedly highbrow talents are paraded so that helpful Hazel may pronounce them suitable for the great American public.

Hazel first evaluates a ballet sequence based on *Romeo and Juliet*. The conflict between the Montagues and Capulets is presented as a matter of competing tastes—one family prefers ballet, the other jazz—as though nothing is more elemental, more productive of fierce loyalty, than entertainment preferences. In contrast with Jane Feuer's analysis of musical competitions in other films, in which jazz beats the classics through the need to make stuffy people and music more folksy and spontaneous, to prompt audiences to embrace what the Hollywood musical does so well, there is no winner here. Hazel declines to choose between them. She tells Oliver, "All I know is what I like." He replies, "So much the better. There are 200 million people who only know what they like." She loves the ballet but has one objection: the outcome is too sad. "I didn't know Romeo and Juliet died." Her surprise not only identifies her as a young woman who is not especially well read but as one who, like millions of others, was indifferent to the release of MGM's prestigious *Romeo and Juliet* (1936). The last personal production of Irving Thalberg before his death, *Romeo and Juliet* was a faithful version of the play and a commercial flop. Hazel converts Oliver to her way of thinking. "If 200 million people want Romeo and Juliet to live, I won't be stubborn."[1]

About the only thing Hazel knows about Oliver's pictures is that they have "class and beauty," just like Goldwyn's own prestige productions.

FIGURE 2. A Hollywood producer (Adolphe Menjou) finds an opinionated young woman (Andrea Leeds) to advise him on what the public wants in *The Goldwyn Follies*.

Her role is really to calibrate tastes, to convince the public that it wants ballet and opera as though it has already, with the skeptical surrogate, evaluated and embraced these classy forms. The producers are on surer ground with the comedy set pieces, which Hazel likes very much but is not asked to judge. The lowbrow Ritzes and middlebrow Bergen and McCarthy are Goldwyn's own insurance against the hazard at the center of the film: that the *Follies* does not simply portray various tests of the public's taste in entertainment but is itself a test, one whose outcome remains unknown until audiences have seen it. Bergen and the Ritzes had already passed tests with moviegoers; the ballet and opera stars had not. *Romeo and Juliet* proved that the public did not want Shakespeare, but it would be up to Goldwyn to prove whether it wanted ballet and opera instead.

The Goldwyn Follies turns a critic of the movies into a fan, but Hazel is not a "better films" maven who seeks to elevate tastes. She also likes a good love story, something "real." The star of Oliver's film, after being jilted by her lover in Venice, is supposed to take up with a gigolo. Hazel nixes that idea. Oliver changes the gigolo to a "human being," a "simple" gondolier. He falls for the star, but "he finds out about her past" and "denounces her." Hazel again protests, because she believes that "love is more important." So love triumphs, in Oliver's film as well as in the *Follies,* when Oliver eventually sacrifices his own romantic interest in Hazel and decides to promote the career of her talented sweetheart, Danny Beecher (Baker). He affirms the values of the Hollywood film: boy gets girl, producer and public get star. Hazel commends his decision: "It was the real thing to do." What counts as real here is the delivery of a resolution that delightfully accords with one's notion of how the world ought to work. She has succumbed to Hollywood's ministrations, speaking now on behalf of its basic entertainment strategies, not as a critic of them or simply an enthusiastic proponent of "class and beauty." The producer who doubts becomes the producer who, in resolving his doubts by consulting the public about its preferences, converts the public to a decided preference for what Hollywood does best.

If every film is essentially a test of the public's receptiveness to it, *The Goldwyn Follies* might improve its chances by coaxing the public's response within the film, but this tactic was just another experiment, like hiring George Balanchine as choreographer. The result of any film was adjudicated not on the screen but at the box office. Reviews in the trade press were enthusiastic but sometimes cautious. According to the *Motion Picture Herald,* "Mr. Goldwyn has underscored the artistic and the beautiful, using the best of materials and talent and presenting them with a certain reverence, perhaps just a bit more reverence than wallop, although it will be a while before the referendum on that issue can be run off." The *Follies* cost $1.8 million and wound up $727,500 in the red, the most Goldwyn had ever lost on a production. It brought to a swift end a string of hits for him. Exhibitors who wrote to the "What the Motion Picture Did for Me" column of the *Herald* provide some evidence of its reception. Most were quite negative about the film or the response from patrons. Comments included "A flop if ever there was one," and "Oh well if this satisfies some Hollywood ego, put it on. We only work here. We don't have to watch the show." Most raved about Bergen and McCarthy, but the response to the ballet and opera was uniformly "too much." The negative reaction to the elite elements may in part have been an effect of the small-town and rural situations of these exhibitors, but one cannily observed, "Can Mr. Goldwyn call one place, 'Metropolitan' included, where grand opera has stood up without aid of charity?" Another remarked that he had simply "cut out the opera, which helped."[2]

Hazel's usefulness is predicated on Oliver's belief in a mass audience so uniform that the tastes of the "200 million" can be represented by a single person. She enjoys everything she sees, but Goldwyn, at least, recognized that tastes vary widely, from the Ritz Brothers to opera, as the film seeks energetically and rather desperately to appeal to them all. In a twenty-seven-page advertising supplement, designed to sell exhibitors on the film as much as to help them sell it to audiences, the editor of the *Hollywood Reporter* instructed them to market "*The Goldwyn Follies* for just what it is—the last word of specialty entertainment for everyone, lavishly produced and presented, smartly balanced for universal appeal." "Entertainment for everyone" did not mean that everyone would like everything. On the contrary, what made the film "smartly balanced" was that it included many "diverse elements" to suit different tastes; that is, "universal appeal" implied only that *The Goldwyn Follies* strategically included *something* for everyone.[3]

The exhibitors' responses, coupled with the commercial failure of the film, indicate that the "referendum" mentioned in the *Herald* review did not pass. *The Goldwyn Follies* tried to stuff the ballot box by dramatizing filmmaking as a collaboration between those who produce movies and those who consume them, by proceeding as though worrying about what the public wants is tantamount to making sure the public gets it. In the end the many somethings of *The Goldwyn Follies* were not enough, or, rather, they were too much, and the union of Harry Ritz and Vera Zorina was scarcely less fortunate a marriage than Romeo and Juliet's. All assertions to the contrary, the film and its failure pointed to problems that would become the talk of the industry by the summer: the idea that Hollywood had lost touch with the public and that its relationship with the public could not be restored until movies spoke more directly to peoples' lives. Goldwyn was exactly right to make his surrogate demand "real" and "human" and "simple" movies; it was just that his film delivered too few of these qualities. Before it was even released, Ruth Waterbury, editor of *Photoplay,* praised its "beauty and charm and originality," "that final essence of chic and showmanship," while holding it up as an example of entertainment that no one wanted. "There is such a thing as so much icing on the cake that you get sick of the entire dish. . . . Please give us simpler and better pictures." She pleaded for films that "give us, straightforwardly and without elaborateness, the dramatic stories of love and faith and home." Two months later she thanked "the hundreds of you" who had written to agree and once again brought up the example of *The Goldwyn Follies,* in which "there's simply too much of everything." Something for everyone had become too much for anyone. The industry itself would soon insist to the public that there was no such thing as the picture that would please everyone, a lesson the *Follies,* despite its frantic solicitation of approval, taught Goldwyn the hard way. And he, in turn, would take its rejection out on the rest of the industry, helping to pave the way for some of the public relations problems that the film itself seemed to work so hard to prevent.[4]

SUCH A THING AS BAD PUBLICITY

The Goldwyn Follies is a remarkable film, but its problems in the marketplace were not. Business was bad, and costs were up. Production budgets had been increased based on favorable returns during the 1936–37 season; as attendance and revenues declined, the film companies found themselves spending more money to make less of it, and they were talking retrenchment. As a result 1938 began in uncertainty. The trade press noted improvement in January over December, which had been the worst month for the film business in the last year and a half, but it reported more grim news in February: a general box-office drop of about 20 percent, a figure repeated periodically throughout the year. By late March, according to a *Reporter* headline, exhibitors were already "preparing for the worst summer season in picture history," which by all accounts, and making generous allowance for hyperbole, they seem to have gotten.[5]

Darryl Zanuck was one executive who blamed the recession for the industry's box-office troubles. "The record shows that the public just hasn't as much money for film entertainment as it had a year ago," he said in May, by way of pooh-poohing the idea that moviegoers had other reasons for staying away from theaters. This perspective, however, was drowned out by a series of well-publicized criticisms of industry affairs and the attention they attracted. Indeed, Zanuck's remark was prompted in part by attacks on Hollywood that Goldwyn himself had issued on April 25, on his return from Europe. In a prickly mood, Goldwyn told reporters that England and France were making inexpensive, high-quality films, and he blasted Hollywood for its excessive costs and overall decline in standards: "People used to be afraid to go to the movies because they thought they might see one bad picture. Now, with double bills, they're staying away because they fear they'll see two." He declared that the public was "on strike against inferior pictures," by which he meant virtually all pictures. The public's absence from theaters, in other words, was not an indirect function of the economy but a purposeful communication, signaling the refusal rather than the inability to pay for the entertainment offered it.[6]

About a week later a group of independent exhibitors took out what became an infamous full-page ad in the *Reporter*. On May 3 the Independent Theatre Owners Association (ITOA) accused the studios of extravagance and poor judgment for casting highly paid stars, "whose dramatic ability is unquestioned but whose box office draw is nil," in "top bracket pictures." The ad christened Joan Crawford, Katharine Hepburn, and Greta Garbo, among others, "poison at the box office." As a bit of intra-industry bickering, the ad might have been harmless enough, but it quickly became nationwide news. Within four days of his interview, references to Goldwyn's criticisms of Hollywood appeared in only four of the forty-nine newspapers in the sample; by contrast, coverage of the "box-office poison" story was widespread. Thirty-three newspapers carried articles and editorials on it within the same time frame, often on the front page, and usually with prominent photos of some of the stars involved. Some newspapers published more than one piece; the *Xenia (OH) Evening Gazette* enjoyed the controversy enough to publish five. Spokespersons for the producers defended the stars; lawsuits against the exhibitors' group were darkly hinted at; Harry Brandt, head of the ITOA of New York, clarified the exhibitors' position. Syndicated Hollywood columnists also drew attention to the story. Ed Sullivan and Hedda Hopper, for example, observed that nothing the exhibitors had said about the declining popularity of the stars was news to Hollywood. Paul Harrison wrote more or less the same thing, adding that the producers were glad for an excuse to reduce their salaries. Trying, one guesses, to be helpful, Louella Parsons came to the actors' defense: "There is nothing the matter with any of these stars that a good picture won't cure." In other words, the stars weren't the problem, just the bad films made by the studios.[7]

These examples help us to understand what Leo Rosten meant when he wrote in 1941 about "Hollywood's incomparable talent for publicity and startling ignorance of public relations." The kind of bad publicity sparked by the ITOA or Goldwyn threatened to veer into bad public relations, which might create damaging impressions—of stars, movies, or an entire industry—with attendant, unforeseeable consequences. The trade press played up the effects of what George Schaefer, then a vice president at United Artists and future chairman of MPGY, would soon castigate as "loose talk." *Variety* blamed the publicity around poison stars and inferior pictures for the "wide-open hissing of poor films," the "vitriolic, vicious, frankly antagonistic razoo" of patrons in theaters. Terry Ramsaye, editor of the *Herald,* wryly mused over the ITOA ad and its aftermath: "campaigning on interior and technical trade concerns in the presence of the box office customers, is possibly not conducive to an impression of allure for the theatre." He thought it about as foolish as when "the studio budget jargon of 'A' and 'B' classification" of films had been added to "the customers' vernacular," teaching them, in effect, that studios actually made bad movies on purpose.[8]

In the *Reporter* W. R. Wilkerson penned a series of articles with titles like "A Call to Arms" and "Shut Up, Hollywood!" These were an effort to scold everyone into discretion when "the industry and its members . . . are facing the damnedest crisis of their lives":

> You're talking too much! You're talking yourself out of business. You've taken your traditional problems into the open and the public has become your judge on matters it never can understand. . . . Exhibitors tell people that some of our important screen stars are dead. . . . In other words, exhibitors are TELLING PATRONS TO STAY AWAY FROM THEIR OWN THEATRES. . . . [Why does a producer] go around town telling people in advance he knows [his new picture] is going to be a crumbo? Has he lost his ingenuity? . . . Why does the same producer knock every other producer's effort?

Wilkerson might have saved his breath. Just two days after his tirade, Harry Warner publicly attacked the other studios for "not playing fair with the public and the exhibitors" by "withholding their important films" until the fall, leading to a "famine of grade A entertainment" over the summer. Warner cited his decision to advance the release of *The Adventures of Robin Hood* (1938) as evidence of his company's good faith dealings with both. A seven-page advertisement followed in the trade papers, including the *Reporter,* in which Warner Bros. accused its rivals of "HOARDING" (a mortal Depression-era sin) their good pictures and thus of contributing to the "slump" in attendance, said to have reached 40 percent in some areas. *Variety* and the *Herald* once again pointed out that Warner was only exacerbating the industry's troubles by "making the public too show-wise." Articles in nine of the sample newspapers publicized his remarks. Parsons also ran a column seconding Warner's concerns. And so the public got to read all about how there would be precious few films worth seeing just in time for the typically slow summer season.[9]

Talk, talk, talk. Discussion about the demerits of double features went on and on. Exhibitors continued to complain about discriminatory trade practices. An active perpetrator of bad publicity and public relations in 1938, the industry also cast itself in the role of persecuted victim. Its spokespersons complained repeatedly about unfair treatment in newspapers and on the radio. Syndicated gossip columnists debated whether Garbo and Leopold Stokowski, the conductor, would marry, but they also criticized individual stars, films, and anything else associated with the world's most unpredictable and conspicuous business. Jimmie Fidler, one of the most powerful and obnoxious of the lot, responded to the industry's complaints by pointing out that he and his colleagues only fed the public's appetite for publicity, good or bad, that Hollywood itself had created. Even as a victim Hollywood bore a share of the blame.[10]

Bad reviews were a perennial problem as well. It was not lost on exhibitors that they paid good money for newspaper advertising, only to see many films disparaged, often on the very same page. "There's no film so bad something good can't be found to say about it," one Philadelphia exhibitor fumed. Ramsaye later described the industry's grievance: "If any Buick was less than perfect, if any cake of Ivory ever sank, we never read about it. But any time, any day, we can read that most any motion picture is a total loss, that Hollywood is a total loss, that its picture makers do not know their art from their elbows." There were calls for reviewers to "report impartially" on the films they saw rather than offer criticism, which was, after all, only a matter of "opinion," and let the public make up its own mind. The ideal reviewer would be something like an adjunct of the film industry, not a watchdog of it.[11]

The industry was not ordinarily inclined to see a necessary correlation between bad reviews and bad films, but 1938 was different. Amid all of the other disturbing reports about the industry, the trade press generally acknowledged that the decline in attendance was not at all helped by several weeks of feeble releases in late spring, "about the worst pictures Hollywood has turned out in many years." In early May *Variety* predicted that the weak product would carry into July, as Harry Warner feared. The business of catering to the public's taste seemed less tangible and predictable than ever, and the usual production decisions and risks, cast at times in the flattering language of sound intuitions and instincts, came to look like "a flock of wild uncommercial guesses as to what the public wants by way of entertainment," according to Jack Warner, as steamed and chatty as his brother. Waves of bad films, bad publicity generated by outside commentators, "loose talk" within the industry, months of poor attendance, confusion about how to proceed—the perfect crisis. Some executives and commentators worried that the public was developing new and potentially ruinous practices in relation to the movies and that new feelings toward them were emerging as well. The industry came to understand, with Goldwyn, that the public—not censors or Catholics or educators or senators—was mad at the movies.[12]

THE MOVIEGOING HABIT

Studies of exhibition, reception, and audiences point out that "the social experience of cinemagoing" has historically been more important than any individual film or films in determining peoples' relationship to the movies. For much of the classical Hollywood period the word *habit* characterized a crucial aspect of that experience, connoting an agreeable relationship with the practice of moviegoing as such. The clarion call of those imbued with the moviegoing habit was, "Come on, let's go to the pictures," regardless of what was playing. Gilbert Seldes, an important analyst of movies and popular culture, as well as a fan, thought that the moviegoing habit more or less explained the fact of cinema attendance. He associated it with the breakdown of judgment and with the play of strong desires and emotional satisfaction: people "go to the movies because they simply and passionately want to go to the movies." "It is upon" this "uncritical and even unintelligent" "attitude that the financial success of the movies is founded." The selection of particular films, based on star or story, was merely a "refinement"; "the fundamental passion is a desire to go to the movies, which means to go to any movie rather than not go at all." The moviegoing habit did not require excellent, or even very good, pictures to sustain it, an indispensable asset to an industry that depended on the production of inferior as well as outstanding entertainment. According to Wilkerson, just "a fairly entertaining program" was sufficient to reinforce the moviegoing routine and preempt questions about "what was playing at the local theatre."[13]

Habits, unfortunately, can be broken. If habit "is the greatest single explanation for the weekly presence of 85,000,000 persons in our theatres," it also helped to explain the absence of others: "Out of repeated discouragement, they have formed the habit of staying away." People who went to the movies habitually were opposed to those who attended individual movies as "shoppers." The movie shopper was a selective consumer, discriminating among films to find ones that appealed. Shopping was often linked to a run of bad films. The scandal of bad films was that whatever the immediate consequences of their unprofitability, they might have the long-term effect of breaking the moviegoing habit. Seldes acknowledged that "if people are not actually pleased with the pictures they have seen and if this happens too many times, the automatic habit of going to the movies will disappear."[14]

Observers anticipated such an outcome by the summer of 1938, when the more or less compulsively enthusiastic industry contemplated the summer offerings with dismay. There were a few huge hits, such as MGM's star-packed *Test Pilot* (1938) and Fox's *In Old Chicago* (1937), as well as Warners' timely *Adventures of Robin Hood*, which led to the usual declarations that "action" was "in." But the popularity of such pictures and of the strange, exquisite *Snow White* (1937) only underscored the weakness of the film industry's performance overall: "business is either great on GREAT pictures, or lousy on all other product." Harry Warner's diatribe against hoarding spoke to fears that the seasonal summer slump, on top of already poor business, would have far-reaching consequences: "far too many people will have lost the habit of regular theatre attendance." According to Joseph Schenck of Twentieth Century–Fox, the summer season had precisely that result. Weeks of poor pictures in early summer "had a damaging effect upon business. Regular attendants at movie houses who might forgive a bad picture this week in hopes of seeing a good one next finally gave up." Shopping itself became a new habit: "The men and women, boys and girls," who once had the "habit of not shopping, are shopping now for what they know to be good. If that's not around, they simply don't go."[15]

By the time the summer of 1938 arrived, the moviemakers' expertise and experience, intuitions and hunches, and even their earnest desire to please seemed to have failed; all anyone really knew about what the public wanted was that the public didn't want what it was getting. The idea of the public "on strike" suggested that many people were declining even to shop. And new behavior implied new attitudes. Between the bad films and the bad publicity, the public was reputed to be distinctly annoyed. The *Reporter* columnist Irving Hoffman urged the industry to diagnose "the fundamental causes and sources of public antagonism" toward Hollywood. A month later *Variety* warned of "an irate public that seems just about tired of paying for inferior film entertainment." The public wasn't just tired; it was sick: "a public nausea . . . is keeping patrons away from box offices." Wilkerson, who routinely begged for "better pictures," and even "BETTER PICTURES," during the first half of 1938, hoped that the producers would start to "feel the pulse of a rather disgusted public." The entire industry was getting poor reviews, not just individual films: "The picture business has been in for an awful panning for the past few months, both from the press and the public, and it has now become the vogue for former ticket buyers to sit around, criticizing Hollywood's seemingly futile efforts to turn out entertainment." "THE PUBLIC IS LAUGHING AT US," Wilkerson thundered in another burst of exasperation, shortly before Doob described the "new nationwide" sentiment that "show-business is racing to hell!" [16]

For all the sweeping pronouncements and hand-wringing, it isn't clear that anyone really knew what the public was thinking. The opinion polls reported occasionally in the trade press tended to be unsystematic and informal (verging on anecdotal), local, and organized around specific issues such as double features. It is possible the public was irate: about extravagant salaries, block booking, and double features, which meant that audiences sometimes had to sit through a crummy film in addition to the picture they really wanted to see, which might also be crummy, about the industry bickering and the lawsuits. It is also possible that the public had no particularly strong feelings about the situation at all. It was troubling to think of a public so upset with Hollywood that it wanted to vomit, but rather less troubling, perhaps, than to imagine an indifferent public, one that had simply picked up other habits and moved on. At least an outraged public still made a place for the movies within its emotional universe. [17]

Where an uninterested public might be won back through some good films and good publicity, an angry public was a job for public relations. The trade press urged "a reeducation of the public in favor of film attendance" and warned against the industry's "life-or-death . . . failure to establish any sort of broad, progressive, permanent public relations policy," even though "the movies and their men and maids bid fair to be as heartily hated" as Standard Oil, AT&T, and J.P. Morgan had been before they had seen the light. The MPPDA handled public relations for "the industry," but it represented the interests of the major companies, which many independent exhibitors and producers often perceived as inimical to their own. "Loose talk" advertised competing interests that were difficult to unify; fractured relations clarified the need for a comprehensive, long-range public relations strategy and precluded it at the same time. Instead, the industry settled for Motion Pictures' Greatest

Year. Hastily organized and executed, MPGY was 1938's most auda-
cious guess, as well as its biggest production. With a cast of thousands
and a superspecial budget, it was action-packed, a stirring drama, and
a farce. Wilkerson's frantic demands for BETTER PICTURES became
the wishful slogan, "Motion Pictures Are Your Best Entertainment."[18]

CHAPTER 2

Exhibitors,
the Movie Quiz Contest,
and a Divided Industry

THE MINDS OF EXHIBITORS

The campaign was first announced in the trade press on July 18, 1938. Details remained sketchy for the next week or so. Lacking a name, a slogan, a budget, and a strategy, it was variously described as a "pep drive," "a nationwide 'go to movies' week," an "advertising campaign," and a "national 'go to the movies' season." By July 27, when some three hundred representatives from all branches of the industry, including independent exhibition, gathered at the Astor Hotel in New York, the general scope of the campaign, as well as many details, had been determined. As its newly appointed chairman, George Schaefer presented the recent box-office troubles as an "industry problem" rather than the "problem of one company or group," which called for a "joint effort" among all its members for the "first time in history." MPGY would run from September through December to inaugurate the 1938–39 movie year. Schaefer presented it as "a great stimulant and challenge to production" and an incentive for "better merchandizing [sic]." It would be conducted from "screen and lobbies" and in a newspaper advertising campaign that was "unprecedented in scope." In addition, a $250,000 movie quiz contest would provide an immediate box-office boost. The major companies had pledged three-quarters of MPGY's $1 million budget—$500,000 from studios and distributors, and $250,000 from affiliated exhibitors. Independent exhibitors were asked to contribute another $250,000, at the rate of ten cents per seat. To help open their wallets, Schaefer predicted a 10 percent improvement in box-office grosses, or $1.6 million per week in additional revenues, and possibly as much as 20 percent over the course of the campaign.[1]

Schaefer's speech sought to rally a spirit of unity among those present and those who would read about the meeting in the trade press. The decline in attendance affected everyone, regardless of interests: all must contribute; all must be spurred to greater effort in making and marketing films; all would benefit. Although the speech was addressed to the industry at large, its proper audience should be understood as independent exhibitors, whose contributions had yet to be pledged and who had played no role in planning a campaign that was presented as the solution to their troubles. In case the meaning of "joint effort" and "industry problem" was unclear, a full-page ad in the trade press, signed by Schaefer, hailed "every exhibitor in the United States and Canada. A warm and cordial invitation is extended to participate in an earnest and industry-wide endeavor to improve business conditions in motion pictures. . . . The effort can only be 100% successful if every individual in every branch wholeheartedly and unselfishly pledges himself to its success." Entitled "The Call to Arms," the ad sought to inspire a collective attack on a common enemy—bad business—and implicitly asked independents to lay down their weapons for the good of the industry, so far as their criticisms of the major companies went.[2]

The Astor meeting took place one week after the Department of Justice filed its antitrust lawsuit against the Big Eight, an action many independent exhibitors had been seeking for years. Campaign organizers denied that the government's suit, long threatened, influenced the decision to launch MPGY, but antitrust actions were potentially quite hard on public relations. If Schaefer and others could persuade independents to demonstrate their allegiance to the industry, and even to pay ten cents a seat for the privilege, the campaign might refute the accusation of monopoly and dispel perceptions of exhibitor grievance without ever bringing them up. Representing MPGY as a united effort, "the first group action of this type" ever undertaken by "the different branches of the industry," was an important focus of the story it told.[3]

Indeed, there were competing accounts of who first proposed MPGY, but organizers favored a myth of origins in which the idea came not from Hollywood, or Hays, but rather from "the minds of thousands of theatre men who have long advocated a united industry drive to herald the beginning of the new entertainment season." At a meeting with New York exhibitors in August, Schaefer "stress[ed]" to those present that "independent exhibitors participated from the very inception of the campaign." It is safe to assume that it did not originate as a collective fantasy of exhibitors, a fantasy of industry unity no less. And independents did not participate from the very first, although their aid was solicited early on, and the desire to enlist their participation shaped the arc of MPGY. According to the only early extant planning document, the men in charge lacked a clear idea about what to do, but they knew who should be doing it. The original planning committee comprised ten executives from the major companies, including Schaefer, Neil Agnew (Paramount), Herman Wobber (Fox), William Scully (Universal), and Gradwell Sears (Warner Bros.) from distribution, and Y. Frank Freeman (Paramount), Joseph Bernhard (Warner Bros.), John O'Connor (RKO), Charles Moskowitz (Loew's), and Spyros Skouras (Fox) from exhibition. Only Columbia was unrepresented among the majors. On July 21 *Motion Picture Daily* ran a big article on the antitrust lawsuit, which listed not only the companies but all the individuals named in the action. With the exception of O'Connor, every member of the planning committee was being prosecuted by the federal government for violation of its antitrust laws, a somewhat inauspicious beginning for a PR endeavor.[4]

On the day of the Astor meeting, Schaefer announced the appointment of a "national exhibitor committee," "represent[ing] all types of independent theatre operation." The committee would work out the details of the contest and raise funds among independents in their regions. It also demonstrated the majors' good faith to other independent exhibitors. Of the seven original members, both R. E. Griffith (Oklahoma City) and M. A. Lightman (Memphis), who was affiliated with Paramount, owned extensive circuits that covered multiple states. Joseph Seider (New York), Edwin Silverman (Chicago), and John Danz (Seattle) each had approximately thirty theaters; only Moe Horwitz (Cleveland) and Nathan Yamins (Boston) operated fewer than ten. The committee included a former president of the Motion Picture Theatre Owners Association (Lightman), a group that opposed federal intervention in industry trade practices, and the president of Allied States Association of Motion Picture Exhibitors (Yamins), a competing organization of independents. Yamins personally testified on behalf of legislation to end block booking and blind selling during Senate hearings in 1936 and 1939. By excluding exhibitors with only one theater, the committee did not really represent "all types" of operation and was skewed toward midsize and large operations. But the inclusion of Yamins might nonetheless have given it some credibility with exhibitors skeptical of the majors.[5]

An undated organizational chart indicates that the national exhibitor committee joined the original organizers to form MPGY's "General Committee." It is not clear what decisions remained for this larger committee to make and what influence the independents exerted within it or, indeed, whether the fusion really meant anything given the distance of most of them from the campaign's New York headquarters. Perhaps the exhibitors' most important task was to lead the fund-raising by example. By the end of the Astor event, the six unaffiliated committee members and twenty-seven other exhibitors had pledged $75,000 of the $250,000 contribution requested from independents. A majority of these exhibitors represented substantial circuits, according to *Motion Picture Daily,* and pledged a total of 744 theaters, with 750,000 seats among them. Independent exhibitors, including many with only one or two houses, eventually enrolled some 4,700 theaters in MPGY, out of an estimated 14,200 independent theaters. This was not quite evidence of a united industry, but evidence is not always a vital element in the amorphous world of public relations. The relevant question is not why so few independents participated in MPGY but rather, given the distrust many of them felt toward the major film companies, why did so many?[6]

THE CARROT AND THE STICK

The answer has to do with the movie quiz contest. While independent exhibitors might have endorsed the idea of an institutional advertising campaign in principle, it was by no means self-evident that they would help foot the bill for something so categorically remote from their own sense of box-office stimulation. The vast majority of film advertising took place at the local level, in newspapers, and was time-sensitive; it strived to bring people into the theater *right now* to see a particular film. The contest, which offered 5,404 prizes, including a first prize of $50,000, belonged to the familiar world of exploitation and was designed to produce the "direct, immediate returns" at the box office that institutional ads in no way guaranteed.[7]

Long before the details were worked out, it was understood that the contest would "be staged in such a manner that attendance at the nation's theatres will be essential" to participate. Contest booklets were available at cost to participating theaters and given free to patrons; submissions had to be postmarked by the end of December (see figure 3). Booklets contained one multiple-choice question, based on picayune details, about each of the ninety-four "quiz pictures," which were scheduled for release from July 29 through October 31. Entrants had to answer questions about thirty films and name the theater where they saw each picture. In the all-too-likely event of a tie, participants also submitted a fifty-word essay about their favorite film, explaining why they liked it. Essays would be read and evaluated by "an honorary committee of prominent persons of unimpeachable character," to be decided on later.[8]

Even if the institutional advertisements didn't change a single mind about the film industry, each theater would gain from every patron who attended, hoping to win $50,000, who would not have gone otherwise. It was expected that die-hard movie fans would participate as a matter of course; the fervent hope was that the contest would attract people who attended irregularly or not at all, or who had stopped going during the recent unpleasantness. Thirty films in seventeen weeks would help to revive regular attendance, or as the Fox West Coast theater chain put it in Los Angeles newspaper ads: "Get the *habit* . . . Join the fun! We mean the $250,000 Movie-Quiz!" The new films inspired genuine enthusiasm within the industry, with such pictures as *Alexander's Ragtime Band, Marie Antoinette, Spawn of the North, Carefree,* and *Boy Meets Girl* scheduled for release between August 15 and September 2. The contest would bring people back into theaters to discover that the "famine" for good product was over and that once again motion pictures were their "best entertainment."[9]

The contest also provided a way to heal certain breaches between the production and exhibition sides of the business. The $250,000 contest was the largest but by no means only giveaway scheme in theaters. Many exhibitors enticed patrons on slow nights with free dishes or with "bank night," "Screeno," and other games with cash prizes. Producers, distributors, and some exhibitors despised these giveaways, which told the public that movies in themselves were insufficient reasons to attend the theater. Exhibitor proponents countered that many movies *were* insufficient reasons, that giveaway nights were often their most profitable, and that industry practices like block booking made them necessary. They blamed producers for foisting inferior product on them and demanded better pictures. Producers and their allies retorted: "Bring back showmanship!"

Showmanship referred to the quality, inherent among those truly called to make and sell motion pictures, of magnetizing the public's

FIGURE 3. Theaters distributed movie quiz contest booklets free to patrons. Author's collection.

interest. Joseph Schenck referred to it as "the art of converting talent into money," but it might be more accurately described, in its most skillful rendering, as the art of turning anything into money. Showmanship was often considered "the life-blood" of the industry, especially in exhibition, because the local application of its principles sealed the final deal with moviegoers and could make or break huge investments. Exhibitors' successful exploitation efforts were recounted weekly in a special section of the *Motion Picture Herald*. Before MPGY the decline in showmanship had become a ubiquitous lament: "No more is exploitation the right-hand bower of the exhibitor." Movies are now just "slapped on the screen" without fanfare or ballyhoo. Since their inception, bank night and its ilk, even more than double features, were widely viewed as a kind of betrayal of the showman's calling; rather than using their ingenuity to coax patrons into theaters, exhibitors simply bribed them with cash and dishes. Exhibitors asked for pictures they could sell in good conscience, while producers and distributors faulted poor selling for contributing to the box-office decline.[10]

The movie quiz contest was a chance to break the stalemate. At the Astor meeting Schaefer did not blame shoddy exhibition efforts for the industry's troubles but gently referred to "a let down in adv[ertising] budgets and showmanship." Organizers presented the campaign and contest as the way to revitalize a dying tradition. Even before it started, industry executives credited MPGY with "reviving the lost art of showmanship among many theatres who haven't put on a campaign in years." In an article prepared by the organizers and published in several newspapers, Schaefer expressed his delighted surprise: "None of us . . . visualized the psychology of showmanship which this united campaign has created. Everywhere throughout the country, showmen are demonstrat[ing] the showmanship principles upon which the business is founded." If a $500 bank night prize or a gravy boat were considered illicit ways for lazy exhibitors to stimulate business, the movie quiz contest would seem to be just a bigger bribe. But the contest created a relationship between films and prizes, as well as a synergy among exhibitors, producers, and distributors. Bank and dish nights dragged people into theaters on the nights of the week they were least likely to attend for any other reason, when exhibitors screened their weakest features. By contrast, the contest drew attention to what was playing on the screen rather than trying to distract audiences from it. Participation in MPGY was evidence of exhibitors' enthusiasm for the business and the films, not their dissatisfaction. The mainstream press mocked bank and dish nights—more bad publicity—which divided the industry into competing camps. The contest might achieve the same box-office goals as other giveaways, while also celebrating the entertainment that exhibitors and studios offered to the public.[11]

In the event that boosting one's own box office, while restoring the public's confidence in the movies, was insufficient inducement to participate, there was always the fear of losing more business. Campaign organizers exploited exhibitor concerns about what might happen if they refused to join. The campaign let it be known: "Non-participating theatres will not be included in the national contest designed to draw continuous patronage to participating theatres," which meant they would not have access to promotional materials, including contest booklets. At their meeting with Schaefer, independent exhibitors in New York weighed the advantages of participation against the perils of resistance. Max Cohen, the president of Allied of New York, urged his fellows to go along, "warning that . . . it would be unwise for any theatre to remain aloof." He did not encourage exhibitors enthusiastically to support the campaign but rationally to acquiesce, so as not to disappoint patrons: "How will they explain to the public which wishes to participate in the contest? How will they meet the competition of those theatres which are in the drive?" In addition to the pleasant prospect of attracting new business, then, exhibitors faced the worrisome necessity of protecting themselves with the audiences they already had. The campaign, as some independents realized, coerced industry unity as much as promoted it.[12]

By far the majority of concerns reported among independent exhibitors pertained to the mechanics—the basic fairness—of the contest. They worried about access to quiz pictures as a result of the very trade practices the antitrust lawsuit sought to redress. A "regimented system" of run and clearance schedules, for example, delayed the screening of films at subsequent-run theaters, sometimes by many months after their release, in order to maximize profits from first-run theaters, most of which were owned by the majors. Campaign organizers tried to reassure independents that they would be treated fairly, which explains the discrepancy between the dates for the contest—September 1 through December 31—and the scheduled release dates for the quiz pictures: July 29 through October 31. The plan ensured that at least some subsequent-run theaters would already have quiz pictures when the contest opened. Organizers further claimed that by November, first-run theaters would have ceased playing them to make way for newer releases. At this point the subsequent-runs would have the contest field to themselves. The case was made that the contest was actually a better deal for subsequent-run exhibitors. As the *Reporter* explained, they typically changed their programs two or more times per week and often played double features; they would enjoy a higher volume of quiz pictures than first-run theaters, which usually changed programs once a week and were more likely to show one feature. A subsequent-run exhibitor who had a sixty-day clearance and changed double-feature programs three times a week could potentially play many more quiz pictures than a first-run competitor. Even exhibitors with longer clearances, it argued, should be able to procure enough quiz pictures to make it worth their while.[13]

Independents often saw the campaign as a project designed for the special benefit of the major companies, however, and were disinclined to take their generosity or good will on faith. At the meeting of New York exhibitors, Harry Brandt, of "box-office poison" ad fame, brought up the issue of "lengthy clearance schedules" and sought time so that exhibitors could "study possible weaknesses" in the contest. A few days before the campaign opened, it was reported that many members of the ITOA of New York worried about "being sold down the river, believing releases of Fall pictures will reach them too late for them to derive any benefit from the $250,000 contest." Shortly thereafter, "several hundred independent operators" in the state declared that they would not join. In mid-August the Allied Theatre Owners of New Jersey adopted a resolution urging members not to participate, both to avoid "imply[ing] undue friendliness with the rest of the industry" and because they perceived the contest as a strong-arm tactic to influence negotiations with distributors for the new movie season, a charge made in other parts of the country as well. It is significant that these decisions to boycott the campaign occurred on the part of state independent exhibitor organizations. By acting together they minimized the potential harm of eschewing the contest as individual competitors, and they professed themselves united as victimized independents against the larger industry that had asked them to join with it.[14]

Participation in the campaign did not secure unity either. Numerous independent theaters in Chicago subscribed, but just three weeks after MPGY started, independent theater owners in that city banded together in a local antitrust action against the major companies and the Balaban and Katz theater circuit, a Paramount affiliate. The suit charged that Balaban and Katz controlled "practically all pictures shown here for [the] first 10 weeks after they open." The Essaness circuit was one of the plaintiffs and its head, Edwin Silverman, one of the members of MPGY's national exhibitor committee. The perception of unity was in many ways illusory at the local as well as national levels. The unfolding of the campaign would do nothing to alter that.[15]

THE QUIZ CONTEST ON THE GROUND

Newspaper theater advertisements provide information about the contest at the ground zero of local exhibition, from the first-run metropolitan movie palaces of the major companies to towns with a single theater. They enable us to see how well the campaign met its promises to independent exhibitors and what opportunities were afforded local moviegoers to participate in the contest. These ads also indicate how and whether exhibitors chose to promote it, at least in newspapers, so it is possible to draw some general conclusions about its importance to exhibitors, which is to say, how important they thought it was to current and potential patrons.

Cleveland, Ohio, will serve as a case study of how the contest worked in a major metropolitan area, where the majority of film revenues was generated. In a city such as Cleveland (sixth in population, with 878,336 residents in the 1940 census) the major companies owned the largest and most opulent theaters downtown and in attractive suburban districts, screened the best new films, and charged the highest prices. A major company often owned subsequent-run theaters as well, while independent exhibitors operated dozens of neighborhood theaters of varying size and prominence. I chose Cleveland because the archive of the campaign treasurer, Frank Walker, provides detailed information about the exhibitors and theaters that participated in MPGY there. Eight independent exhibitors paid for twenty-one theaters, numbers that were manageable to research and represented a range of independent situations, from exhibitors who enrolled a single theater to others who operated small- and medium-sized chains. Moe Horwitz, who served on the national exhibitor committee, was based there, which afforded an opportunity to see how one of the organizers promoted the contest. The next section looks at exhibition situations from the newspaper sample, where I find that the experiences of exhibitors in Cleveland had much in common with those of their peers in other cities and towns.[16]

Not surprisingly, people who attended the movies in Cleveland had little difficulty finding thirty quiz pictures to enter the contest and were sold it from the start. Cleveland's most important theaters were Loew's

State, the Hippodrome (Warners), and the Palace (RKO). The State and Hippodrome received the top new releases and ran them for at least a week; the features at the Palace were new, typically weaker, A pictures, supplemented with live entertainment. From these theaters films usually moved to one or more of the five others owned by Loew's (Stillman, Park, and Granada) and RKO (the Allen and Keith's 105th), before eventually turning up at neighborhood houses. None of the eight prime theaters ran double bills. According to advertisements in the *Cleveland Plain Dealer,* six of the eight began MPGY on Thursday, September 1, with quiz pictures, including two of the most anticipated: *Marie Antoinette* at the State and *Alexander's Ragtime Band* at the Allen. *Four's a Crowd, Racket Busters,* and *Rich Man, Poor Girl* were also playing. In addition, Keith's 105th was screening *The Amazing Dr. Clitterhouse,* a quiz picture released on July 29, which would soon make its first appearance at independent neighborhood theaters. All of the theaters advertised their quiz pictures, in most cases via the contest's signature medallion: "THIS IS ONE OF THE MOVIE QUIZ $250,000 CONTEST PICTURES" (see figure 4). The next day Loew's and RKO began promoting the free contest booklets as well.

The *Plain Dealer* did its part. On September 1 the movie critic W. Ward Marsh published a celebratory article in support of the contest, campaign, and the "Grand and Glorious" films: "the producers" are spending so much money "because they want to smash through to the public consciousness the fact that this is to be a great year. . . . The best part of it is this: these 94 all look to me as if there was not a single 'B' picture in the lot. Ninety-four smash hits early in a season are enough to put this film industry over again." He directed readers to the advertisements and to theaters for more information on the contest. The next day the paper followed up with an editorial, predicting "better cooperation between producer and patron and a better quality of screen attractions" as a result of the campaign and contest. Between the efforts of the major theaters and the enthusiastic support of the *Plain Dealer,* Cleveland residents were apprised of MPGY and the contest at their inception and encouraged to expect great things from them.[17]

Four independent theaters that advertised in the *Plain Dealer* were also playing quiz pictures on September 1, but none so promoted it, even though all had subscribed to MPGY. The Alhambra, with *Letter of Introduction,* screened a mix of the better films from Columbia, Universal, and RKO as singles on second-run and duals of these studios' B pictures in their first Cleveland screenings (along with many new

FIGURE 4. Important Cleveland theaters owned by Loew's, Warner Bros., and RKO promoted the movie quiz contest at its inception. *Cleveland Plain Dealer*, Sept. 1, 1938, 8.

films from Republic). The other three independent theaters with quiz pictures offered them at the bottom of double bills. The Circle, which also played new B pictures on double features, paired the quiz picture *Bulldog Drummond in Africa* with an older film from 1938, *Tropic Holiday*. The other quiz picture to play in Cleveland on opening day was *Mr. Chump*, at the Euclid and Yale theaters, which both screened it with reissued films, *The Charge of the Light Brigade* (1936) and *Bullets or Ballots* (1936), respectively.

These double-feature programs are interesting in light of Marsh's exuberant comment, right on the same page, that it looked as though "there was not a single 'B' picture" among the ninety-four contest films. *Bulldog Drummond in Africa,* an installment of Paramount's established adventure series, and *Mr. Chump* were unabashed Bs, as their place on the billing suggests. Indeed, Marsh's review of the former, published the next day, hardly put it in the "Grand and Glorious" class: "A potboiler of the most lurid order, it belongs to the 'Hair-Breadth Harry' era of invincible heroes and buzz-saw villains." Moreover, the reissues of much older films on two programs were reminiscent of the warnings about bad pictures over the summer and how exhibitors had dealt with them. There was something of a reissue craze in 1938, with once popular and now "obsolescent features" consistently making their way back to screens. Reissues were an important part of the Cleveland moviegoer's diet in September and beyond, with such films as *Dracula* (1931), *Scarface* (1932), *A Farewell to Arms* (1932), *Man's Castle* (1933), *King Kong* (1933), and *Mr. Deeds Goes to Town* (1936) playing, often at multiple neighborhood theaters. That *Mr. Chump* was treated as secondary to the reissues with which it was paired suggests that the "famine" for good entertainment was not quite over for independents.[18]

According to the *Plain Dealer* ads, nine different quiz pictures were showing in Cleveland on MPGY's opening day, although readers were in a position to recognize as such only the films at the downtown theaters owned by the majors. More came that weekend: on Friday, first-runs *Three Loves Has Nancy* at the State and *Boy Meets Girl* at the Palace, while *Carefree* opened Saturday at the Hippodrome. Meanwhile, *The Crowd Roars* received a third Loew's screening at its Park and Granada theaters. On September 4, thirteen independent theaters, including four that subscribed to MPGY, were playing *Little Miss Broadway*, which had been released on July 29. The Shirley Temple vehicle ran almost exclusively as a double feature. Only two independent theaters, the Astor and Heights, advertised it as a quiz picture, and they did so in

Sunday ads only. Both theaters belonged to Moe Horwitz, and *Little Miss Broadway* was his first quiz picture. He was no doubt prepared for the advent of the contest and led the way in promoting it among independents. Four days later, independents were back down to just two quiz pictures, one *Little Miss* and a *Chump*. This would remain the pattern at independent theaters for the rest of the month, as quiz pictures waxed and waned, and individual films often arrived at several neighborhood theaters almost simultaneously.

By the end of September diligent Cleveland moviegoers, contest booklets in hand, would have been able to see more than the thirty films necessary to enter, primarily because of the weekly arrival of new quiz pictures at the State, Hippodrome, and Palace and repeat engagements of others after September 1 at the remaining Loew's and RKO houses. At this point, among the independent theaters subscribing to the campaign, eleven quiz pictures had played on thirty-three different programs, for an average of fewer than two quiz pictures per participating theater. The actual number of quiz pictures that any of these theaters received in September ranged from none at all (five theaters) to four at the Circle. Three of the eleven pictures played at an independent theater for the first time after the start of the contest; four of the eleven, all Bs, had their first Cleveland showing at the Circle.

This arrangement looked rather bleak for participating independent exhibitors who wanted to cash in on the contest during its first month, when the campaign attracted most of its publicity and ran its big institutional ads. But this was simply how distribution worked. Major first-run theaters played the best pictures upon release; independent theaters waited for them more or less at terms the majors set. For example, *Sing You Sinners,* a well-reviewed Paramount film with Bing Crosby and Fred MacMurray, opened at Loew's State on September 30 and then went straight to Loew's Stillman on October 7 for another week, before making its leisurely way to Loew's Park and Granada for a week's run at the end of the month. The practice of husbanding top films among different theaters within a chain, which also happened in other large cities, enabled the major companies to squeeze more profits from them while allowing its premiere local theater to continue to screen new product. *Sing You Sinners* first arrived at two independent neighborhood theaters on November 12, six weeks after it had opened in the city. In cities like Cleveland, where the major theaters played only single features on a weekly program change, a few better-situated independent theaters were sometimes first to screen lesser films that the majors didn't want, such as *Bulldog Drummond in Africa* at the Circle. Warners' three subsequent-run neighborhood theaters, the Colony, Uptown, and Variety, generally screened films earlier than most competing independents in Cleveland, the kind of favoritism that exasperated many independents and earned the scrutiny of the Justice Department.[19]

Access to contest pictures for independents who participated in the campaign worked pretty much as promised in September, insofar as the films that had been released in late July through mid-August were already trickling into many of their theaters. Eventually the trickle became a steady stream. Thus, *Sing You Sinners* may not have arrived at any participating independent theater until November 20, but it nonetheless played at sixteen of them, the last play dates beginning on Christmas Day, before the close of the contest. By December 31 all but three of the independent theaters subscribing to MPGY had played more than thirty quiz pictures, the minimum number that subsequent-run theaters were ultimately promised they would receive. At the end of October no participating independent theater had played more than fifteen quiz pictures and many far fewer. But by the end of the contest, twelve had played more than forty, and seven of these played fifty or more. The Riverside, which screened double features and changed programs three or four times a week, led the pack with sixty, which means that it played almost two-thirds of all contest films, or more than were screened in some small cities.[20]

Four independent theaters that had not received any quiz pictures in September still achieved the quota by the end: the Union and Mall theaters squeaked by with just over thirty apiece, while the Haltnorth, a Horwitz theater, wound up with forty-five and the Metropolitan forty-six. None of the eight prime theaters of the majors played more than fourteen quiz pictures during the contest. For the vast majority of participating independent theaters, then, this turn of events supported the campaign's promise: they would receive many more contest pictures, especially if they played double features, than downtown first-run houses. For the most part they also did better than Warners' neighborhood theaters, with thirty-seven quiz pictures apiece, if only because the latter played more single features than the independents (the Colony showed no duals at all).

What of the theaters that did not receive thirty contest pictures despite having paid for the privilege? The Circle played twenty-three overall, the Alhambra sixteen. Like the major theaters, the Circle and Alhambra usually changed their programs once a week, while as a rule the other participating independents changed theirs three times. The Circle was the largest independent theater in the city (1,875 seats) and part of Community Circuit Theatres (CCT), a local chain. The Circle played fewer important subsequent-run quiz pictures—only *Algiers, Alexander's Ragtime Band,* and *You Can't Take It with You*—but it played the first more than a month before the other independent theaters (and held it over for a second week) and the last still ahead of them. Likewise, the Alhambra (1,500 seats), one of three Cleveland theaters enrolled in MPGY by Martin Printz, played more programmers and Bs for the first time in Cleveland than second-run hits, but it screened the Deanna Durbin film *That Certain Age* two weeks before other neighborhood theaters got it, including those owned by Warners. The Circle and Alhambra got the good films early and the bad ones first and played them all longer. In other words, they got fewer quiz pictures because they were *advantaged* in relation to other independents.

Another participating theater to have received fewer than thirty contest pictures was the Eclair, but not because of a favored place in the subsequent-run hierarchy. J. H. Schulman enrolled just the one theater; the pledge put its seating capacity at five hundred, one of the city's smallest. After September 18 it advertised in the *Plain Dealer* only on Sundays, not a good sign, but its films could be tracked in another daily paper, the *Cleveland Press.* The Eclair received a grand total of fifteen contest pictures, or half the number that patrons needed to see to enter. Its first quiz picture, *Little Miss Broadway,* arrived on October 26, the latest date for any participating theater, some fourteen weeks after the film opened in Cleveland. The other participating independents received prominent quiz pictures from at least five of the major studios; by contrast, the Eclair received seven from Fox, including *Little Miss Broadway* and *Alexander's Ragtime Band,* but the rest were Bs. It played a number of Republic films and many westerns, along with two Polish-language films during the course of the contest. It is hardly likely the contest did much to improve its business.[21]

The lack of contest pictures at the Eclair had nothing to do with the contest; that is, it was evidence of a long clearance schedule and constraints on booking in general. The Eclair was more typical of independent theaters nationwide that pledged but did not get a sufficient number of quiz pictures than were the Circle or Alhambra. The Eclair should never have joined the campaign if it did so to aid its own box office in the short term rather than out of a selfless impulse to help the film industry, of which it was a very marginal member, spread good feelings. Despite industry rhetoric about the subsequent-runs and how they would all benefit, they were not created equal either. There was a great deal of uncertainty about the details of the campaign and contest before it commenced, and the owner of the Eclair might have joined in confusion or in optimistic good faith, thinking perhaps it would help the theater acquire pictures in a timelier fashion, at least for the duration of the contest. It may seem that Schulman was the only benighted exhibitor in Cleveland to have joined in error, that the campaign for the most part rightfully attracted only those independents in a position to benefit from the contest. Only around one-fifth of Cleveland's approximately one hundred independent theaters paid to join, which suggests that most exhibitors were wary of MPGY. But records show that other Cleveland exhibitors pledged to the campaign; they just never paid up. At least four independent exhibitors with just one theater apiece later reneged on their pledge, as did another who had signed up three theaters. Clearly there were exhibitors who had second thoughts about joining or perhaps found they were simply unable to afford it.[22]

Based on the advertisements in the *Plain Dealer*, even independents who paid did not think the contest especially worth their while either. Campaign organizers urged exhibitors to advertise the contest on a daily basis in their regular newspaper ads. The participating independents in Cleveland scarcely advertised quiz pictures at all, and when they did, it was almost always on Sunday only, even though advertising a film as a quiz picture did not have to add to the size and cost of the ad. The Riverside, which received a bonanza of quiz pictures, promoted just eight of them as such, the most of any CCT theater. The Circle promoted none. The Lexington, Norwood, Union, and Eclair did not advertise any quiz pictures, and three other theaters advertised only one or two during the four months of the campaign. Horwitz supported the contest to a slightly greater extent in his theaters, but the most even he advertised was eleven of forty-six quiz pictures at the Astor. This hardly counts as enthusiastic support. The Alhambra, alone among participating independents, continued to promote the contest until the end, although it did not do so continuously. At the others the frequency of the advertisements declined over time. Only four participating independent theaters advertised any quiz pictures at all in November or December, and three of these were owned by Horwitz. In fact, the most consistent advertiser of quiz pictures among Cleveland independents in the *Plain Dealer*, the only independent to advertise them at all in December, on

Sundays, all the way to the bitter end, was the Broadvue, one of the theaters that reneged on its pledge to the campaign.

The major theaters advertised their quiz pictures far more frequently than independent subsequent-runs, but even their ads tended to peter out toward the end. Cleveland's two largest theaters, the State and the Hippodrome, promoted seven of the eight quiz pictures they received between them in November and December. But where these theaters had advertised them virtually on a daily basis during MPGY's first two months, they typically did so inconsistently, here and there, during the second half of the contest. The remaining Loew's theaters did not bother promoting some of their quiz pictures at all during the last two months, and by mid-November the RKO theaters, including the first-run Palace, had stopped advertising their quiz pictures altogether. The Warners subsequent-run theaters advertised some quiz pictures in December, but the Uptown and Variety stopped during the last three weeks of December and the Colony during the last two. Even if the majors' first-run theaters had been willing to turn their backs on the campaign later—as they increasingly played new releases, and quiz pictures moved on to subsequent-run theaters—surely independent theaters would have promoted them aggressively if Cleveland moviegoers had cared much about the contest.

A point to mark here is that first-run theaters were not supposed to have been screening any quiz pictures at all beyond the first week or so of November, let alone until the very end of the contest. This is what it meant for the campaign to have been organized around releases from July 29 through October 31; the prediction, more like a promise, to subsequent-run exhibitors had been that the contest field would be theirs for the final two months of the campaign, which would compensate them for having to wait for quiz pictures while the major theaters screened new releases in September. The notion that quiz pictures would simply disappear from first-run theaters shortly after October 31 was wishful thinking for two reasons. First, very successful pictures were often held over at the theaters of the majors. Extended first-runs sometimes created a backlog of new films. Beyond that, MPGY could estimate but not dictate release dates; some of the quiz pictures were not ready on schedule. Thus while first-run theaters nationwide began in November to show anticipated releases such as Paramount's *If I Were King* (1938), Warners' *Angels with Dirty Faces* (1938), and MGM's *Citadel* (1938) and *Out West with the Hardys* (1938), new quiz pictures also continued to arrive on their screens through December. This was true in smaller towns and cities especially, since even the prime theaters did not necessarily get big new films immediately on release, but it held good for the metropolitan markets as well. On December 14 in Cleveland, for example, Loew's State played Goldwyn's *The Cowboy and the Lady* (release scheduled for October 21, delayed until November 17), and the Park screened *The Great Waltz,* its fourth showing at a Loew's theater. RKO's Palace also had a new first-run, *Listen, Darling* (release scheduled for September 23, delayed until October 21). *Sweethearts,* with Jeanette MacDonald and Nelson Eddy, did not come to Cleveland until December 30, its revised release date, more than two months behind schedule. This delay was topped only by Columbia's *Thoroughbred.* Sharp-eyed Edith Fellows fans would have noted that this proposed quiz picture was never released at all.

MPGY made half its promise good to most of the independent exhibitors who participated in Cleveland. They received ample quiz pictures for their patrons to enter the contest, without ever having to go to another theater. It was their fate, however, to play staler quiz pictures, ones that had already knocked around, sometimes for a whole month, at the various theaters of the majors. The whole conceit of the *quiz picture* could not flatten out important distinctions. For the purposes of selling independents, organizers behaved as though the contest automatically functioned like the moviegoing habit of old. The identity of films as quiz pictures suggested that no one was more or less valuable than any other, that each represented one-thirtieth of a ticket to "fame and fortune." The emphasis throughout was on quantity, not quality or timing. But there simply was no equivalence between first-run screenings of MGM's *Too Hot to Handle,* which rejoined Gable and Loy after the spectacular success of *Test Pilot,* and subsequent runs of Fox's *Gateway,* a dull programmer with Don Ameche and Arleen Whelan, or Columbia's *Juvenile Court,* a weak B. However much the film industry sought to cultivate moviegoing habits, the system of distribution and exhibition recognized that moviegoers were also shoppers, and it was set up to encourage them to shop earlier and more often at certain theaters than at others. The movie quiz contest primarily dramatized the everyday dynamics of distribution. It was supposed to turn the inherent disadvantages of the system for subsequent-runs into a boon during November and December. Instead, these theaters were often, as usual, just playing older films, except now some of them were paying extra for the same old deal.

In the end CCT paid only 25 percent of its pledge, even though its theaters received plenty of quiz pictures overall. The circuit held off payment until after the contest was over, which enabled it to evaluate the extent to which MPGY fulfilled its promises to subsequent-run exhibitors and to ascertain the value its theaters gained from the campaign and contest. Of course, its ambivalence toward the campaign was already evident in the decision to enroll only eight of the seventeen theaters with which it was credited in the *Film Daily Yearbook*. This was not because its other theaters were too disadvantaged to receive enough quiz pictures. By joining the campaign but not fully supporting it, CCT behaved strategically. It was governed by its own calculation, and recalculation, as to benefits more than to the needs of the industry as a whole or even to the promises it had made, to the extent of leaving other indies to cover proportionately more of the cost.[23]

It is not possible to know how many Clevelanders entered the contest, how popular it really was with audiences. If the contest did motivate audiences less than local exhibitors had hoped, as might be judged by the lackluster promotion of it in the *Plain Dealer* ads, Clevelanders who did want to participate were generally well served. They had lots of films to choose from, new releases as well as return engagements, weeks or months down the line, at downtown movie palaces and neighborhood theaters, just like always.

WHAT THE CONTEST DID FOR ME

Like their counterparts in Cleveland, independent exhibitors in cities and towns across the country joined MPGY and in some cases did not play enough quiz pictures to justify their subscription. Those with chains sometimes did not enroll all of their theaters, limiting their financial exposure to an uncertain venture and resisting pressure from campaign organizers to throw their full support behind the industry. From necessity or disenchantment, many independents remitted only partial payment or reneged on pledges altogether. Others paid in full but then declined to promote their quiz pictures, while sometimes those who did not contribute advertised them freely. Many exhibitors thus took advantage not only of the major companies but of other independents, whose lots may have been as hard or harder than their own. Far from unifying exhibitors, with the industry as a whole or with each other, the contest brought into focus the competition they faced and the scramble to turn a profit during hard economic times.

MPGY may not have inspired uniform excitement among exhibitors, but it was promoted in the ads of one or more theaters, at least for a time, in every sample newspaper. The fervor with which it was brought home to local patrons varied a great deal. Cleveland was anomalous in one way: elsewhere, the vast majority of participating exhibitors, majors and independents alike, began by advertising the movie quiz contest energetically, especially when they played quiz pictures early. This probably had less to do with a commitment to MPGY's broader public relations objectives than with the immediate goal of cashing in on the attention the campaign and contest were receiving. Regardless of affiliation, theaters overwhelmingly promoted the campaign and its "Motion Pictures Are Your Best Entertainment" slogan much less than they called attention to the $250,000 contest and the quiz pictures playing at their theaters. Exhibitor enthusiasm for the contest did wane over time, however, and the advertising of quiz pictures usually declined during the last four to six weeks. Theaters that continued to promote the contest typically stopped doing so on a daily basis, and promotion disappeared altogether among many independents. In some small cities it was impossible to tell in December newspaper ads that local independent exhibitors had ever supported the campaign.

Sometimes theaters did promote the contest all the way through. This was true in Frederick, Maryland, where Warners had a local monopoly on exhibition. Because of the town's proximity to Baltimore, its three theaters did not receive important new releases immediately, but its largest, the Tivoli, was ready to go with big quiz pictures of an earlier vintage when the campaign opened. As in many smaller markets where an individual or company owned multiple theaters, the Opera House had its own niche, playing better Bs and a few returns of the more popular quiz pictures at reduced prices. The Frederick was usually open only on Saturday, a sign of lingering bad times. It played mostly westerns and screened just one quiz picture, the much deplored *Meet the Girls*. Because there was so little overlap among films, and theaters changed their programs more than once a week, patrons in Frederick were able to see more than sixty quiz pictures locally during the contest, even in the absence of double features. The Tivoli and Opera House screened quiz pictures until the end of December, and they were diligently advertised as such from start to finish. Even the single, sorry offering at the Frederick was touted as a quiz picture.

In situations where an independent had multiple theaters and effective control of the local market, even exhibitors less secure in their campaign stake than the Warners theaters in Frederick knew they would offer enough quiz pictures to make the contest feasible for their customers and stood to reap all the benefits themselves. If such exhibitors could build interest in the contest right away, if enough patrons invested in it, the contest might indeed boost their business to the end. In Charleston, South Carolina, the Pastime Amusement Company enrolled only two of its four theaters in MPGY. As often happened, especially outside major cities, the start of the contest appears to have taken them unawares; the Garden and Gloria both played quiz pictures on September 1 but did not begin to promote them in the paper until September 4. Together they played forty-six quiz pictures as single features, all first-time local screenings, and from this point avidly promoted them until contest's end. The Victory and Majestic, Pastime's smaller, unsubscribed theaters, played twenty-five repeat and new B quiz pictures between them, which were advertised freely as such. By enrolling its prime theaters at full seating capacity, the Pastime paid based on where it stood to gain the most financial advantage from the contest; by promoting quiz pictures at theaters for which it had not paid, the company got something for nothing. The Palace, a fifth Charleston theater, got only eight quiz pictures, all but one as repeats. It did not subscribe and declined to mention the contest at all.[24]

Local control of exhibition did not always result in enduring support for the contest. Indiana-Illinois, an independent chain of twenty-seven theaters, owned all four theaters in Elkhart, Indiana. The chain pledged its largest theater there, the Elco (2,200 seats), as well as *either* the Orpheum (650 seats) *or* the Roxy (280 seats), to the campaign (another strategy by which independents sometimes joined without overcommitting resources). The company advertised all four theaters as MPGY participants in the *Elkhart Truth*. Even before the town's first quiz picture, the omnipresent *Little Miss Broadway*, arrived at the Elco on September 4, an almost full-page ad announced tie-ins with local manufacturers in support of "your best entertainment" and a chance to win free tickets. One month later, another ad reminded "Mr. and Mrs. Movie Goer" to pick up contest booklets and touted upcoming quiz pictures at all theaters. Despite screening sixty-four different quiz pictures through December, the theaters dropped all mention of the contest from movie ads after November 21.[25]

Elkhart patrons apparently lost interest in the contest—or never much cared—and so did the theaters. It is possible that interest waned because patrons had seen enough quiz pictures to enter, but it was only on November 10 that Elkhart theaters had played thirty quiz pictures. Audiences would have had to be extremely diligent or gone elsewhere to see them. It is more likely that the contest did not grab them, that patrons who needed a reminder to pick up free booklets a month into it were indifferent. The theaters in Frederick and Charleston may have advertised the contest until the end because their patrons cared more about it than those in Elkhart and other communities. The Warners theaters might also have felt an obligation to carry the promotion through regardless, to not give up on Motion Pictures' Greatest Year. But this sentiment was not uniform even among the theaters of the majors. The two theaters in Gulfport, Mississippi, were owned by a Paramount affiliate and followed the same course as the Warners houses in Frederick. The theaters in nearby Biloxi, which belonged to the same affiliate, did not. Biloxi's Saenger played fifty-three quiz pictures and advertised the contest avidly in the *Daily Herald,* but the Buck Theater, which played fourteen quiz pictures, mostly Bs, scarcely mentioned it at all. In this instance contest advertising was less about promoting the new season's releases and reviving patrons' interest in the movies as such than about trying to maximize attendance at the prime local theater, which played stronger pictures and charged higher admission prices.

The independent Nogales Theater in Nogales, Arizona, also had a lock on local exhibition and was an enthusiastic promoter of the contest. Its situation dramatizes the risk taken when the only theater in a community tried to offer patrons the same opportunity easily available to moviegoers in larger cities. Nogales, the smallest city featured in the sample newspapers, had about five thousand residents and was some sixty miles from Tucson. Its eight-hundred-seat theater belonged to a small independent chain owned by Nick Diamos. In the fall of 1938 it played everything from superspecials to Bs, including the bulk of Fox's pictures. There were four changes a week, usually singles on weeknights and double features for the Friday and Saturday programs, which often included a western from Republic or Grand National. Less characteristic of the general American small-city market were the Spanish-language movies it ran on some weekend matinees. On August 31 the Nogales ran a big ad in the *Herald* announcing the opening of MPGY and telling readers to "Get Ready for the 'MOVIE QUIZ' CONTEST $250,000 in Cash Prizes! Watch for Details." It also urged them to listen to "[Governor] Stanford's Proclamation of a greater movie season" on the radio and identified various Nogales businesses that would tune in to the broadcast, the kind of local tie-in that campaign organizers applauded as a hallmark of showmanship. After September 1 the Nogales dropped the contest ad for a few days, while still promising readers that "Motion Pictures Are Your Best Entertainment"; the contest ad was back from September 5 to September 13 before disappearing again. For the whole month of September readers watched for details in vain. The Nogales finally promoted the contest again on October 5, before announcing the arrival of its first quiz picture on October 9, Fox's *Straight, Place and Show*.[26]

From here on the Nogales advertised quiz pictures routinely until the end of the contest. The only ones it did not promote as such were two B westerns with George O'Brien, *The Renegade Ranger* and *Painted Desert*. This was unusual, given that films from all studios, across the spectrum of quality, stood an equal chance of being sold as quiz pictures by theaters. In other words, the contest was not used to entice patrons to inferior films or to alert them to quality pictures that made "Motion Pictures Are Your Best Entertainment" ring true; conversely, there was no discernible tendency to bypass contest advertising for weak films that betrayed this slogan or for top films that could be sold on their own merits. In Nogales it looks as though these B westerns were thought to appeal more to audiences on their own. In the end the Nogales squeaked by with thirty-four quiz pictures among some one hundred Hollywood films it played during the four months of the campaign. Local audiences would have had to see almost every one of them, or make the long trek to Tucson, in order to enter the contest.

In Tucson they would have had eighty-six different contest pictures to choose from at five theaters. Fox owned the Fox and the Lyric, and the State was a Paramount affiliate. Tucson received so many contest pictures because all theaters changed their programs at least twice a week and ran double features; the theaters of the majors absorbed not only the important releases but the B quiz pictures as well. Their promotion of the contest became uneven during the final month, and the Lyric, which received fifty-two quiz pictures in all, virtually stopped promoting them in early November, again perhaps so as not to advertise business away from the chain's ritzier Fox. Diamos also owned the seven-hundred-seat Plaza in Tucson, which was likewise enrolled in the campaign. The Plaza fared worse than the Nogales. By the time its first quiz picture rolled around, on November 1, the other Tucson theaters had already screened sixty-four of them, and the Plaza had stopped all promotion of the contest and campaign some six weeks previously. Beginning with the "B-minus" *I'm from the City,* which it played at the bottom of a double bill with *Dos Cadetes,* a Spanish-language film, the Plaza received twenty-three contest films, all on their third-run. In Nogales residents got scarcely enough quiz pictures to enter the contest; in Tucson they had plenty of films, but Diamos's theater was not an important vehicle for delivering them to moviegoers. It may also tell us something about his patrons, and their relative interest in the contest, that none of the five quiz pictures screened with a Spanish-language film received top billing.[27]

The scenario in Tucson was repeated in competitive situations in other locations. In general, the prime theaters were the earliest and most persistent promoters of quiz pictures, whether affiliated with the major companies or not. These theaters received the best films, the ones most likely to render the contest a pleasant bonus rather than an excuse for attendance, and they usually began receiving quiz pictures straight-away, while competing subsequent-runs and their patrons often had to wait. Many disadvantaged exhibitors who joined MPGY gave up on it when quiz pictures did not break their way. For example, Great States, a Paramount affiliate, owned half of the eight theaters in Alton, Illinois, and environs. Quiz pictures hopped from one of the chain's theaters to another; each received about fifty. Two independents agreed to join MPGY, but only the Ritz paid. It advertised free quiz booklets in the *Alton Telegraph* on September 7, but two months passed before it received its first quiz pictures, *Little Miss Broadway* and *The Amazing Dr. Clitterhouse,* the kind of amazing double feature that sent do-gooders running to telegraph their congressmen. The Ritz promoted these and its next quiz picture as such, but that was it, even though it received another twenty-five of them through the end of December.[28]

The Hollywood Reporter's assurance to subsequent-run theaters that they would be able to play many more quiz pictures than first-run theaters simply did not speak to the range of exhibition situations. Nor did the campaign's assertion that the contest was "especially designed for the smaller theatres who change from two to five times a week and show many more pictures than the large theatres." As we have seen, such statements were relevant and accurate for many, but not all, independent subsequent-run theaters in major metropolitan markets like Cleveland, where the first-run theaters of the majors played single features for a week at a time or more. But in Rochester, New York, double features at the majors' first-runs meant that they played more quiz pictures than many independent houses, except those in the Schine circuit, which controlled more than one hundred theaters in several states.

Less-privileged subsequent-run theaters with multiple program changes may *ultimately* have played more contest pictures than any individual major theater with only one change, but this was small consolation if the films arrived after December 31. And what mattered in smaller cities across the country—in Tucson and Alton, but also Missoula, Salem, Ashland, Madison, Hays, and so on—was that the prime theater or theaters played more quiz pictures than anybody else, and they played them first. These theaters consumed so many films because they changed programs two or more times a week and often played double features, like their weaker rivals. They were frequently owned by or affiliated with the major companies and not subject to block booking, which operated as ever during the contest and constrained access to quiz pictures for many independents. Large independent chains also had significant leverage over their smaller rivals to contract for better pictures.[29]

The contest went unmentioned in only one sample newspaper's theater ads. Independent exhibitor Fred Beedle subscribed both theaters in Canonsburg, Pennsylvania, to MPGY. They played seventy-nine quiz pictures during the contest, more than in many towns with twice as many theaters. There were no duplicates in Canonsburg: the Alhambra screened as single features thirty-three of the top quiz pictures, which arrived in a surprisingly timely fashion given the town's proximity to Pittsburgh. The Continental played all manner of Bs on straight double bills at three changes a week. Canonsburg was the kind of situation the majors might have pointed to in order to defend the fairness of their trade practices to independents and the benefits to the public. Theater ads never refer to the contest, but in late September, well after the arrival of quiz pictures, they incorporated the campaign's slogan, "Motion Pictures Are Your Best Entertainment." By November the slogan was a fixture, whether or not the theaters were playing quiz pictures, and it continued to appear into January, after the contest and campaign had ended. Theaters elsewhere sometimes used the campaign slogan in advertising, but the Canonsburg theaters were the only ones for whom touting the campaign—the public relations goal of selling the movies as such—even in so attenuated a form, wholly substituted for promoting the contest: the publicity angle designed to hustle audiences back into theaters right away.

The contest was assumed to be the reason independent exhibitors would join MPGY, and the Canonsburg theaters were in a perfect position to capitalize on it. Beedle may have gauged a lack of interest or worried about disappointed losers and figured the less said about it, in a town where movie exhibition served the public well, the better. He also may have been unwilling to implicate his theater directly in something that looked like other Depression-era giveaways: the bank nights, Screenos, Movie Sweepstakes, etc. There was some idea that MPGY and its crop of superior films would put the brakes on these practices. The *Arizona Star* celebrated a return to the days "before bank night, car giveaways, dish nights, buck nights, and other forms of enticements were used to draw the patrons through the turnstiles" and mentioned the faith of local exhibitors that "for the next few months, at least . . . the pictures alone will be good enough to get the customers back in line." Midcampaign the *Reporter* described a broader "trend": the "most salient, cumulative result of the Movie Quiz contest" was a movement "definitely away from the promiscuous 'giveaways' of recent years. . . . 'Bank nights' are disappearing rapidly." This alone would have given campaign organizers reason to rejoice.[30]

It was simply not the case, however, that routine giveaways disappeared on September 1. On the one hand, giveaways operated as usual at theaters that did not join MPGY. In Kansas City, for example, the Oak Park promoted giveaways of beauty ware, silverware, dinnerware, and even goldfish to entice patrons to see their quiz pictures. Theaters that joined were not immune from these practices either. On MPGY's opening day the Gibraltar chain's three theaters in Casper, Wyoming, slyly apprised readers of "800 Reasons Why You Should Attend the America, Rialto, or Rex" that night, a common sort of phrasing at theaters trying to evade antilottery laws or perhaps avoid paying licensing fees for Bank Night. The ad neglected to mention MPGY or that two theaters were playing quiz pictures. Even theaters affiliated with the majors held giveaways, although less frequently than independents. The State, one of four theaters owned by a Paramount affiliate in Chattanooga, bolstered weaker quiz pictures such as *Meet the Girls* and *Personal Secretary* with cash incentives. Another Paramount affiliate, the Sunset in Fort Lauderdale, routinely gave away trips to Havana, Cuba, with theirs. Both theaters in Hays, Kansas, the Fox-owned Strand and the independent Star, used giveaways throughout the campaign. On Thursdays the Strand offered something called "Work Night." The duties were mysterious but presumably not onerous. A few days before the contest ended, its ad cajoled:

Now Showing
WORK NIGHT Salary $125.00
Also 2 features.

This sort of ad, in which unnamed films are afterthoughts to cash prizes, drove producers and the trades crazy. But to have sold *There Goes My Heart* as a quiz picture instead would not have entirely sorted out the confusing priorities implicit in the contest and all other giveaways. Efforts to bolster attendance with such prizes during MPGY indicate that many exhibitors thought the contest was not an adequate lure in their communities and, more ominously, that the films were insufficient in themselves to win patrons back.[31]

INDEPENDENTS REBEL

From the start campaign organizers worried that many exhibitors would not make good on their pledges. By September 7 independents had pledged 3,369 theaters for a total of $281,000, but fewer than half were paid in full. Ultimately they pledged more than $50,000 above their quota, but as of November 11 only $221,548.77 had been collected; some five hundred independent exhibitors nationwide had not paid up, and many others submitted only partial payment. Letters were sent to theater owners begging them to honor their pledges, but the vast majority of those who had not paid as of mid-November never did. The total eventually received from indies for MPGY was $239,889.11.[32]

In early September Harold Franklin, a former exhibition executive and MPGY's business manager, speculated that independent exhibitors who had subscribed but not yet paid were probably waiting "until they play the [contest] pictures." The contest was at the heart of letters that exhibitors wrote to cancel pledges or complain. Small exhibitors from rural areas to big cities commonly realized they would be unable to get enough quiz pictures before the contest ended. For example, N.J. Brossoit, of the Shell Theater in Tacoma, Washington, reneged on his pledge because his theater had a one-hundred-day clearance, and he had not known when he subscribed that "the contest would be nearly over before we could show any of the contest pictures." According to ads in the *Tacoma Times,* the Shell was the only one among eighteen theaters in the city to get no quiz pictures at all before the contest ended.[33]

MPGY was organized so quickly, and the details worked out so close to its inauguration, that many independent exhibitors were poorly informed about it. The Nogales's pattern of advertising—heavy promotions of the contest punctuated by disappearances of all mention—suggests that the exhibitor likely had no clear idea exactly what quiz pictures would arrive at the theater or when they would start to do so.

In late October H.C. McNulty from Whitehall, Montana, wrote that he would gladly send a check for his pledge if he could get enough films, but "last week I sent in 14 dates to MGM for booking in Nov[ember] & Dec[ember] and only got two movie quiz pictures." An article called "What the Exhibitor Must Do" advised exhibitors to subscribe to the campaign, get a supply of booklets, and sell, sell, sell—all straightforward enough—but the other tip, the simple-sounding directive to "arrange to book at least 30 of the 94 quiz contest pictures," belied the complexities and constraints of the system. Some exhibitors tried and failed to make adjustments to their schedule. One from Salem, Oregon, noted, "I have talked to other exhibitors. . . . They too . . . have made an effort to have clearances shortened that they might receive benefits from this campaign; these efforts have been unsuccessful." The letters reflect the anger of independents who, according to *Variety,* were protesting "from coast to coast" the "refusal of prior run houses to waive any protection or clearance and permit smaller houses to get the films earlier in order to keep faith with patrons."[34]

Rural and small-town exhibitors faced a different problem from that of their urban peers. G.E. Widger of Ione, Washington, near the Canadian border, wrote a few weeks into the campaign that he expected to screen just ten to twelve quiz pictures at his two-hundred-seat theater during the contest. He would not pay because his patrons "can't afford to go 50—or 100 miles in order to see the thirty necessary" to enter. In isolated communities with only one theater, an exhibitor who promoted the contest but then could not play enough quiz pictures might end up with frustrated or angry patrons.[35]

In more populous areas a shortage of quiz pictures meant frustrated and angry exhibitors. Two Georgia exhibitors, with three small theaters, had pledged to participate but wrote at the end of September to cancel. They claimed they had subscribed without knowing what the quiz pictures were or what they would get "under the usual hold back accorded the small towns. We find we have less than 20 percent of the [quiz] features booked between now and the end of the contest." Theaters in a nearby town had already played three or four quiz pictures, "and our patrons are going to these places to enter [the] contest. You can readily see this seems to be helping [us] out of business." Other exhibitors likewise contended that the contest "hurts us more than helps." A. Adolph of Salem, Oregon, felt betrayed by the change among his regular customers, "folks who had been my friends and patrons" but stopped coming when he was unable to play quiz pictures. Even with three program changes a week and some double features, the State did not get its first quiz picture until October 28, and by the end of December it had only played twelve. He claimed to have spent one hundred dollars on promotional materials, money he could not get back, "only to find that it was taking business away from my house and sending them to the first run accounts." Hence the lament that the campaign produced "no benefits whatever except for the boys who are already in the dough."[36]

Such letters reveal the flipside of the fear that remaining "aloof" from the contest would drive patrons away. Even exhibitors who supported it might watch their patrons desert them for theaters in a position to capitalize immediately on interest stimulated by early campaign publicity. Moviegoers in Salem could see more than enough films to enter the contest because there were two first-run Warners houses, as well as other theaters with quiz pictures, to accommodate them. Contributing to the campaign in the case of some small exhibitors meant paying to increase the business of their rivals, including the major companies, who already had all of the natural advantages that early play dates for the best new releases, contest pictures or otherwise, conferred.

Some exhibitors indicated that they had pledged with the understanding that quiz pictures would be made available to them. One from Texas wrote that he "was promised quite a few pictures in this Campaign," but they had not been delivered. It makes sense that some exhibitors might have joined MPGY with the expectation that they would receive concessions on lengthy clearance schedules or block booking, at least for the duration of the contest. The majors were still working on a self-regulation plan for distribution to persuade the government to call off the lawsuit, and generosity regarding the scheduling of contest pictures, as a show of good faith, might have helped to build good will among independents. In this light, enrolling in MPGY might have seemed a clever, inexpensive way for disadvantaged exhibitors to improve their situations. There was so much confusion about the contest amid the haste of launching the campaign that exhibitors took a leap of faith in participating. But any exhibitors with a long clearance who assumed that, say, *Little Miss Broadway* would miraculously show up on their screens September 1 were sorely disappointed.[37]

Franklin sought to control the damage. He promised delinquent exhibitors that they would be treated fairly. He offered refunds to those who paid and did not receive thirty pictures; few, apparently, were eager to trust him. Instead, subsequent-run independents fought to make the contest conform to their needs. Having failed to persuade disobliging competitors to shorten clearances, a grassroots effort emerged to have the contest deadline extended into 1939 so that more independents would be able to play at least the thirty films necessary to enter the contest. Just two weeks into MPGY, Schaefer wrote in a confidential letter that it was "quite possible" the contest would be extended until March 1, and *Variety* speculated a few weeks later that an announcement of the extension was imminent. But other exhibitors protested. In the end Schaefer announced that the four-month timeline had been "advisedly chosen" and changing it would "not be keeping faith with the public." The decision not to extend the contest, not to keep faith with independent exhibitors, offered them another reason not to fulfill their pledges.[38]

Although the majority of exhibitors who canceled invoked the unfairness of the contest, another complaint was that patrons were simply uninterested. A New York exhibitor with three theaters wrote in late October, asking to be relieved of his pledge: "In joining you, we thought that this campaign would really mean something to the Box Office, but after trying it out for the past month and a half, we find that it has not helped our business at all." "No one appears to be interested," commented a small-town Texas exhibitor. C. M. Olsen, of the Minne Lusa in Omaha, reported that "this Quiz contest has done nothing for me so far. . . . My janitor cleaned up over half of the books which were thrown on the floor, so you can see what interest has taken place." Someone else mentioned booklets that "we can't even give . . . away" and poor returns, despite having actively promoted the contest. An exhibitor from Thompson Falls, Montana, wrote a week before the contest ended to say that despite buying advertising accessories and distributing quiz booklets, "we are unable to create any enthusiasm among our patrons," and he could not pay. But he was soon leaving to join the Montana legislature and would "use every opportunity I can to help the motion picture industry in Montana. In that way I may contribute more in services to the industry than the amount I pledged," in effect offering to settle his account with political influence rather than money.[39]

The contest, which was to be the exhibitors' incentive to join, became the ready-made excuse for withdrawing. As we have seen, the CCT circuit in Cleveland did not make much effort in newspaper ads to interest patrons in the contest, but owner Max Lefkowich complained strenuously when he offered to settle his account for $247.96, 25 percent of a pledge that already involved fewer than half the theaters of the chain. "No doubt you know this [the contest] is the biggest flop that ever was. As far as we are concerned there wasn't more than five or ten people that asked for the programs during the whole period. . . . It didn't mean $25.00, total increase in receipts to us in all of our theatres." He noted that his "associates" disagreed with his intention to pay anything at all. Of the six unaffiliated independents on MPGY's original national exhibitor committee, only Griffith, Seider, and Yamins pledged every theater and paid in full. Horwitz declined to pledge two of his seven Ohio theaters, the Globe in Cleveland and another in Cuyahoga Falls, claiming that they "played pictures anywhere from six months to a year after release date," and thus the contest would yield "no benefit" to them. He paid his pledge for the others. The son of John Danz sent in a check for $591.30 to cover the costs of seven of the eighteen theaters the circuit had pledged. He did not criticize the contest but cited "late availabilit[y]" of quiz pictures as the reason for dishonoring the commitment. Silverman did not bother to explain why he paid only $2,500 of his $3,180.70 pledge. He may have regretted paying that much, given that he wrote to request a refund on unused contest booklets, a request that was apparently denied for fear of offering an inducement to exhibitors to withhold them from patrons. Even Lightman tried to enroll most but not all of his theaters, but as an affiliate they were enrolled automatically by Paramount.[40]

An MPGY pledge was treated as a promise, not a contract, and an industry that had such testy relations with independents found itself repeatedly cajoling and negotiating and compromising with them. Whether or not the contest was as big a failure as they claimed, it offered many independents the freedom to dictate to Hollywood for a change. Many more exhibitors reneged on their pledges, but there are no letters to explain. It is likely that others who paid in full early on, often before MPGY began, also found themselves shortchanged by a contest and campaign that had promised to benefit the industry as a whole and them in particular. Whatever general support independent exhibitors may have felt for the film industry's effort to improve the stature of the movies, they participated because they wanted to increase the size of *their* audience or just coax it back. MPGY appealed to a single community of exhibitors nationwide, but it could not create one. The contest proved that the industry was not at all united; as many independents had feared, it reinforced the privileges that accompanied chain ownership and affiliation with the major companies—privileges the lawsuit sought to address—but now at the literal expense of those who paid only to watch their business go to competitors.

The complaints of exhibitors largely remained within the industry. If MPGY was organized to enlist the support of independents, its purpose was not to leave them with warm, fuzzy feelings about an industry they knew well. The other cornerstone, the institutional advertisements, allowed the organizers from the big companies to shape public discourse about MPGY and "the movies" in the nation's mainstream press. Now we turn to how the campaign addressed its primary audiences—the public and the press.

CHAPTER 3

The Campaign and the Press

THE FILM INDUSTRY SPEAKS ITS MIND

The proposed solution to the damage caused by the intra-industry bickering and the surplus of bad films was not, in the end, for Hollywood to "shut up" so much as for it to "talk back," to "give our side . . . to the public." The film industry budgeted $575,000 for institutional advertisements, almost twice the amount ($315,000) set aside to administer and award prizes in the movie quiz contest. The vehicle for delivering its story was some eighteen hundred daily newspapers in the United States and Canada. As local forms of address, newspapers spoke directly to readers from within the communities where they attended movies. The planning committee had discussed "the very judicious use of radio advertising," but exhibitors, whether affiliated or independent, deeply resented the competition from radio, which had become Americans' favorite form of recreation by 1938, according to a *Fortune* survey. Exhibitors routinely criticized the studios for letting movie stars appear in radio-play versions of current movies and on other programs, and independents would have been even less inclined to join MPGY if it meant enriching radio in the process. Newspapers were not competitors for the entertainment dollars of the public and likewise saw radio as a rival. Everyone, from exhibitors to producers and the executives in New York, was dissatisfied with newspaper coverage of Hollywood that exaggerated its faults. A timely expenditure of $575,000 would help to generate support for the campaign and perhaps stimulate long-term co-operation between the media.[1]

The task of creating the ads fell to Donahue & Coe, an agency that counted MGM and United Artists, the companies most associated with quality films, among its clients. Most film advertising sold the concrete product, here and now, at the local level. By contrast, the institutional ads did not tout particular films or stars, which "represented individual company possessions," but were designed to remind the public of the value of the whole enterprise known as *the movies*. Movie advertising was known for its abundant and frequently unjustified use of superlatives, the super-colossal syndrome. It operated as though, to paraphrase the Philadelphia exhibitor who objected to unsympathetic film critics, "there was no film so bad" that it wasn't also the industry's most outstanding production in some way or other. The institutional ads would generate new terms of public address by creating a promotional language that followed "the path of dignity" and avoided "sensationalism and show," bringing a measure of restraint to a business long associated with extremes. Ramsaye enthused about the ads: "the institution" of the movies "must have stability, continuity of performance, resources of substance and a character of substantiality. After all, the motion picture, for all of its often proper use of ballyhoo, is not a circus which folds its big top and moves on." As the prominence of such terms as *greatest* and *best* in campaign rhetoric suggests, however, old habits die hard. An uneasy tension between publicity and public relations, between old-fashioned hoopla and moderation, was at the heart of MPGY.[2]

Eleven institutional ads were created, two of which ran in virtually every daily English-language newspaper in the United States, as well as in Canada, where Loew's and Paramount owned theaters. The first ad usually appeared on September 1 or 2, the second a week later. (Another ad, devoted to the contest, appeared in October.) By industry standards the institutional ads were huge, their size arguing for their importance. The first usually ran about three-quarters of a page; the second was smaller, no more than two-thirds of a page as a rule, but still dominant. Most were visually rather dull. In some the dominant visual element was simply the title, such as "Two Hundred Million People *Can't Be Wrong!*" Others had small line drawings. Three included realistic representations of people. In general the graphics were designed to call attention to but not distract readers from the message, which was delivered over several paragraphs, roughly four hundred words per ad. The ads could not be comprehended at a glance; unlike regular theater advertising, where any text was punchy and short, their job of educating the public required the reader's time, attention, and cooperation.[3]

The ads touched on some familiar themes, especially regarding the recreational benefits of the movies. Entertainment remained the first principle of Hollywood filmmaking, in keeping with the campaign's slogan. Ever mindful of conditions outside the theater, the ads proposed that movies provided a healthy, necessary "escape" from a "reality" that was "harsh" or "drab" or both. The movies made "the world a better, happier place to live in," largely by distracting moviegoers from it. They "transport you from the commonplace workaday world into new worlds of wonder." Six of the eleven ads stated that in the theater "entertainment, relaxation, freedom from care are yours in overflowing measure," and the rest extended the same promise in slightly different, if equally florid, language. Will Hays and industry executives had been making this case for years. The entertainment function of film was seen as the basis of its popularity and profitability, and even a campaign that was supposed to represent an innovation in communicating with the public could hardly avoid sounding the old notes.

And yet there was more to the movies than an encounter with the content onscreen. "Going to the movies" served a social function that made the theater "one of the world's most important institutions." Part of the satisfaction of moviegoing was sharing "a group experience," the kind that radio, a medium associated with the privacy of the home, did not provide. Whatever the individual pleasures and distractions it afforded, moviegoing was "a national habit," a regular, even ritualistic activity that bound people as a people. At the same time, the theater brought them concretely together—situated them—at the local level. In the theater, neighbors and strangers met in a public space that combined the personal pursuit of entertainment with the equally pleasurable "affirm[ation] that man is a social being."[4]

The ads actively promoted not only the theater where movies were consumed but also the industry that produced them. Several drew attention to the "thousands of men and women" employed in "one of the world's great industries." The title of one ad, "It Could Only Happen in the Movies," brings to mind implausible coincidences and inevitable happy endings, but it actually referred to the collaborations motion pictures made possible, not only of artists and craftsmen but also of scientists, technicians, and researchers. In the ads the production of motion pictures was about hard work and innovation rather than glamour. The ad "276" alluded to the number of different "arts, industries and professions" involved in filmmaking, emphasizing the creation not only of films but of jobs, a common way to promote consumption and corporate service during the Depression. Movies, in other words, may release us, the audience, from the "workaday world," but their production depends on the workaday activities of others, not only the "rarest talents" of stars and writers but ordinary "bricklayers and carpenters," most of whom labor "anonymously—behind the scenes," just as we do. Significantly, the word *Hollywood* does not once appear in the ads, while references to the *Motion Picture Industry* are everywhere. *Hollywood* evoked the insubstantial culture of movies, the people and behavior that fueled gossip columnists and inspired reformers. The *Motion Picture Industry* communicated permanence and respectability, highlighting the solid economic structure behind the shadows on the screen.

References to the motion picture industry ran the risk, however, of turning the familiar world of the movies into something distant and impersonal; the ads resolved this problem by insisting, ad infinitum, that the most important participants in the enterprise of filmmaking are "you," the customers. When the title of another ad asked "what is your 'stake' in motion pictures?" it answered as though "you" are actually a stake-holder in them: "everybody who goes to the movies enters a partnership with the producers and the motion picture theatre-owners. . . . Yes, the 'movies' are *your* business as much as ours!" Two other ads indicated that the movies are "the chief cultural possession of the average man and woman" and "the beloved property of everybody." As "a part of the daily life of the people," the movies were a collective possession, one that hard times could not take away. Things may not be "so hot" for "Joe Doakes and his girl, Marge," the protagonists of one ad. They have "been pushed around a lot," but at the theater "everything is changed. . . . Whatever they want, the movies get it for them," whether it is a swing band, a love story, or an African adventure. In this ad the movies provide not simply an escape from the unpleasant realities of the Depression but serve as a bastion against the feelings of powerlessness it inspires. At the movies "Joe Doakes is boss." And so, of course, are *you*. "Reconstruct an historic place—re-create an historic battle—build a volcano! . . . It is *you* who order these things." "It is *you* who develop" everything from the selection of stars and stories to "new twists of action, of camera work, of pace and tempo" (italics in originals). The public is presented here not as passive consumers of popular entertainment but as the active producers of it. "The 'movie' is . . . subject to the approval of the box-office, a referendum as accurate as that of the ballot-box itself." As in an election, the will of the people is the ultimate authority.

The impulse to call on *you* in the ads embraces both the universality of the moviegoing experience and your concrete particularity. So although Joe Doakes suggests a generic everyman, and Marge an everywoman, the ads go out of their way to deny that there is such a thing as a mass public. This impulse is especially evident in the most important of the eleven ads, "The Average Movie-Goer Speaks His Mind" (see figure 5). It was one of two ads that ran in every city or town with a daily newspaper (the others were created for cities with multiple papers). It always appeared first and was the larger of the two. If the "average" moviegoer in the 1930s was, in fact, widely assumed to be female, like Hazel Dawes of *The Goldwyn Follies,* the Average Movie-Goer and Joe Doakes ads look beyond this presold market and strive to make the moviegoing experience appear more central to the lives of men. The former ad emphasizes that moviegoing is a family activity, just as Joe and Marge imply that a trip to the theater makes the ideal Depression-era date, on their way to becoming an average moviegoing family in their own right. The spokesman in the Average Movie-Goer ad is the man of the family, but the ad invites identification from both sexes, the elderly, young, and middle-aged, while representing class amorphously enough to include the working and middle reaches, by way of suggesting that movies, indeed, have something for everyone.[5]

The Average Movie-Goer ad reflects a broader interest in what the "average" person was thinking at this time and who could speak for him. Surveys such as the Gallup Poll, which first appeared in 1935 as "America Speaks," brought "a modern public . . . face to face with itself" in the guise of a "quantified average" rather than as a collection of diverse individuals. As Sarah Igo notes in *The Averaged American,* a study of how surveys changed the way people thought of society and of themselves as members of it, the idea of the *average* invoked the specter of a "mass subject," given that surveys often seemed to make a heterogeneous public speak as though with a unified voice. The Average Movie-Goer, by contrast, argues on behalf of the wide range of tastes and opinions among people—on behalf of differences, in other words, not of flattening them out. He begins his discourse by talking about his love of apple pie and how hard it is to believe that "there are folks who honestly don't like it at all." He doesn't like liver and bacon, which he knows others adore. So, too, with the movies. He and his neighbor disagree about the merits of a star; he sometimes thinks his wife may be

THE AVERAGE MOVIE-GOER
SPEAKS HIS MIND

FIGURE 5. The most important of the institutional ads, "The Average Movie-Goer Speaks His Mind," suggested the breadth of the movies' appeal and the range of audience tastes. *Rochester Democrat and Chronicle*, Sept. 1, 1938, 15.

"losing her judgment" when she raves about a picture he and his son don't like. But this is good news. He realizes that "we all have our likes and our dislikes. We're all different—thanks be! A dull world it would be if we weren't." The point of this folksy wisdom is that just as disdain for apple pie is no reflection on the pie, disliking a particular film does not reflect on its quality but points instead to fundamental differences in taste that contribute to the pleasurable variety of life.[6]

The appreciation of differences and its consequences for moviemaking are sounded repeatedly in the ads. "Two Hundred Million People Can't Be Wrong," one title tells us, but it is also the case that two hundred million people can never agree. The speaker in this ad is "The Man Who Runs Your Favorite Motion Picture Theatre," and he sounds a lot like the Average Movie-Goer. The exhibitor notes his patrons' wide range of responses to films: "Within the space of a couple of minutes I have heard the same picture enthusiastically applauded and severely criticized, the same stars praised and 'panned.'" Two hundred million people are not wrong to dislike particular films, just different. And the film industry has not made a mistake, or lost touch with the public, in producing films that are not to your taste; it has simply appealed to a portion of the public that does not include you. The ads cleverly acknowledge the criticisms against the film industry's products, criticisms that helped to motivate the campaign; by insisting on the active critical function of moviegoing, they defuse those criticisms at the same time. No movie, the exhibitor concedes, "will please everybody, everywhere," rejecting the fantasy of a mass audience so perfectly homogeneous in *The Goldwyn Follies* that one member of it can speak for the preferences of two hundred million people. The important thing, the Average Movie-Goer reminds us, is that "taking them all together, I figure that the 'movies' give more pleasure to more people at a lot less cost" than anything else. Or as the exhibitor puts it: "motion pictures, by and large, hit a mighty high average of pleasure-giving." The ads dismiss the impossible demands of a mass audience and promote, instead, the concept of averages, an unempirical meaninglessness that allows these spokesmen to celebrate the range of individual tastes and assert, without need of proof, that the movies in general manage to satisfy most of them. The shift to an audience of diverse moviegoers makes the case that the only way to please everyone some of the time is not to please you all of the time. Just as a democratic system doesn't mean you always get the elected officials you voted for, democratic filmmaking doesn't always result in a film you want to see.

If the point of *The Goldwyn Follies* is so to cater to the tastes of an impossibly uniform public that critics turn into fans, the ads acknowledge that criticism is inevitable. As the Average Movie-Goer says, "Sure, I criticize the pictures. I pay my money and that's my right." By turning fans into critics, the ads confer on the public a function that was also the province of professionals, the reviewers who generally cast their objections to a film in terms of its failings—in other words, blaming the pie. The campaign ads strike at the foundation on which objective criticism depends. Criticism, in these ads, is just a matter of opinion; it says more about you than about the movies you watch. It is a result of personal likes and dislikes rather than universal truths, which is precisely why, according to the title of another ad, "YOU are your own best Movie Critic."

Criticism and the reasons for it are also treated as a service that helps movies in general to improve. "This very diversity of taste, this healthy difference of opinion, has challenged us to fresh endeavor—to constant research and experimentation." The movies evolved by way of striving to accommodate the vast range of preferences. The very thing that makes them such a gamble is embraced as their signal achievement: it is the differences among people that make them "the great entertainment they are today," in the words of another ad. And it is "the responsibility of the audience to see that they get their money's worth—to approve work well done—or to voice disapproval—and thus to help the theatre management interpret public reaction accurately." Far from fostering either private, passive enjoyment or impersonal sociability, the theater emerges as an energized public space that facilitates active engagement with and disputes over what appears on the screen. The ads also invited readers to send in their "opinions, criticisms or suggestions about motion pictures" directly to campaign headquarters in New York. The eager solicitation of feedback corresponds to the idea of public relations as a "two-way street," in which the public must be heard and understood, not merely informed and persuaded. It was not enough to "depend on your own judgment" as your own best movie critic. "Make it heard, make it felt."[7]

Such criticism has a genuine impact, according to the ads. The Average Movie-Goer tells us: "I kind of figure that it's the criticism of average folks like me that's largely responsible for the pictures getting better and better all the time." The account of cinema's improvement over time was too deeply cherished a notion, too ingrained a mantra, for the ads to consider it simply a matter of opinion, the way that they treat objections to or endorsements of particular pictures. Significantly absent from the ads are references to the Production Code and its effects. Credit for "better and better" films is given to "average folks," not to the public groups that threatened and cajoled the industry. Or as another ad put it: "The *audience* is responsible for the amazing growth of the cinema. . . . It is the *audience* demanding as the price of attendance, always higher standards in stories, acting and direction" that has kept movies vital (italics in original).

Never before had the film industry produced such definitive and widely circulated claims about the centrality of the public to the filmmaking process. The ads insist that the public is the most crucial of the industry's thousands of collaborators, that motion pictures are a direct result of its directives to the industry, and that it bears responsibility for their quality and content. Overall, that responsibility has been discharged with distinction, as evidenced by the continual improvement of movies. And the film industry has honorably discharged its obligations as well, given that the movies satisfy and enrich a vast collective of moviegoers who are idiosyncratic and demanding in their individuality. The uniqueness that the Average Movie-Goer stands and speaks for, rather than failures of judgment on the part of the nominal producers, accounts for the range of films, as well as discrepancies in their reception. It is this fact that lets movies off the hook when you don't like them. The movies, one of the cornerstones of mass culture, are in fact proud advocates for your individuality.

MARGINAL MOVIEGOERS

Some moviegoers were more individual than others. Daily foreign-language newspapers also were enlisted in the campaign, but they received one institutional ad instead of the usual two, and the Average Movie-Goer ad was not used. Instead, they ran "Two Hundred Million People Can't Be Wrong!" on September 1 or, rather, "Zweihundert Millionen Menschen können sich nicht irren!" *(New Yorker Staats-Zeitung und Herold)* and "Duecento Milioni di Persone Non Possono Sbagliare!" *(Il Progresso Italo-Americano).* In the *Jewish Daily Forward* the Hebrew title translates as "An Entire World Is Not Crazy." The "two hundred million" in the title refers to the number of people the film industry claimed attended the movies worldwide each week. To make the only ad that highlights international attendance the one to communicate the industry's message to readers of foreign-language papers was, in effect, to differentiate them from the national community of moviegoers. It implies that the campaign proposed a slippage between the Average Movie-Goer and the average American. With its "just folks" language, unpretentious clothing and decor, and general atmosphere of white middle-class stability and small-town home life, the Average Movie-Goer ad strived for readerly identification. And even if one could not locate oneself within the ad, it accommodated that response, too: everyone is different. But the readers of the foreign-language press were apparently too different. The switch indicates a belief that the homogeneous, small-town appeal of the Average Movie-Goer might fail to engage ethnic metropolitans, that he and his family are natively American in a way they wouldn't understand.[8]

Interestingly, *La Presse Montréal* was treated the same as English-language dailies; in it readers encountered the usual family of five under the words: "Un Habitué de Cinéma Dit ce Qu'il Pense." To the American film industry at least, French Canadians were somehow really Canadian in a way that readers of Italian or Hebrew newspapers in the United States did not really count as average or American. Ethnic and racialized subjects could not "embody America," Igo observes in *The*

Averaged American, but "could only represent themselves." For these readers the repudiation of a mass public of moviegoers was potentially exclusionary. If the campaign's principal spokesman for diversity does not speak for them, the force of the Average Movie-Goer's claims on behalf of difference might rest in no small degree on his looking so much like his imagined audience. The relevant particularities in the case of ethnic Americans are less those inhering among individuals than those between groups, the native and the foreign. The average movie-goer is already American, not someone for whom movies might play a role in the process of Americanization, as silent films had purported to do for earlier generations of immigrants.[9]

The African American press was not part of even an abridged institutional advertising campaign. These were weekly papers and thus were excluded altogether from the MPGY appropriation; an exception, the *Atlanta Daily World,* was simply ignored. Most weeklies were published in rural communities, where theaters were sparse and industry profits a fraction of those in larger towns and metropolitan areas. Weekly African American newspapers, such as the *Chicago Defender, Pittsburgh Courier, Cleveland Gazette,* and *Washington Afro-American* were, by contrast, city-based. Their exclusion underscores the sense that African Americans were the great afterthought of the film industry, the "phantom audience" Anna Everett calls it, a market to be exploited rather than a public to be solicited.[10]

Some of the African American papers did not mention the campaign; the rebuff from the industry would scarcely have inclined them to promote it for free. But MPGY was prominently featured in the *Washington Afro-American,* which ran three institutional ads. Lichtman Theatres, a white-owned chain of twenty houses catering to African American patrons in D.C., Virginia, and North Carolina, advertised heavily in the paper, and owner A. E. Lichtman was the likely sponsor of the ads. The Average Movie-Goer addressed the *Afro-American*'s readership first, with one difference: the image of the white family was replaced with a photograph of a black one (see figure 6). The newspaper also ran the only other ads that featured realistic images of people: Joe Doakes and Marge and a postman, who delivers "A Message to You" from the industry. Both ads were likewise transformed, except that the white Joe Doakes became the black "Joe Worker," an indication that the white ad's name for universality was not that universal and that the generic middle-class appeal of the Average Movie-Goer and his family could be explicitly broadened, creating other possibilities for identification.[11]

FIGURE 6. An unofficial version of "The Average Movie-Goer Speaks His Mind" ad promoted the campaign to African American moviegoers, who were not at all considered "average" by Hollywood. *Washington Afro-American*, Sept. 10, 1938, 5.

Lichtman theaters, which received plenty of quiz pictures, promoted them heavily in their movie ads. In the kind of quid pro quo that campaign organizers counted on, the Average Movie-Goer ad ran next to an article that plugged the contest at Lichtman theaters; the article also touted the theaters' policy of hiring "courteous colored workers" and screening "the cream of the movie output." The institutional ads ensured that the industry's public relations message, and not just its big bribe, reached African American audiences in Washington. The doctored ads told them that the film industry cared about their business in particular, that their desires and ambitions shaped production. The choice to remake these three ads, rather than to use others that were visually race neutral, betrays the suspicion that for all their talk about *you*, ads that lacked black faces would not seem to speak to the experience of African American patrons. The ads might repudiate a mass audience, but Hollywood made films for white people.[12]

The difference in images has interesting implications for the text of the ads, which is unchanged. The Average Movie-Goer ad suggests that African Americans are generally happy with the entertainment they receive. And when they are dissatisfied, there is the lesson of the pie. One might think here of objectionable racial stereotypes in Hollywood films, a source of discontent that received no little coverage in the *Afro-American* and other weeklies. They offend some people but make others laugh. According to the ads, speaker and reader should conclude that "We're all different—thanks be!" But the ads also appear to make promises the film industry was scarcely prepared to keep. For example, as with Joe Doakes and his girl, "the movies get" "whatever" Joe Worker and Marge "want." What one writer wanted, in the following issue of the *Afro-American,* was for films to stop appealing to "nearly every group imaginable, except to colored people." In "$250,000 Movie Contest Shows Lack of Sepias," the columnist Louis Lautier praised the quality of quiz pictures in general but deplored the failure of Hollywood to film stories of interest to African Americans. He did not care much about the "cameramen [who] go into darkest Africa," an example of the movies' contributions from the Joe Doakes/Joe Worker ad, but rather asked for a film based on the true story of an American slave revolt aboard the *Creole.* The end product "might be offensive to sensitive Southerners, but it could not be as offensive to them as 'The Birth of a Nation' was to colored people." Here was a chance to prove, as "A Message to You" maintained, that the "very diversity of taste" and "healthy difference of opinion" really "challenge" the film industry "to fresh endeavor."[13]

The ads in the daily press celebrated the wonderful diversity of the public, arguing for a moviegoing experience guided by personal likes and dislikes rather than by objective standards, on which grounds the industry's products might be found wanting. But in the context of the *Afro-American,* as with the foreign-language papers, it was impossible to relegate the industry's message about differences simply to individuals and not also to groups. When the average black moviegoer imagined the range of responses to individual films, he might think of racist characters or stories biased toward a white audience, as well as quibbles over the appeal of a particular star. Relativism has its limits, and a taste for pie is not really the same as a taste for dignified representations or equal opportunities, nor were the implications of such preferences for the film industry identical.

The point is not to observe that the ads might foster identitarian responses and criticisms regardless of the industry's intentions. It was hardly news to the film industry that many African Americans were discontented with depictions of the race onscreen, and this audience did not need an advertising campaign to make them aware of their frustration, as letters from readers in these papers indicate. Rather, the ads in the *Afro-American* render explicit what was left unspoken in the industry's general endorsement of diverse tastes and opinions and commitment to catering to them, the foundation of the ads that appeared in daily papers all over the country. It was one thing privately to acknowledge that of course all movies did not appeal to all people, that what went over on Broadway often failed to perform well in the hinterlands, or that "father" and "mother" and their children did not necessarily share the same tastes in stars or stories. But it was another to advertise such facts. If there was no such thing as a mass audience or a movie that could please everyone everywhere, then the ads, taken to their logical conclusion, undermined one of the industry's most important rationales for excluding controversial topics from the screen. Controversy asks people to take sides; it results in dissatisfied moviegoers. But the ads make the case that some people already leave the theater dissatisfied, that everyone is dissatisfied some of the time. Dissatisfaction is a normal, indeed necessary, element of the democratic filmmaking process. There is no reason not to film the story of the *Creole*.

This was not a contradiction that the industry was prepared to admit. About halfway through the campaign, the *Afro-American* published another article by Lautier that included some comments made by A. L. Selig, from MPGY headquarters in New York, on the necessity of "keeping away from delicate controversial subjects" in film. Lautier thought the comments relevant for understanding "the attitude of Hollywood" toward better parts for black actors and more relevant stories for black audiences. According to Selig: "To reflect contemporary thought in motion pictures is treading on dangerous ground. . . . Of the 84,000,000 people who attend picture theatres a week in these United States, will be found millions of varied beliefs and trends of thought. . . . It has been definitely established that audiences demand that the pictures they go to see should be entertaining according to their idea of what is entertaining to them, and deeply resent any intrusion of propaganda, no matter how subtly interwoven in the story." Millions of people have millions of different ideas and opinions; this is one of the central points of the institutional ads, the very reason movies cannot please everyone. But infinite variety apparently comes together in a single point of agreement—what counts as entertainment, which is opposed to something else that counts as propaganda, which has something, apparently, to do with "contemporary thought." Having established that dissatisfaction is an inevitable part of moviegoing, because there is no mass audience, the campaign tries to take it back. The industry must behave as though there were.[14]

The institutional ads implicitly headed off arguments on behalf of films that reflect "contemporary thought," as the industry had in the past, by incanting "entertainment, relaxation, freedom from care," the appeal to thoughtlessness. If, as one ad indicated, "going to the movies" is "a habit that survives wars, strikes, political upheaval and national crises," it did so, the mainstream position held, precisely by avoiding such divisive topics. The ads acknowledged the inevitability of dissatisfaction, but controversial films actively cultivated it. With the call to pleasure and "your best entertainment," MPGY reminded the public that movies were still the joyful medium of irrelevance. The ads both denied but also portended change. The film industry did not much care what African Americans wanted, but they were not the only critics or moviegoers to ask for films that dealt with important social issues or problems relevant to a world in crisis. The cry for films that mattered was all but deafening by the end of 1938, despite the industry's desire to suppress it. We will return to the controversy over controversial films later on, to find that the campaign itself inadvertently prompted revisions to the idea of what constituted entertainment.

THE GOSSIP COLUMNISTS

The success of the industry's institutional ads depended in part on the extent to which newspapers translated their promotional messages into editorial content. Many dailies answered the industry's $575,000 appeal to their balance sheet, or sincerely championed the value of the movies to their readers and communities, with articles and editorials in support of MPGY. The campaign and its coverage tell us something about the relationship between these media, which shared neither the competitive nor the symbiotic dimensions of film and radio and about which less has been written.

Given just a few of the events that competed for newspapers' attention during September—the Sudeten crisis and imminent prospect of war in Europe; the persecution of Jews in Germany, Austria, and Italy; Thomas Dewey's highly publicized prosecution of the racketeer James Hines in New York and the subsequent mistrial; a hurricane on the East Coast that killed some five hundred people; and, of course, FDR's policies and the ongoing economic crisis—that something as comparatively trivial as MPGY received as much coverage as it did indicates that film was not the only medium to seek to provide customers with some "escape" from the harsh reality that was evident elsewhere in their pages. Part of this escape was achieved through syndicated Hollywood columns. Numerous columnists turned up in the sample newspapers, including Louella Parsons and Hedda Hopper, Ed Sullivan and Jimmie Fidler, and lesser known figures: Robbin Coons, Hubbard Keavy, Sheilah Graham, Paul Harrison, Erskine Johnson, Harrison Carroll, Frederick Othman, Harold Heffernan, and Alexander Kahn. Walter Winchell's acerbic "On Broadway" column, which often included bits about the movies, was represented as well. The columnists worked for such organizations as Hearst's International News Service and King Features, Scripps-Howard's United Press and Newspaper Enterprise Association, and the Associated Press. They could be counted on to take some notice of the campaign, and their good will was likewise solicited but hard to engineer. Criticism of the movies and periodic, sometimes vitriolic, attacks on particular personalities, projects, and studios were their stock in trade. The columnists tended, at least at times, to present themselves as champions of the public, too, protecting its interests against the fallible judgment and sometimes downright stupidity of the producers. The industry was only moderately successful in securing their cooperation. Some favorable copy appeared, but they did not seem to feel especially constrained from criticism. On the whole, they proved themselves unwilling to become mouthpieces for the industry and treated MPGY as cavalierly as they would any other Hollywood production.

The Broadway Committee, which handled publicity for MPGY in the world's most important movie market, reported on September 6 that a column had been "planted" with Sullivan, but his next published words on the campaign were hardly industry-sanctioned. He wondered whether the contest "will make friends or enemies for the cinema moguls. . . . The questions submitted are so simple that you can be permitted a mild bafflement," but the tie-breaking essay is "where the howls will originate, because if a lot of them have the correct answers and yet lose a $50,000 prize because the judges prefer one letter to another it is just going to be too bad. . . . Theater managers will have to hide up in the projection booth to escape irate patrons hunting for them with shotguns." Hysteria aside, Sullivan's point was valid. For exhibitors who were still ambivalent about the campaign, here was a timely reminder that they, not producers or campaign organizers, were on the front lines when it came to a disgruntled public. Sullivan based another column on humorous answers to hypothetical quiz questions. For example, of *Rich Man, Poor Girl* he inquired, "In the boating party in this comedy, what falls overboard and is lost? Answer: The plot and the M-G-M stockholders." This was not the sort of coverage the Broadway Committee had in mind.[15]

Eventually the industry got its Sullivan plant. A sober appreciation, "Movies Are Big Business" came out two months into the campaign. "It is not enough to tell you that movies are your best entertainment. . . . The why and wherefore should be demonstrated." The column purported to provide a factual account of moviemaking for the upcoming year, enumerating the productions in the works and costs associated with them and impressing upon readers that "only steel, agriculture and the automobile industry top" motion pictures. He praised the industry for its willingness to "gamble" "on anything as subject to fluctuation as public taste." The column's other contribution to building good will was to explain that because so many films "have to be made for you," not all of them "will be great," "but you will see an amazing number of fine pictures and it is on these that Hollywood should be judged, because the rest comprise the slack that is inevitable." "It is asking too much for each of the six pictures each week to be an epic, isn't it?" Here was a less attractive version of the case that the film industry's products hit "a mighty high average." Drawing attention to bad pictures counted as a helpful defense of the industry, so long as they were justified away. A poor film such as *Rich Man, Poor Girl* is not, for example, a result of the trade practices that made B pictures so profitable but rather a function of the industry's responsiveness to insatiable audience demand.[16]

Jimmie Fidler was similarly schizophrenic in his treatment of the industry during MPGY. Fidler was the most gratuitously nasty of the columnists and, with a twice weekly radio program, a special thorn in the industry's side. Not even a featured role in the Warner Bros. quiz picture *Garden of the Moon,* playing renowned gossip columnist Jimmie Fidler to the tune of $50,000, with a contract for additional films, was enough to shut him up. He attacked MGM and the most expensive quiz picture: "With some very flowery speeches about their wish to 'cooperate for the best interests of the industry,' the czars of M-G-M have announced that they are canceling plans to roadshow 'Marie Antoinette' at premium prices and that they will release it in the usual way. Pretty, but it doesn't ring true. The real reason for the change in policy,

I'm convinced, is that the much-touted 'colossal' is laying an egg at the box-office." A few weeks later he was onboard, promoting the new season's releases and his own interests:

> For two years, I've been contending that poor pictures were the real reason for the great movie depression—and today's facts are proving my contention. Hollywood has suddenly snapped out of its lethargy and started turning out top-notch entertainment. . . . It's time to call off the feud. Hollywood has done its part and it is now up to the public to show its appreciation by picking up the theatre-going habit where it was dropped. . . . All kidding aside, there is a bushel of truth in Hollywood's new slogan, "Motion Pictures are your best entertainment."
>
> But I'm wondering how many of the exhibitors who a year ago were hysterically blaming "poison stars," frank-spoken critics, radio and everything under the sun excepting poor pictures now have sense of humor enough to laugh at their own folly as they realize that better product and better showmanship have solved their problem.

Fidler named several quiz pictures as evidence of his acumen, as though by making good entertainment the studios were finally listening to him. At "popular prices" even *Marie Antoinette* is "packing them in." He pronounced the "feud" he helped to foment over, calling on the public to make peace by rekindling the moviegoing "habit," precisely the goal the campaign sought to achieve. All this good will was undercut by the unexpected attack on exhibitors, who had, in fact, blamed bad pictures for their troubles as loudly as anyone, even frank critics. The column supported the campaign, or at least the studios' contribution to it, but it also demonstrated Fidler's superior investment in his signature venom, the basis of his own entertainment value.[17]

Sullivan's and Fidler's affirmations of the industry and its films were about as good as MPGY got. In early August Parsons came through with a little pitch for the contest and the "first rate" movie season it celebrated, "bringing untold happiness to many, many millions." But Winchell remained snide about Hollywood and had little to say about MPGY, except to point out a few days after Parsons's plug that the original campaign slogan, "Movies Are Your Best Entertainment," had been changed because of the unfortunate acronym "MAYBE." Paul Harrison introduced readers to the campaign under the heading "One Million Dollars for Hooks and Lures." He cautioned: "In all I've read and heard about this drive for better business, nothing seems to have been said about better pictures." A few months later, Hedda Hopper turned her sense that pictures *were* better into an indictment of the campaign and industry. She began by remarking Hollywood's absence of "feelings, ideals, sincerity." "Instead of spending money to improve pictures, it's spent on posters, banners and movie quizzes to inform the world that 'Motion Pictures Are Your Best Entertainment.' When all that is really needed to prove that is a few good pictures. Of late there have been some swell ones." She named a handful. "With pictures such as these, the public needs no advertisements to point out that motion pictures are your best entertainment. So, what's the percentage?" MPGY was the industry's latest error in judgment. The only public relations needed was quality entertainment.[18]

Robbin Coons, an Associated Press columnist, offered a similar critique:

> All the movie studios are in on the big "educational" campaign designed to make you—and many others—come and see the new season's flickers. . . . I hope the campaign works so that all the producers and exhibitors can be happy again—even so happy as they were in the good old days when people flocked to the boxoffice through habit and came back again no matter what manner of celluloid tripe they had been served.
>
> That will be fine. It will be finer if all these highly touted new flickers turn out to be as fine as they're supposed to be. . . . I've seen a few that can go down on anybody's list right now.
>
> On the other hand, I'm thinking like a great many other people that the best way to convince people about their "greatest entertainment" is to make the picture so goldarned entertaining that they can't deny it. Get a picture like that, sell it with showmanship, and the picture and the public will take care of the rest. . . . It used to be a trusty maxim of this business—"There's nothing wrong with the movie industry that good pictures can't cure." The present come-on-and-see campaign is inspired by a realization that something more is needed, some general stir-up of the old public enthusiasm for the screen. But back of it all, that old maxim still holds true.

The references by Hopper and Coons to good pictures must have seemed a high price for the criticisms of its means of promoting them. The only way to prove the truth of the campaign slogan was to make good films. For Hopper, good films made the campaign unnecessary. Coons was not so sure; he believed that "something more is needed," but at the same time, the public would support truly entertaining pictures, properly sold. At any rate, the days when the "habit" could be sustained by "celluloid tripe" were over, so whatever else the campaign promised, the pictures had better be as good as it said.[19]

It is impossible to know what impact columnists had on public perceptions of the campaign or on the industry, the movies, and the stars in general. Readers might well have enjoyed the rantings of a Fidler or a Hopper without being guided by their views, just as audiences went to the movies even though they were probably wise to the fact that each new picture was not the greatest ever made. But the industry thought the columnists mattered. Two weeks into the campaign, *Variety* reported enthusiastically that two Pittsburgh dailies had suppressed negative comments about MPGY by gossip columnists. The *Press* omitted the section of Sullivan's column in which he anticipated an angry public, armed with shotguns, and the *Post-Gazette* dropped an entire column by Othman, who complained that a third of the quiz pictures "would send people out of . . . theaters mad at the industry rather than appreciating the quarter of a million bucks it's awarding to lucky patrons." I only know about Othman's column because of the *Variety* story; this particular column did not appear in any of the three sample papers that carried him: the *Detroit Free Press, Washington Post,* and *Xenia Evening Gazette.* But none of them ran his column on a daily basis. Indeed, it was common practice for newspapers to publish "daily" gossip columnists anywhere from several times a week to sporadically. The *Detroit Free Press,* the only sample paper to carry Sullivan, also did not run his column every day. It published neither of his hostile columns about MPGY but carried the favorable "plant." Coons's assessment of MPGY ran in only one of the seven newspapers that sometimes carried his byline. It is impossible to know whether these papers purposefully withheld columns critical of the industry as tangible evidence of its cooperation with the campaign, although the Detroit example is suggestive, and the paper had been criticized earlier in the decade for dropping gossip columnist Sidney Skolsky at the request of local exhibitors. Regardless, if one of the campaign goals was to silence the carping of columnists, MPGY was not a success, even about MPGY itself. There were, however, better ways in which newspapers could support (or hinder) the campaign than by censoring (or publishing) frivolous columnists. They could promote the industry's effort in feature articles and editorials that treated the campaign as a serious, newsworthy endeavor.[20]

THE DAILIES HAVE THEIR SAY

MPGY's budget included $10,000 for five "campaign representatives" to meet with newspaper editors and publishers in 155 cities. According to Howard Dietz, director of advertising and publicity for MGM and the chair of MPGY's advertising committee, their assignment was to solicit "criticisms, suggestions and discussion of motion pictures. Our idea was to acquaint the press with the importance of collaboration, to convey the industry's feeling of its responsibilities and to point out that these had much in common with those of the newspaper," but not to indulge in any "special pleading." They sought to persuade the press that the industry's "intentions are thoroughly sincere and deserve cooperation" without having to ask explicitly for support. If the representatives strived for subtlety, campaign organizers enjoined local exhibitors to secure cooperation more directly. MPGY's theater committee badgered them: "Nearly 100 cities report that exhibitor committee has visited newspapers and secured promises of unusual editorial support; special stories; full page ads; editorials, etc. Have you done this?" The Comerford circuit, with which Frank Walker was affiliated, exhorted managers to "acquaint the publishers with the fact that out of the million dollars raised by the industry, which includes a large sum from your theatre, half . . . is to be spent in newspaper publicity nationally and each daily paper will undoubtedly get their share of this huge amount. . . . This visit should find your publishers in a very receptive mood" and afford an opportunity to arrange for "special stories localizing this activity," as well as "constructive editorials" on motion pictures. Exhibitors would make their financial contributions and the quid pro quo arrangement clear to local newspapers; their theaters and the industry in general would reap the benefits.[21]

The efforts to solicit newspaper cooperation frequently paid off. Thirty-one of the newspapers in the sample ran at least one article on the campaign between September 1 and September 18 (the end of MPGY's third weekend, about ten days after the second institutional ad appeared). Almost half of them published two or three. The *Alton (IL) Evening Telegraph* and *Detroit Free Press* ran four or more articles; the *Salt Lake Tribune, Wilmington (DE) Morning News,* and *Fremont (NE) Daily Express* each threw their support behind MPGY with special sections that included articles, photographs, and ads from local businesses. With the exception of the *Kansas City Star,* every paper in which more than ten theaters advertised daily published an article on the campaign during this period (the *Star* published an editorial on it). In general MPGY received more coverage in newspapers from larger cities than from those in towns with the fewest theaters. This trend was most evident in the biggest cities, including New York, Chicago, Pittsburgh, and Los Angeles, which were not part of the sample. At the other end of the spectrum, the *Nogales Herald,* the only sample paper from a city with just one theater, published nothing at all on MPGY, even though the local theater advertised in it daily and promoted the contest heavily. Half of the towns with two operating theaters (Boulder, Ft. Lauderdale, and Santa Fe) published at least two articles on MPGY in their newspapers, while the other half (Bismarck, Canonsburg, and Hays) ran none at all, despite the participation of theaters in all six towns. While the lack of support in some small towns might have rankled local exhibitors, the cooperation of papers in large cities was more important to organizers and the interests they represented. These papers enjoyed greater circulation, and the important theater holdings of the major companies were concentrated there.

Not one of the articles published in the sample newspapers could be considered hostile to the campaign or to the industry. On the contrary, ringing endorsements were the rule overall. The remarkable consistency among the articles indicates that much of the content came from the campaign's own publicity machinery. During MPGY's first two days, the same article, with small variations, inaugurated the campaign in five newspapers. Each version began with more or less the same announcement as "Campaign to Boost Movies Is Underway":

> In every city, town and hamlet in the United States, there will start today a celebration of what "moving picturedom" confidentially considers "Motion Pictures' Greatest Year." This celebration will be touched off by the first appearances of a comprehensive and factual advertising campaign in daily newspapers. The campaign will be a cumulative statement of the essential character of motion picture entertainment in the social and cultural life of the people.
>
> It will bring forcefully to the attention of motion picture patrons the earnest and highly specialized efforts of Hollywood writers, directors, actors, and technicians in providing America with its most popular form of entertainment. A total of well over 2,000 daily newspapers will be used in bringing this essential character of motion picture entertainment to those who enjoy it as well as to those who are at present not enjoying it.

The one unusual refinement to this opening occurred in the *Daily Missoulian*. Someone there apparently read the article with enough care to realize that by launching a nationwide campaign, "moving picturedom" probably had meant to say that it "confidently" rather than "confidentially" considered this Motion Pictures' Greatest Year.[22]

Such a laughable error speaks to the haste with which the campaign was put together and the perhaps too-eager cooperation of newspapers in publicizing their benefactor's claims. The article was designed to attract editors and publishers, as well as to inform the public. It begins with MPGY but moves immediately to the importance of daily newspapers in "touch[ing] off" the celebration, via the ad campaign, whose "factual basis" the paper attests to. The newspapers cooperate insofar as the industry's story in the ads—the "essential" place of the movies in our "social and cultural life"—becomes the papers' story about the industry. By highlighting the contribution of "well over 2,000 daily newspapers" (a Hollywood number, not a factual one) in bringing the industry's virtues to the public, the article provided a bonus promotion of sorts for the papers they used.

The article acknowledged that America's "most popular form of entertainment" was currently not so popular with everyone. For those who needed a less abstract lesson about the place of movies in their lives, the basic mechanics of the contest were described. The article touted it as "one of the greatest and most interesting of national brain-twisters," which "will start a four month puzzle life" for patrons. By no means all newspapers relied so heavily on the industry's own rhetoric about the contest, which treated questions about the most trivial, even tedious, details of films as an exciting mental challenge, a kind of counterweight to frequent attacks on movies as insults to adult intelligence. But on the whole they were diligent in promoting the contest to readers if they published any articles on the campaign at all.

Indeed, it was common for newspapers scarcely to mention anything other than the contest, downplaying or bypassing the public relations angle, capitalizing in their own way on what was most sensational about MPGY in an era when such contests were something of a rage. For example, three of the four articles in the *Alton Evening Telegraph* focused exclusively on the contest, and the first drew attention to it as well. Such coverage helped exhibitors by "localizing" publicity and promoting attendance in lieu of abstract claims about the industry's merits. Several newspapers remarked the participation of their city's own theaters. The first of two MPGY articles in the *Bristol (VA) Herald Courier*, both of which focused on the contest, promoted the role of four local theaters, all Paramount affiliates, in bringing it to residents: "Bristol theaters have entered a nation-wide $250,000 cash prize contest . . . and their patrons will be eligible to compete for these prizes. . . . All theatres in the city will have booklets containing complete information." Residents of Bellingham, Washington, read that "four leading moving picture theaters" had come together to sponsor the contest and that exhibitors provided a concrete local service. In the words of the mayor, "In our own city the moving picture theaters have a strong place in the community, and provide employment for a large number of citizens." For the most part, however, the focus on the contest drew attention away from the campaign's broader goals; put another way, the public relations message always threatened to be overwhelmed by the publicity enlisted to disseminate it. The third and final newspaper ad, promoting only the contest, exemplifies this tension. In this version of the ad the noisy usher with his giant sack of gold sacrifices whatever restraint the institutional ads had managed to achieve (see figure 7).[23]

In competitive situations attention to the contest often operated to the exclusive benefit of the major companies. In New Brunswick, New Jersey, all three RKO theaters together promoted the contest and the quiz pictures they were playing on September 2. The *Daily Home News* ran one article on MPGY, devoted exclusively to the contest: "Cooperating locally are the RKO State, Rivoli and Albany. . . . When visiting one of these showplaces, ask the management for a contest booklet in which all rules and questions are published." Here coverage of MPGY amounted to an advertisement for a single major company, with none of the broader institutional benefits that a campaign to build good will for the movies in general was supposed to create. The *Daily Home News* had not reported the mid-August decision of Allied Theatre Owners of New Jersey to recommend its members boycott the campaign for fear that it would benefit the majors at the expense of independents. More typically, in Alton, Illinois, where two independent theaters pledged but only one paid, the city's Paramount-affiliated theaters were actively advertising themselves as "official $250,000 Movie Quiz Contest Theaters" by the time the *Evening Telegraph* ran the articles promoting the contest. Only the Paramount theaters had played quiz pictures and would do so until the end of October. The articles ostensibly in support of the campaign functioned as supplementary advertising for the company best positioned to cash in on the contest right away.[24]

Only the *Providence Journal* did not mention the contest in its article. It reported instead on an official proclamation by the governor of Rhode Island, who selected September 12 "for special observance of 'Motion Pictures' Greatest Year'" and urged "the citizens of the State to participate to the 'fullest measure in the celebration and presentation of the splendid pictures which have been prepared by the motion picture studios.'" The *Journal* may have covered the endorsement in an effort to treat MPGY in the context of something like an actual news story rather than as a favor engineered by paid advertising. Needless to

FIGURE 7. Contest advertising sometimes undermined the more dignified tone sought by campaign organizers. Harold B. Franklin Collection, Margaret Herrick Library, Academy of Motion Picture Arts and Sciences.

say, such proclamations were not spontaneous outbursts of enthusiasm from movie-loving politicians; the task of securing them from state and local officials often fell to exhibitors as well, who were instructed to use "the most influential means at [their] disposal." The proclamations not only supported the campaign's claims about the movies but also proved that the film industry enjoyed the warm support of some politicians at a time of active hostility toward it among others.[25]

Even though most articles focused on the contest at the expense of the campaign's loftier goals, they drew readers' attention to an enterprise in which the film industry had invested a million dollars and its reputation. So did editorials, the coveted prize of organizers. In mid-October MPGY's advertising committee claimed that 610 editorials had been published. An MPPDA analysis declared that 95.7 percent were favorable to the industry, 1.6 percent neutral, and only 2.7 percent adverse, demonstrating that the campaign's message was getting across, at least to those charged with delivering it. Harold Franklin distributed a simple bar graph with the data to "all regional chairmen, circuit heads, exhibitors, managers, and publicity directors," along with a column from *Film Daily,* which noted that although it was impossible to translate favorable editorials directly into box-office terms, benefits "promise to materialize as improved press, and hence public, relations." "Never before," Dietz enthused in a report to Schaefer, "has such an overwhelming manifestation of the good intentions of journalism toward the screen been so evident." Money well spent.[26]

A thirteen-page booklet, prepared for exhibitors, demonstrated the importance of the editorials. It included almost seventy excerpts from editorials published in the first two months of MPGY, including four from the sample newspapers. They came from all regions of the United States, and two were from Canada. Twenty-three states were represented, with more from New York and California than from others; city and small-town editors both had a voice. The booklet alerted exhibitors to the positive attention the campaign was generating and of the newspapers' good will toward the industry, that MPGY was worth their financial contribution and their further promotional efforts.

The editorials in the booklet often drew heavily from the language of the institutional ads and industry press releases. Several remarked on the harmony demonstrated by the different branches involved in the campaign, without examining too closely the basis of the industry's claims about it. None of the excerpts drew attention to the antitrust lawsuit or the conflicts that for years had divided the industry; instead, they applauded the "unprecedented" "co-operation" of producers, distributors, and exhibitors, who had at last "united" in a common purpose. Big numbers were bandied about to impress on readers the commitment of exhibitors of all stripes to MPGY. According to an editorial in the *Massillon (OH) Independent,* sixteen thousand theaters were participating; the *Hollywood Citizen-News* put the figure at seventeen thousand theaters, "every one in the United States and Canada." Articles in the sample newspapers made similar claims. For example, the *Waterloo (IA) Daily Courier* stated that "all American motion picture producers and theatres" were "co-operating in sponsoring the contest," a specter of industry-wide harmony of which campaign organizers had not dreamed. In reality, not even all the theaters in Waterloo sponsored it. Whatever these editorials and articles say about the incautious handling of material grounded in press releases, they suggested a stronger endorsement of the campaign among exhibitors and others than actually existed. The exaggerated impression of unity was beneficial to those who had organized it.[27]

Frequent references to the entertainment value of the movies were to be expected. The shortest excerpt, from the *Illinois State Journal,* read simply: "The advertising campaign launched by the picture industry to stimulate theatre attendance has for its slogan: 'The movies are your best entertainment.' Isn't it the truth?" Several newspapers commended the industry on the improvement of recent pictures and on the "amazing progress" it had made over the years. The vast majority was also adamant that "moving pictures do more than entertain." Hollywood might be remote, but movie theaters were always situated within particular communities, and they were treated as important civic institutions in the big city as well as the small town. "Whether on Broadway or on the back concessions," the *Telegraph-Journal* of Saint John, New Brunswick, in Canada wrote, "the movie house is a community centre," due largely to the breadth of the movies' appeal and their affordability. The *Boston Evening Transcript* agreed with the proclamation of the mayor, who called theaters "community centers which are the common meeting ground of all our citizens, young and old." To call the theater a community center and associate it with the prerogatives of citizenship was to insist that it performed a valuable, if vague, service that yielded benefits having nothing to do with the entertainment on the screen.[28]

The economic value of theaters was not slighted either, and several editorials described the contribution to the community in rather more substantial terms. "It is hard to conceive of a business center without a motion picture theater." The movies not only provided inexpensive entertainment, but "trade follows the silver screen." Theaters anchored local business districts, bringing patrons downtown during the evening, when otherwise they would stay at home. According to the *Stockton (CA) Record:* "Picture patronage and shop window viewing go hand in hand." Theaters supported local economies in other ways. A matter-of-fact excerpt from Lawton, Oklahoma, tallied the number of employees (forty) hired by the heads of the local movie theaters and the annual taxes the exhibitors paid ($18,000) and marveled that the film business could offer "the public the most inexpensive wholesome entertainment that it is possible to buy." These ways of thinking about the place of "the movies" were not particularly new. Since the early days, small-town exhibitors had fostered specific, lasting ties between their theaters and the community. But it was one thing for exhibitors to insist on these connections and quite another for theaters to be widely celebrated as necessary local institutions by an older and more venerated institution—the newspaper.[29]

The movies and the film industry assumed national importance as well. Several editorials described their influence on the economy, just as the ads had done, by creating employment: "Two hundred and eighty-two thousand men, women, and children depend on the movies for their livelihood," and another "237 industries are more or less dependent for existence" on them. More important, the movies "stimulat[e] the buying appetite" among millions of moviegoers, who naturally covet the things they see in films, creating markets for them at home and abroad. One did not need to work for the film industry, or even be particularly interested in its products, to experience its impact: "When the implement worker goes to his local movie-house he is supporting an advertising agency which as it reproduces a typical American farm scene, demonstrates the efficiency of the product of his factory to farmers and planters on the several continents." As "aggressive salesmen of American products," "the working silent partners of all American industry," the movies had the unique ability to sell "goods," as they did everything else, "on a colossal scale."[30]

The editorials were also pleased to call attention to one business in particular that the film industry was aiding: the newspaper business. The dailies often made use of MPGY, turning the institutional ad campaign to account at a time when their ad revenues had fallen steadily and many papers were consolidating or folding. In 1938 it was not at all unusual to see editorials that urgently promoted the value of advertising, a bald example of the newspaper's opinion-molding function subject to its bottom line. A few institutional ads may not have been enough to make or break individual papers, but by aggressively promoting both the decision to conduct the ad campaign in all North American dailies and the size of the appropriation, the film industry not only savored the showmanship such an announcement entailed but created surplus value for newspapers that may, as much as anything, have helped to bring about such a show of editorial support. The *Homestead (PA) Messenger,* for example, quoted an MPGY official on the ways films benefit business, before turning to the ways that newspapers benefit business:

> The value of newspaper advertising was clearly defined by the theatre executive.
> "We believe newspapers will enable us to reach the public with our message . . . more effectively, quickly and efficiently than any other medium."

The executive added "another compliment," not the part where he said that "'the newspapers have . . . on many occasions treated us unfairly,'" "'criticiz[ing] our industry for things which pass unnoticed in other[s],'" but his comment that their differences were "'minor'" in view of the "'cordial relationship'" that exists between the media, which "'warrants this mark of confidence by us.'" No greater sign of cordiality could be given than the film industry's spurning of "other" media, which really meant one medium: "After devoting considerable money to radio and other forms of advertising, the movie men have come to a full appreciation that their messages in the daily newspapers bring better results." MPGY argued not only for the importance of the movies to community and national well-being but also for the indispensability of newspaper advertising in selling these ideas to the public.[31]

With the campaign, the film industry also sought recognition as a serious and stable business that was not "the creation and the field of endeavor of zanies." A most gratifying aspect of the editorials, then, had to do with their frequent acknowledgment that the film industry belonged within the ranks of big business. For years Hollywood had boasted of its stature within American industry, and the editorials took up the cry: it "rank[s] among the greatest of the nation's enterprises in capital invested, in employment provided and in importance to the consuming public." The best evidence for its importance was the decision to launch MPGY. The recession of 1937–38 had daunted but not defeated the film industry. To meet the most recent economic crisis by spending money rather than by retrenchment, to demonstrate such "confidence in the future" and in itself, made the film industry "a shining example to other industries" and "to the rest of the nation." An editorial from the *New York Journal and American,* said to have "appeared in nearly all the Hearst papers," applauded the campaign for "giv[ing] powerful impetus to recovery programs in all industries," evidence that "the motion picture industry is capable of TAKING THE LEAD in the inevitable march of American industries back to normal and prosperous conditions." This was the sort of editorial attention and acclaim usually reserved for the bedrock American industries, automobiles or steel. In these editorials an industry better known for timidity than courage, one that was frequently criticized for its systematic avoidance of controversy, was reborn with a "tradition" of "bold, aggressive action" and "bold initiative." The boldness had nothing to do with the content of its films but rather with its daring investment in public relations. The editorial celebration of the film industry's courage and acumen was an exemplary public relations prize. Even if the nation's editors did not begin to hang on the pronouncements of Nicholas Schenck or Harry Warner, as they did Henry Ford's, the editorials disseminated a new impression of Hollywood, associating it both with a kind of radical thinking, necessary to dispel the climate of economic uncertainty and gloom, and with a model of conservative corporate citizenship, from which other American industries might well take their cue.[32]

Finally, many editorials supported the grounds on which the industry's claims to be "your best entertainment" ultimately rested: its "devot[ion] . . . the year round to learning what the public wants and to meeting the demand." As in the institutional ads, the industry is not presented as all-knowing but rather as a solicitous student of public preferences, possessing an exemplary "alertness to public opinion." The excerpt from the *Burlington Free Press and Times* was the only one to take as its subject the visit of the industry representative to discuss the movies. While the editor recognized that the purpose of the call was "primarily for . . . establishing better public relations," he believed that "the producers of films were sincerely interested in improving them, because they are coming to realize that it is what the majority of the people want." If the movies are "growing up," as he indicated at the end, it is because the producers are "getting acquainted with their audiences." Like Joe Doakes, "the public" is, as the title of one editorial put it, "the boss of motion pictures." For the *Cairo (IL) Citizen and Bulletin,* the institutional ads were great because they "reflect the opinion of the average man and woman and child who, after all, make the pictures what they are." A few editorials emphasized the challenge of making films to appeal to a wide variety of tastes: "The industry never loses sight of the fact that tastes are not all alike." Therein lies the miracle of its success, that it can "carry pleasing and highly satisfactory entertainment to the great majority of patrons." There is little to distinguish here between the editor and the Average Movie-Goer.[33]

Picking up on the fine print of the institutional ads, the *Sioux Falls Daily Argus-Leader* advised its readers on how to cooperate with the industry: "suggestions from the public will be invited. The people will be asked to criticize the films and to tell what in their opinion the industry can do to make its programs more entertaining and more worth while." A handful of editorials similarly treated the contest less as a gimmick to boost attendance, the way any bank or dish night was, than as a serious effort to increase the industry's knowledge of its customers. Yes, the contest was "a diversion, which will be immensely profitable to some," but it was also "a test of public sentiment. The industry knows that the public is boss and wants to know what the boss has to say." The *Cadillac (MI) Evening News* likewise believed that the contest would be used to "acquaint producers with trends and ideals of motion picture patrons"; the *Indianapolis News* described it as "an authentic survey of popular taste in movie entertainment." The contest would indicate thirty films of choice for millions of patrons, and the fifty-word essays on their favorite films might provide new information about how people responded to certain pictures—what they really enjoyed—rather than just confirming which movies they went to see. When the campaign was first announced, Schaefer had suggested that it would enable the organizers "to measure both patron and reader interest before and after the proposed contest and gather knowledge from which theatres naturally will benefit," another little effort to induce independent exhibitors to join.[34]

Fourteen newspapers in the sample ran editorials related to MPGY during the campaign's first two months. The editorials came from all regions of the country, except the Southwest, and from cities of all sizes. They reflected the views of the booklet's handpicked editorials in some respects but not all. None of them, even in the smallest cities, touted the value of theaters and movies to the local community. The industry's importance on the national scene was emphasized in a few. Film was called a "great" and "enormous" "industry," and attention focused on the thousands of people employed in it and the millions amused by it. There was otherwise little passionate promotion of the film industry as a serious and impressive business. The *Kansas City Star* mentioned the antitrust suit but only to say that the recent "alarming, if not colossal" decline in attendance concerned the industry far more. It commended the studios for their effort to turn out "better pictures." The *Frederick (MD) Daily News* offered a version of Ed Sullivan's apology for poor ones. The movies need to "appeal . . . to a great average of American taste and understanding," and it gave the size of "the output" as the reason "the product cannot be consistently great." Only two papers, already cited from the booklet, mentioned the industry's efforts to get to know audiences and to solicit criticism. Both also went on at some length about the movies' progress, including favorable comments on "clean" entertainment, with the *Burlington Free Press and Times* reviewing past transgressions in rather grim detail. All of this was edited out of the excerpts. Three editorials emphasized the advertising campaign and again championed the industry's faith in newspapers over radio and even its own movie screens as the means of handling it. On the whole, the tone of these editorials was favorable and flattering but lacked the euphoria that characterized many in the booklet.[35]

Unsurprisingly, the booklet contained no negative editorials on MPGY, but one in the sample was hostile. The *Hays (KS) Daily News* noted the launch of the advertising campaign but dispensed with the idea that the industry could simply advertise its way out of difficulties. The *News* did not assume the arrival of superior entertainment but demanded it: "One thing the picture industry must do is make better pictures." It expressed contempt for "contests of all kinds," the "quick-money schemes" that both theaters in Hays used to "bulge receipts" on slow nights. These games "have no relation whatsoever to their business . . . of entertaining patrons with pictures worth going to see. . . . Failure to confine their efforts to this demand of the public is the right answer to the question they themselves are asking, 'What's wrong with the picture business?'" The scolding in defense of the public is a swipe not only at poor showmanship and poor films but at the whole public relations enterprise, the industry's misguided approach to winning back the public.[36]

In a friendlier vein, an excerpted editorial from the *Charleston (WV) Gazette* suggested "that any who might have 'quit the movies' in a moment of pique venture back for at least one sample." In other words, patrons should no longer be mad at the movies, could no longer be if they experienced the new season's entertainment and properly understood the movies' social, cultural, and economic role, the great part played by "an institution far transcending a mere industry." The image of the film industry that emerges from the advertisements and the favorable editorials, especially the excerpts in the booklet, is of a united enterprise that performs a great public service, a forward-looking business that leads but also that listens, a benign institution that the public in some sense owns. Editorials that did not enter into the spirit of MPGY were relegated to an insignificant place on the bar graph. The film industry "had decided to go to the public with its story," and newspapers from across the country stepped in to interpret that story, for the most part endorsing the industry's accounts of itself and adding their sense of what it ought to be doing, while also addressing their needs as a medium facing challenges of its own.[37]

If the task of the contest was to provide an immediate stimulus to the box office, the institutional advertisements and the favorable press coverage they generated were designed to give the short-term gains something more substantial and lasting to build on. The booklet of editorials provided exhibitors with evidence that many of the nation's newspapers were willing to cooperate with the larger goals of the campaign, and Howard Dietz was no doubt sincere when he celebrated the good will in the press that MPGY had created. But exhibition was a local practice, and exhibitors surely knew whether or not their own dailies had penned favorable editorials and articles. In the event that positive coverage had not been forthcoming, it is hard to imagine that rave responses anyplace else would have compensated for it, that contributing independents in Alton or Nogales would have been impressed by the enthusiasm expressed by the *Portland News-Telegram* or the *Montreal Gazette*. Perhaps the purpose of the booklet was to inspire them to try (again) to enlist the cooperation of the local papers and to throw their all into promoting the campaign at home. Or perhaps it was merely supposed to reassure them that MPGY was not the debacle many in the industry suspected.

At any rate the actual impact of favorable MPGY editorials and articles on public perceptions of the industry is really no clearer than the impact of criticisms made by gossip columnists. Despite the trouble and expense of the campaign, the thing most likely to improve the public's attitude toward the movies, as the *Hays Daily News* suggested, was the movies themselves. The question remains of what role the ninety-four movie quiz contest pictures, Hollywood's self-proclaimed "finest array of productions" ever, played in MPGY's efforts to shore up ailing box offices. To what extent might these films have helped or hindered the larger purpose of the campaign, to reignite the public's commitment to Hollywood and its products? How did they work as public relations devices?

The quiz pictures were in the works before MPGY was announced, let alone launched; many of them, and certainly the most ambitious, were under way in advance of the bad publicity that helped to fuel the industry's sense of crisis. But the box-office troubles had registered well before 1938 began, and the dirty laundry was there before industry spokesmen took it upon themselves to air it. The crisis of confidence that made MPGY necessary found its way into these productions. Above all, the campaign and the industry's struggles created a vital context for the promotion and reception of these films; the industry might insist that "motion pictures are your best entertainment" and that *you* are "boss," but it was up to the films to prove it. It is difficult, of course, to evaluate the entertainment value of these movies on anything but the most personal grounds, although exhibitor reports, reviews, box-office tallies, and a handful of extant contest essays provide useful hints. A number of films confront the issue of the movies' value to the public and weigh their obligations to it. They solicit the public as collaborators and dramatize Hollywood's allegiance to gratifying it. In other words, these films should be considered not only as entertainment, or as the products of particular studios and individuals, shaped by diverse strategies and goals, but as promotional efforts, a more sophisticated level of institutional advertising. It's time to see what audiences found awaiting them in theaters during Motion Pictures' Greatest Year.

PART TWO

The Films

CHAPTER 4

"The Finest Array of Productions"

NINETY-FOUR FILMS

In many ways the campaign films resembled any three-month slice of Hollywood product at the transition to a new season. There were films across a range of budgets, from costly spectacles to programmers and the cheap Bs that produced reliable profits, if little glory, thanks to block booking and double features. Superspecials were very much in evidence: *Marie Antoinette, The Great Waltz,* and *Sweethearts* from MGM; *Alexander's Ragtime Band* and *Suez* from Fox; *Men with Wings* and *Spawn of the North* from Paramount; *Carefree* from RKO; *You Can't Take It with You* from Columbia. Four were left over from the 1937–38 season: *Alexander's Ragtime Band,* which became the highest grossing film of the year, was released on August 19, *Marie Antoinette* and *Spawn of the North* a week later, and *Carefree* on September 2, each welcoming audiences back to the majors' urban theaters at the start of the campaign, after the typical summer decline in attendance.

Among the eight majors, only Warner Bros. did not release any million-dollar productions during MPGY. The company long known for economy had gone wild during 1937–38 after the recovery of the previous year, bringing out no fewer than seven pictures costing more than $1 million each, including its most expensive film to date, *The Adventures of Robin Hood.* The recession brought the studio back to earth; Warners made only two films costing more than $1 million for the whole of the 1938–39 season. It released thirteen films as part of the campaign, five fewer than during the same three-month period in 1937. The average cost per picture was significantly higher for the MPGY films ($475,230 vs. $353,444), a consequence of producing fewer low-budget films and focusing instead on films of moderate cost (six in the $500,000–$600,000 range), to attract without dazzling audiences back into theaters. For MGM and RKO, the other companies for which the financial data are available, the difference from the same period in the previous year was less pronounced. RKO produced the same number of films for MPGY (eleven), MGM one more (thirteen), with each also distributing a film for an outside producer. RKO's production costs dropped from $392,090 to $348,727 per film, with seven pictures (vs. five) under $200,000; just two big films accounted for almost half the cost of all in both years. MGM's costs rose by an almost equivalent amount, from $928,500 to $969,153 per film, including four films at $1.5 million or higher (vs. three). RKO, not yet out of bankruptcy, continued to fight for its place among the top five companies, while MGM remained the industry's stunner, spending and risking big in spite of the recession.[1]

United Artists and Monogram released the fewest pictures as part of the campaign. Five independent producers distributed through UA. The pictures were typically costly, all As, with such stars as Janet Gaynor, Fredric March, Gary Cooper, Merle Oberon, and Charles Boyer, while Sabu headed the cast of Alexander Korda's *Drums,* the one British film in the campaign. The four offerings of Monogram, the only independent production company to join MPGY, were just as typically cheap, all B films. But they were its better Bs, with Boris Karloff, Anne Nagel, Jackie Moran, and Frankie Darrow. It was the only company not to have all of its feature film output over three months included in the campaign. Monogram's contribution would not help to bolster the industry's reputation for quality, but its participation usefully broadcast that independent companies could cooperate with the Big Eight, despite the latter's close, often exclusive, and mutually beneficial ties.[2]

Moviegoers might also have been struck by a certain familiarity in the approach to programming the campaign films, which were treated in publicity as though all were part of the heralded new 1938–39 season. The "finest array of productions" encompassed the usual range of genres, a mix highlighted as evidence of the movies' breadth of appeal— its *something for everyone* philosophy, according to an article based on an industry press release, which sometimes appeared as "Patrons Dictate Plots for 94 New Release Pictures." Straight comedies and comedy dramas abounded; every major except Columbia had at least one musical; the western was represented by RKO and Paramount (Monogram's westerns were not part of its campaign offerings); crime films continued to be a staple at Warners and Columbia, and every studio except MGM made at least one, mostly low-budget affairs; there were several mysteries too. For prestige there were costume biopics. For thrills there were action pictures. For a good cry there were melodramas. For confusion these categories often overlapped. There was little here to suggest that Hollywood was exactly reinventing itself.[3]

Film genres enabled classical Hollywood studios to strike a balance between competing imperatives: to standardize enough to operate efficiently and economically while satisfying audience demand for novelty. They gave rise to familiar narrative and stylistic conventions; repeated, with variation, film genres met audience expectations while providing something new. Thus "Patrons Dictate" noted the gangster film was getting another makeover, now adopting "a more serious or sociological angle," thanks in part to the success of *Dead End* (1937). *The Amazing Dr. Clitterhouse,* for example, counts as a gangster film, but the off-casting of Edward G. Robinson and the plot offer unusual touches. Robinson played a brilliant doctor with a lucrative practice. Hiding his identity, Clitterhouse joins and eventually commands a gang of thieves in order to study criminal physiology and psychology. Claire Trevor, as his fence, furnishes a romantic angle. He is well liked by most of the gang, and there are some deft comic touches, building on Robinson's turn in the innovative and successful gangster comedy, *A Slight Case of Murder* (1938). *The Amazing Dr. Clitterhouse* was well reviewed overall, and was Warners' third most profitable MPGY picture, but some critics noted that Robinson's past roles made it difficult to accept him as a cultured man of science. Another sort of gangster film, *Algiers,* is a kind of limit case of Hollywood's inability to mass-produce anything. It is a virtual duplication of the French masterpiece *Pépé le Moko* (1937), whose plot revolves around the criminal Pépé (Jean Gabin), who is lured from the safety of the Kasbah to his death when he falls in love. Producer Walter Wanger could copy an excellent French film because French films hardly mattered in the American market. It would seem new, even exotic, to audiences. Indeed, the fact that it was so much a copy made it one of MPGY's most original films. But Wanger could only make this same/different film once.[4]

A remarkable feature of the campaign films was the number of series represented. A successful series could achieve an ideal, inexpensive balance between standardization and novelty, allowing studios to recycle popular characters, as well as general storytelling conventions, while creating new situations for them. It could develop a fan base across a number of presold films, giving these B movies unusual traction. While disparaging expensive failures, the exhibitors' "box-office poison" ad had lauded the success of the cheaply produced Charlie Chan and Mr. Moto films, as well as the Jones and Hardy Family series, and demanded more. *The Hollywood Reporter* noted in November that series had "become rampant," with twenty-five in the works. Fox led the way in series production under Sol Wurtzel. Apart from pictures starring Jane Withers, a popular child star, its strategy was to make every B part of a series. Five of Fox's fourteen quiz pictures were from a series, including *Mysterious Mr. Moto,* with Peter Lorre, and *Safety in Numbers,* the third Jones Family installment of the year. Fox inaugurated three new series during MPGY: Roving Reporters with *Time Out for Murder;* Big Town Girls with *Meet the Girls;* and Sports Adventure with *Speed to Burn.* Fifteen of the ninety-four contest films were listed as series pictures, including westerns, mysteries, crime films, and comedies. *Freshman Year* and *Swing That Cheer* were the initial offerings of Universal's new Collegiate series. The *Reporter* speculated that series might become the "Solution to [the] 'B' Problem." The campaign gave series pictures a kind of added value, advertising not only the current film but those to come, while also promoting the idea of the series as such. Columbia and Warners were the only studios not to have any series pictures in the contest, but they didn't miss by much. Warners' *Nancy Drew—Detective* and Columbia's *Blondie* both came out in November. Unfortunately, series production was already pronounced "on [the] downgrade" by late December. They were great in theory but hard to sustain in practice. Fox, it turned out, was eliminating all but the Motos, the Chans, and the Jones Family films, just another little miscalculation during a volatile year.[5]

While the campaign insisted that motion pictures in general "are your best entertainment," it also claimed that ninety-four particular pictures made it the industry's "greatest year." Although certain more ambitious or expensive films tended to be highlighted, as usual, what made the fall of 1938 different from previous seasons was that the contest "compelled the producers to announce all films to be released" over an extended period for the first time, turning ritually vague claims of merit into promises about the concrete entertainment value of a list of actual films, each cited by name in the booklet. These promises were amplified by a cooperative press and echoed repeatedly in the business-as-usual promotion of individual movies. In other words, the campaign films, alone and as a package, were in a position to prove—or disprove—to moviegoers the slogan on which the industry believed its fortunes rested. The risk of the nationwide public relations campaign was not . simply that it might fail to stimulate attendance but that its failure had the potential truly to embarrass the industry. The campaign films might support the idea that those who made the movies possessed sound judgment and labored in a productive partnership with the public. Or they might instead demolish the industry's claims to know anything at all about the public and what it wanted, as the abrupt termination of Fox's three new series suggests. The invitation to test the premise that "motion pictures are your best entertainment" against audience members' own reception of every picture put out by the majors challenged the foundations of the film industry, whose purported obligation to do no more than entertain rested on its capacity to do at least that.[6]

THE DEATH OF GLAMOUR

Beyond the novelty of the contest framework there was something distinctive about MPGY movies, the way they aspired to please, and how they were sold individually and in clusters to the public. Indeed, 1938 was an extraordinary year in Hollywood filmmaking, and the series pictures are an important part of the story. Many of Hollywood's pieties, that glamour was a bedrock of the movies' appeal, that audiences wanted above all to escape from their own lives into a different, more attractive and luxurious cinematic world, disintegrated in light of their presumed resistance to many of the old formulas. There was a turn to new types of stories and characters and stars. These developments were not a product of MPGY but rather an effect of the conditions that inspired it, from the desire to rekindle the interest and affection of patrons to the pursuit of greater economy during the downturn. As such, it was a stroke of good fortune, as well as an opportunity, that a trend already falling into place by the time the campaign was announced—toward films that purported to feature ordinary, true-to-life characters and situations and to be driven more by story than spectacle—proved so well suited to the purposes of an institutional project that sought to convince the public of the industry's abiding loyalty. In other words, MPGY coincided with a new, well-publicized, and warmly welcomed change that facilitated the industry's claims to meet the needs of the public, by putting something like the public itself on the screen.

The "box-office poison" ad, and the furor it caused, is illustrative in this context. The ad is usually remembered, if at all, in relation to the careers of the stars denounced in it: the beginning of the end for Joan Crawford at MGM and a backdrop for Katharine Hepburn's flight from failure in Hollywood to Broadway and redemption in *The Philadelphia Story*, with which she relaunched her movie career a few years later. But for the industry the ad's significance had more to do with the suggestion of a broader shift in tastes away from some of the staples of 1930s filmmaking, a suggestion that could not help but give the film companies pause as they performed their own box-office tallies.

The ad named seven "stars" "whose public appeal is negligible," although it hinted darkly at "many, many others." In addition to Hepburn and Crawford, they were Greta Garbo, Mae West, Kay Francis, Marlene Dietrich, and Edward Arnold. Arnold's presence on this list was an anomaly to say the least. Unlike the rest of his derided colleagues, Arnold was a notable character actor. He had received top billing in his previous two pictures, including the expensive, unsuccessful *Toast of New York* (1937) at RKO, and exhibitors may have resented that his name was now expected to carry a film as though he were a star. He was not, as newspaper coverage of the controversy indicates. The vast majority of articles in the sample newspapers did not even bother to mention his name and only did so if the names of all were listed. The exhibitors' criticisms of Arnold were not really news, unlike their objections to the others.

The press coverage focused on the actresses, among the most famous and highest paid female stars of the decade. What these women had in common, in addition to their gender, was their glamour—even West, who inhabited its campy extreme. Amid the Depression and its deprivations, the 1930s is often considered the zenith of Hollywood glamour, which was particularly associated with female movie stars and their highly publicized effects on fashion and standards of femininity. The topic of glamour generated considerable interest in fan magazines, and the names of all the "poison" actresses appeared in discussions of it. A 1931 article in *Photoplay* informed readers that "charm" was out; instead, "You Must Have GLAMOUR!" and it identified Garbo, Dietrich, Crawford, and Francis, among other actresses, as examples of the "new fad." The article was less decisive when it came to defining the term: "Glamour is as elusive as Garbo being interviewed." That Garbo emerged as the enduring icon of Hollywood glamour, its "very quintessence," was not unrelated to the "magic spell of mystery" she had woven about herself; Garbo and the glamour she embodied shared a basic and compelling inscrutability.[7]

Articles about glamour often pointed readers to the literal definition of the term, only to marvel at its inadequacy. "The dictionary doesn't give a very complete definition of it. 'Enchantment,' it says, and that's perfectly true. 'A charm or spell, as one which deceives the sight.' . . . And that may be true, too, but it isn't all." The glamour of *glamour* had to do with its intangibility, a property it shared with the films that circulated it. Writers attempted to demystify it but often had to acknowledge their inability to do so: "I personally haven't been able to get the straight of the thing." "Nobody knows what glamour actually is." To explain would begin to deglamorize it. An article published under Myrna Loy's name voiced her thoughts on this "important but terribly confusing" topic: "That is one of the nice things about glamour as a subject for conversation; you don't have to know what you are talking about." Paragraphs later, efforts to establish its essence foiled, she ended back where she began, still confused: "It is something which we can appreciate without knowing what it is."[8]

The suppleness of the term meant that Hollywood could always be glamorous, but how one defined it could change to accommodate new styles and personalities. It might be about excess and ostentation in one incarnation, the "milk bath type of glamour," and about good taste and restraint a few years later. Glamour distinguished stars from ordinary people but was also democratic: fans could cultivate it with the proper instruction and effort. Glamour never disappeared—the term had long since become a virtual, vital shorthand for the lure of Hollywood and the movies—and yet in 1938 it faltered to an extraordinary degree. The word *glamour* was not mentioned in the exhibitors' ad, but many articles on the controversy from a variety of sources drew attention to it anyway in reporting on the actresses' declining popularity. Headlines for the newspaper articles differed, but many offered some variation on "Are Glamor Girls Slipping at Box Office?" with photos of three or four of the actresses (see figure 8). *Business Week* summed up the whole controversy, predicting dire things for summer theater attendance, with the article "Glamour under Fire." Even fan magazines wondered whether "the day of the glamor girl" had "gone by." The verdict on the ad was that it had established the public's disenchantment with glamour itself.[9]

The exhibitors made a point of saying that they had no complaints about anyone's talent; they objected only to the films' failure to make money, despite the stars' "tremendous salaries." Whatever else glamour

Are Glamor Gals Slipping?

FIGURE 8. Attention surrounding the "box-office poison" debacle focused on glamorous female stars, as in this frequently printed composite image. *Elkhart (IN) Truth,* May 5, 1938, 19.

was, it was usually expensive; its appurtenances included such things as elaborate wardrobes and splendid sets, and the more highly paid the star, the more costly the picture in general. As has frequently been noted, movie stars were supposed to function as a kind of "insurance policy" or "probable guard against loss" for expensive films. The economic fact of a star's past popularity with the public, having propelled her or him to stardom in the first place, offered some measure of security for the studios' future investments. The ad offered a rather different account of the situation: "the studios find themselves in the unhappy position of having to put these box office deterrents in expensive pictures in the hope that some return on the investment might be had." In other words, expensive pictures had now become the insurance for overpriced stars, but the protection was not paying out.[10]

The exhibitors applauded Paramount's "cleverness and consideration" in settling Dietrich's contract without making her final picture. They fretted over Kay Francis, Warners' highest paid star at $5,250 a week, who nonetheless appeared in B pictures. Better known for her wardrobe than her acting, Francis's "entire career was based on fashion and glamour." She sued the company in 1937, claiming that a part she had been promised in *Tovarich* (1937) went to Claudette Colbert and that Warners had reneged on its contractual obligation to provide her with superior stories. She dropped the suit, but her complaints were not unjustified. As Warners' spending grew more lavish overall in 1937–38, the budgets for her films plummeted, the better roles going to Bette Davis. After the suit Warners kept Francis busy in inferior productions to squeeze what profits it could from her, and perhaps to try to humiliate her into quitting, before letting her contract expire in September 1938. Given the volume of her output, it was virtually certain that she would have a film represented in MPGY, and she was the only one of the six "poison" actresses who did. *Secrets of an Actress* was not a picture to restore her reputation. Francis played Fay Carter, a road-company actress who decides to conquer Broadway with the help of a besotted architect cum aspiring theatrical producer (Ian Hunter). Recycled from her previous potboilers, the plot develops around a romantic triangle, with Hunter, yet again, nobly bowing out, to George Brent this time, whom she really loves. But unlike *Stolen Holiday* and *Another Dawn* (both 1937), Hunter does not kill himself for Francis: he simply lets Warners' disloyal, overpriced liability go.[11]

The star most likely to be defended against the charges was Crawford. A few of her films had underperformed (not doing "the business expected of a Crawford picture"), but the producers had themselves to blame for casting her in such poor vehicles: "There is nothing wrong with Crawford that a good picture won't cure." Of the seven stars, only she had been systematically marketed to the public as a figure for it; audience identification was the cornerstone of her success. With "a screen personality [created] from scratch," Crawford, once a "shopgirl" herself, had become the "Shopgirl's Dream," the attractive, modern, working-class woman who made good in many films. While the box-office problems of Garbo, Dietrich, and Hepburn were sometimes linked to their qualities as people and to their standoffishness with the public—declining interviews, shunning publicity, and, in Dietrich's case, "becoming too engrossed in her glamor"—Crawford was notoriously cooperative with the press and gracious to fans, acknowledging her obligations to the paying customers who had made her a star.[12]

Still, after ranking in the top ten of the *Motion Picture Herald*'s annual exhibitors' poll of "Money-Making" stars from 1932 to 1936, she dropped off the list in 1937. It was observed that Crawford's transition from "a dancing lady to a grand lady" might have harmed her. "Making good" in her films often meant being rescued from drudgery and obscurity because her taste, manners, and comportment raise her above others of her class. That is, Crawford could embody the "shopgirl's dream" because her own extraordinary qualities had surmounted the all but unbridgeable gap between dreaming it and living it. Even in *The Bride Wore Red* (1937), a notable failure that one writer rechristened "The Exhibitor Saw Red," her character chooses obscurity only after rejecting an upper-class marriage. Anni Pavlovitch (Crawford) is a singer in a dingy café, where she meets cynical Count Armalia (George Zucco). He gives her clothing and money for a two-week resort holiday to prove his theory that only luck distinguishes aristocrats from peasants. His friend Rudi Pal (Robert Young) believes that breeding is all; deceived by Anni/Crawford's noble bearing, he falls in love. Anni ultimately prefers Giulio (Franchot Tone), a peasant indifferent to these distinctions. Anni bears out both the count's theory that aristocratic behavior is made not born and the film's theory that such behavior can be learned at the movies. When the count first admires her "charming manners," she tells him, tartly: "I go to the movies. I watch the ladies of your world." Anyone can watch and learn; that Anni can do more than watch is a function of being in a movie instead of just seeing one. Luck may be all that distinguishes aristocrats from singers, or stars from shopgirls for that matter, but luck in the form of serendipitous counts and simple peasants who look and sound like Tone, her real-life Hollywood husband, is a quality far more readily available in the movies than out of them.[13]

Crawford survived the "poison" controversy, but under the contract she signed with MGM just before it erupted, she was already to receive $25,000 less per picture. She may have been the shopgirl's dream, but in 1938 there developed something more like an interest in the shopgirl's reality, and the "box-office poison" ad helped the industry, its critics, and anyone else with an investment in the movies to give voice to it. The editor of *Photoplay* observed that the stars named in the ad had "one thing in common":

> They all play people whom the average movie-goer could never imagine himself being. . . . How can we put ourselves into the place of Dietrich, who, swathed in fur from neck to ankle, suffers over whether she shall deceive her husband or her lover? Mae West amused us at first, but we couldn't keep on indefinitely imagining ourselves back in the '90's flirting with crooked politicians. . . . And Miss Francis is really somehow too removed from us in her eternal velvet evening gowns. Garbo took up playing long-dead, unknown queens and courtesans. Edward Arnold has played few modern roles since his stardom, nor Hepburn either, and Miss Crawford's excursion back into American History in "The Gorgeous Hussy" was anything but exciting.

Even Crawford, true to type as an innkeeper's daughter who becomes the official hostess for President Andrew Jackson, was growing away from her audience. The ad identified the stars that exhibitors wanted more of, "the Myrna Loys and Gary Coopers and Sonja Henies," names that were among the top-ten big-money stars in the poll of 1937. Their appeal, along with that of Shirley Temple, Clark Gable, Robert Taylor (the top three in the *Herald*'s poll), and other ranking favorites, was that "they are human, understandable, co-operative, and kind." There was nothing standoffish about them; they are all "regular fellows," "your kind of folks, and mine."[14]

The demystification of Hollywood stars has previously been linked to damage mitigation. Scandals over immoral behavior and negative attention to extravagant salaries and lifestyles, potentially dangerous during the lean years of the 1930s, required them to appear to be more like "us." In addition, the transition to sound conferred new "reality and intimacy to the film-going experience" in the 1930s; star voices helped to bring once inaccessible ideals down to earth. More and more, stardom combined "the spectacular with the everyday, the special with the ordinary." What is striking about 1938 is the effort put into stripping away the special and spectacular, as well as the emphasis on the popular revolt against such qualities and the sort of stories that suited them, the tales of gorgeous hussies and mistresses, in a virtual sprint to the commonplace. The "just folks" approach became the way to explain the difference between the stars on the wane and those whom the public continued to embrace: "The fans are fed up on glamor and want their stars to be real human beings." People were now assumed to demand stars who were mirrors of themselves. Glamour may have been potentially available to all, if the fashion and fan magazines were to be believed; however, in 1938 the democratic channels more urgently ran the other way. An ordinary humanness was something even movie stars could achieve. Another flurry of publicity highlighting the normal lives that stars lived—the preference for cozy dinners at home over night-clubs, the joys of parenthood, a disdain for late parties—was of the sort that pleased nagging critics of movie morals, but it had to do now with convincing ordinary moviegoers that stars had exactly the same habits, yearnings, and responsibilities they did.[15]

Just as the "poison" actresses came in for special attention from the press, so, too, did Henie and Loy in the months following the ad's publication. Between them, "you couldn't ask for two more human gals." Henie is not as well remembered today, and if a champion Olympic athlete from Norway does not quite seem like "just folks," there was at least a consonance between the smiley European ice-skater she played in several films for Fox and the smiley European skater she was. The MPGY film *My Lucky Star* made a point of cultivating Henie's human image, at the insistence of Zanuck. Kristina Neilson (Henie) works as a wrapper in a department store. She is sent to nearby Plymouth University as a kind of living mannequin; outfitted with a fabulous array of winter outfits, she changes clothes several times a day, promoting the store to other students while keeping her employment a secret. Unfortunately, the young clothes horse attracts a lot of hostility. Her admirer, Larry Taylor (Richard Greene), finally explains that not everyone is rich like she is. Larry knows she is "a regular fellow" underneath all the fancy clothes, but she needs to "show" it. Happily, being a champion ice-skater is no barrier to this goal. Henie is another (if lesser) "aristocrat of talent," the quality that made Fred Astaire deservedly, indeed, democratically different from everyone else without making his superiority to us uncomfortably uppermost. Kristina skates on behalf of the college, and once she stops parading her clothes and starts behaving like a regular coed, everyone starts buying them. When she is mistakenly implicated in a scandalous love triangle with George Cabot Jr. (Cesar Romero), the son of the department store's owner, she can negotiate the settlement with his wife, who recognizes her innocence without sharing it: "You're just a nice, sweet, wholesome kid," the antithesis of glamour's aspirations.[16]

By 1938 Loy's career had come to embody the trajectory describing the changing taste in stars. She began in silent films, playing glamorous exotics and sirens, but the "movies guessed it wrong," as an article about the actress in *Life* gleefully put it in 1938. "The one thing no one ever thought of was to cast her just as she was, just a charming, quiet, well-bred American girl." The turning point was *The Thin Man* (1934); never mind that Loy's Nora Charles had money and glamour to spare. The famous legacy of that film was to romanticize marriage, to make the usual thing somehow extraordinary. In other movies she domesticated the unusual, as in *Test Pilot*—MGM's million-dollar *mea culpa* for *Parnell* (1937)—in which Loy as Gable's wife, fresh from a Kansas farm, literally brings him down to earth. By then she was being celebrated as the embodiment of "the idealized image of woman, as wife, sweetheart, and mother." The article in Loy's name that meditated on the nature of glamour a few years earlier would have been unthinkable in the delicate year of 1938, when she came to represent the sweet virtues of normalcy (see figure 9). By then she was reported to have claimed that she "wouldn't know what glamor was if it were mailed to me in a Christmas package."[17]

In 1937 Loy was voted "Queen of the Movies," with Gable as her king, by readers of more than fifty newspapers in a poll conducted by Ed Sullivan. Her claim to the throne was only strengthened following the "box-office poison" ad, and the popularity of Loy and Henie was exploited right into the campaign. Their faces often beamed at readers in a September series of articles that appeared in many daily newspapers, announcing that the "'Natural Girl' Is Queen Now!" Natural girls like Loy and Henie had deposed the "Glamor Girl of yesterday," who "Does Fadeout." The juxtaposition of glamour and nature reinforced what was implicit in the idea of glamour as something you could learn: to acquire it was in a sense to be false to yourself. "A glamorous person appears to be something which she isn't!" *Naturalness* was seen as a refinement of self, an expression of one's own personality, the other a gilding over it. Glamour was identified with phoniness, whether it involved wearing "layers of purple eye shadow to try to look wan and pale" or "walking shoes" that couldn't really "be walked in." The

FIGURE 9. In the MGM campaign film *Too Hot to Handle*, Myrna Loy, here with costar Clark Gable, embodied the qualities of the "natural girl," even while playing a celebrated pilot.

natural girl "stays away from high fashions, the flights of fancy which are worn by all and sundry today and gone tomorrow." Being natural had to do with much more than appearances. The natural girl's "manners are simple, sincere, healthily natural," and they were reflected in her common sense, quiet good taste, and self-sufficiency. The emphasis on health redescribed glamour as something like illness. The emphasis on the natural and normal turned it into a kind of freakishness.[18]

With a whole host of suggestions about how to accomplish the right look and feel of the thing, naturalness was, of course, as manufactured as glamour. Being natural, embracing genuineness more or less genuinely, was never as simple as just being yourself. And 1938's enthusiasm for the *natural* looked a lot like the praise for "a healthy, solid and substantial glamour" in 1935. The *natural* may have been another turn of glamour's many screws rather than a wholesale rejection of it. But the rhetoric of the time presented naturalness and glamour as different, indeed, utterly incompatible, ends. Glamour as such, "Hollywood's most marketable commodity," had become a very hard sell by the time MPGY rolled out.[19]

The natural girl was put before the public as a figure for it. Women sought to emulate her, readers were told. Men and women liked her and wanted to be liked by her. It was "unexpected" to "find" the natural girl "in the places where affectation has been a virtue rather than a fault," most pointedly, in Hollywood, but this wonderful creature abounded there, including some lesser-known actresses that studios wanted to promote in their MPGY films. The "box-office poison" ad had only exacerbated the studios' never-ending quest to discover "new faces." In addition to Loy *(Too Hot to Handle)* and Henie, MPGY natural girls included Marjorie Weaver *(Hold That Co-ed)*, Margaret Tallichet *(Girls' School)*, Arleen Whelan *(Gateway)*, and Anita Louise *(The Sisters* and *Marie Antoinette)*, among several others who were not specifically featured in the articles. All exemplified modesty, simplicity, and good taste. The claim for Paramount's *Men with Wings* was a sign of the times: "In Hollywood, where the 'glamour standard' takes the place of the 'gold standard,' vivacious Louise Campbell has the distinction of being the girl who was given her big chance because a producer believed she 'lacked glamour'!" In April, Whelan, a former manicurist on whom Fox pinned high hopes, was promoted as "one of Hollywood's newest and most glamorous 'finds'"; in September her "naturally feminine figure" "typif[ied]" the "new ideal" against which "the painfully thin, languidly drooping figure of the passé Glamor Girl" was harshly judged. The description of Whelan's slim figure hardly differed from one story to the next; the change lay in what one should call it, in what would sell. Of the French actress Annabella, a recent import who appeared in *Suez,* an article subheading informed: "Hollywood Sought to Make a Glamor-Girl out of Annabella—And Very Nearly Ruined Her Screen Personality. Now She's to Be Herself, and as a Result Is Due to Become Star." As with Loy's evolving screen persona, Annabella's transformation was not treated as evidence of the film industry's ability to adapt to changing tastes but rather of its incompetence, its insistence on trying to make stars into something they are not.[20]

The article on Annabella was an effort to banish glamour by decree. She was hardly a "natural" with American audiences newly primed for their stars to be "regular folks" like us, folks who mostly have, for example, a last name. Even among the more natural natural girls the new style was hardly a guarantee of stardom. In the end, by far the most important "new face" to be featured in MPGY was the only one to be associated with glamour to the exclusion of almost everything else. The big news about *Algiers* was Hedy Lamarr, or Hedy *Glamarr* as she was nicknamed, an exotic European beauty in her first American role. Much of the discourse around the movies at this time, including the industry's own, loudly repudiated glamour, but under the right circumstances there was eagerness enough to embrace the talismanic appeal of this Hollywood mainstay. There would always be room for a Lamarr amid the promotion of other kinds of faces, always a commitment to satisfying a diversity of tastes. The obscurity of Weaver, Tallichet, Whelan, Campbell, and Louise today, as well as some of the other young MPGY actresses we will meet, implies that the category of "the natural" was not in and of itself a natural sell or that Hollywood was not especially adept at marketing it, in the 1930s at least. It indicates the extent to which a certain otherworldly glamour is the enduring legacy of stardom in this decade.[21]

HUMAN FILMS

Lamarr was an exception in 1938, when the industry latched on to the public's ostensible preference for stars who were more like real people, in stories that might happen to such people. The effort to respond to, while also crafting, new allegiances, to run with a trend already in the making, shaped many aspects of MPGY. Early reports on the campaign acknowledged that glamour was a crucial feature of the movies and that audiences needed a reminder of its importance. One emphasized that the purpose of MPGY was "to sell the glamour of motion pictures, to sell the entertainment value of motion pictures, and to make people motion-picture minded," as though these goals were inevitably linked. Despite such announcements, however, there was actually very little selling of glamour at all. With all their verbiage, the ads themselves refrained from mentioning the word. Indeed, the campaign's principal spokespeople—the Average Movie-Goer and his family, Joe Doakes and Marge—pretty much killed glamour in its tracks.[22]

The Average Movie-Goer ad evoked, instead, the movie families that were so attractive to studios, exhibitors, and, apparently, audiences in 1938, when the "family type" picture took its place alongside comedies, musicals, and crime films as a category of new releases. Among the many series pictures in production this year was the family series, the most important of all. The trend originated in 1936, with the first of many Jones Family films for Fox, which followed the comic adventures of John Jones (Jed Prouty)—a goofy, Babbitty, small-town druggist—and his brood. The actors who portrayed the family were a set of "plain-looking people, without a glimmer of glamour," the better to represent "average Americans." MGM gave the family series a measure of prestige with the Hardy films. The Hardy series was born with *A Family Affair* (1937), an inexpensive film about a sober small-town judge, played by the A-list Lionel Barrymore, and his tribulations at work and home. In it, Judge Hardy risks winning reelection by delaying a popular aqueduct project as the law requires. Powerful enemies manufacture evidence of the infidelity of his married daughter, Joan (Julie Hayden), and blackmail him. The climax comes at the nominating convention, when the judge denounces the project and defends his daughter. He stands before the people "not as a candidate" but as one of them: "a fellow citizen, concerned in the things you're concerned in. And as a father." His credibility with his peers restored, they nominate him by acclamation.[23]

A Family Affair turned a neat profit and met with some acclaim of its own among small-town and rural exhibitors, some of whom wrote to the *Herald* to embrace it as the right kind of movie for their patrons, a modest story about modest people, that outperformed some of its overblown competition: "A grand picture for small towns . . . the type we need in these small communities," and "another of those down-to-earth features of a typical American family that is better entertainment than many of the so-called specials." Following Fox's lead, MGM developed a series after recasting parents Barrymore and Spring Byington, who was serially busy as Mrs. Jones over at Fox. Louis Stone, as the new judge, remained earnest, but the maudlin Joan simply disappeared as the series explored the more comic side of family life. It became enormously popular, and not only among the small-town residents it purported to represent. The fourth film, *Love Finds Andy Hardy* (1938), opened in major first-run theaters nationwide and landed eighth on *Variety*'s list of top-grossing films of the year, despite costing only $212,000 to make.[24]

The series gave evidence of being as warmly acclaimed by the public as Judge Hardy had been at the end of *A Family Affair* and on more or less the terms he established. The Hardy family came before the public as members of it, as fathers, mothers, sons, and daughters. The repetition inherent in the series format made the characters familiar, that is, something like family. Analyzing the chemistry of the family series in general, *Theatre Arts* concluded that the feeling of "*auld acquaintance*" produced "an equity in audience sympathy"; the "stability of family relationship" became an acceptable alternative to the "novelty" that moviegoers usually demanded. Verisimilitude and representativeness were the signal accomplishments of the Hardy films. They "admirably treated" "the problems of a normal American family" and offered audiences "the 'pleasures of recognition'": "the characters are all cozily identifiable as people you know. Your neighbors, your family, yourself when young, and the incidents of the stories are of the simple, homely kind." Company publicity exploited this angle. In one ad for *Love Finds Andy Hardy* MGM congratulated itself on "creat[ing] a real American home that audiences know and understand"; a promotional article offered the film as "an intimate inside view of the life of an average American family." The Hardys' "joys and sorrows are the joys and sorrows of the 'just folks' who pay their money at the boxoffice." While the industry fumbled along generally, trying to figure out what would please the public, the Hardy films were "getting closer to the pulse of the great American audience" than any others, according to another commentator, who urged more pictures just like them.[25]

What was so exceptional about the Hardy films was their ordinariness, their simplicity and sincerity, however expertly cultivated, which seemed to repudiate what Hollywood had long stood for, everything it had championed, the things for which it was either celebrated or reviled by others. They possessed homely qualities that not even eruptions into song by the lovelorn Betsy Booth (Judy Garland) could compromise. Despite arriving in Carvel in a chauffeured car, the daughter of a famous actress, Garland as Betsy was simply another manifestation of the series' lack of affectation and claim to normalcy. After all, her repeated lament in *Love Finds Andy Hardy* is that she has "no glamour." The Hardy films were not seen as escapist entertainment but as mirrors reflecting back to audiences the drama and comedy inherent in their daily lives. Betsy sings beautifully, which differentiates her from us, but she also sings to express her insecurities and a hopeless crush, wistful feelings that we recognize. We are all individuals; there are things we all share. The popularity of the Hardy series was held up as evidence of the audience's delightful at-homeness with the characters, either as the people they knew or the people they were, and that nothing was more pleasurable for moviegoers than the surprising intimacy of watching their world on the screen.[26]

"The World Is Ours," a short film made to promote MPGY in theaters nationwide, could not do otherwise than represent a "typical American family," in recognition of "the great success of the 'family' style of picture" with the public. This one vacations in Hollywood, visiting studios and seeing stars. Like the institutional ads, the short film teaches us all about the social, economic, and entertainment value of the movies. Charley Grapewin played the skeptical grandpa who more or less believes that cinematic progress stopped with "The Great Train Robbery" (1903). He is finally converted to contemporary movies when he learns to share his grandson's (Johnny Walsh) love of Andy Hardy. In fact, "The World Is Ours" was originally reported to star the Hardy cast, a clever mobilization of the first family of the movies to promote the eager consumption of them. But either because of time constraints or the campaign's promise of studio neutrality, other actors, including Anne Shirley as the teenaged daughter, were cast instead in a different story. Ads for "The World Is Ours" at theaters often mentioned the quantities of stars featured in it, but the cast was also promoted as a "new Movie Family."[27]

Other new families joined them to capitalize on a trend that met with audience favor and was economical as well. In addition to Columbia's Blondie series, which ran for more than a decade, one of Monogram's four contest pictures was *Wanted by the Police* (1938), the first of its Murphy Family pictures. Republic improved on mere verisimilitude with the Higgins Family series, whose cast included an actual family: married character actors James and Lucille Gleason and their son, Russell, also a recurring Jones Family cast member. And MGM, the studio best known for superspecials and extravagance, itself inaugurated another inexpensive but important family series in time for MPGY. *Young Dr. Kildare* starred Lew Ayres as the committed doctor who goes to New York to learn and practice medicine and Lionel Barrymore as his mentor, Dr. Gillespie. *Young Dr. Kildare* counted as a family series, even though Jimmy Kildare's first action is to break up the family, when he decides not to join his father, Stephen (Samuel S. Hinds), in his small-town medical practice, despite the wishes of his parents and sweetheart, Alice (Lynne Carver). But Jimmy does not leave them behind; they join him at the first sign of crisis, and when his career at the hospital is threatened, the only alternative he can imagine is to return home to the life they planned for him. Hinds, as the older Kildare, is a dead ringer for Lewis Stone as Judge Hardy; both were tall and slender with noble gray heads, sonorous voices, and a certain earnest demeanor. Both characters also share a folksy kind of professional common sense that is not at all inferior to the wisdom of New York's finest minds. In "The World Is Ours" Hinds was, in effect, cast as the Judge Hardy *manqué;* he played the father of the "typical American family" that goes to Hollywood, a plug for MGM's newest icon of paternal normalcy.[28]

Ads for *Young Dr. Kildare* presented it as MGM's attentive response to the public's desire for such films and series, invoking the Hardy Family to establish the studio's credentials. "BY PUBLIC REQUEST! To the public which has asked for sincere, human stories of real people, we present this well-told drama. It begins another heart-storming series by M-G-M, producers of the famed 'Hardy Family' pictures." "WHAT EVERYONE HAS BEEN ASKING FOR! Here is a sincere story of real people, rich in warm human appeal." The clamor invoked and raised here was the chorus of 1938. It was the better part of marketing to treat one's films as evidence less of intuiting the public's desires, or taking its "pulse," than of listening to what it had to say and giving the public what it asked for. Such films and advertising bespoke respect for a public that rejected artificial characters and stories and chose substance over spectacle, as well as the self-regard of a company that had identified and met this need.[29]

Like Standard Oil and AT&T, one columnist mused in 1938, Hollywood had "succeeded in alienating public affection," but also like these companies it could be "humanized" and "popularized"; it could strive to "win" back "friendship." The public's estrangement from the movies was blamed in part on the moviemakers' estrangement from the public. "The men at the top," many of them immigrants from poor backgrounds, once "had the 'common touch,'" the editor of the *Reporter* reflected, but were now "affluent and removed from the folks they used to know" and "not as well equipped to touch the plain, wholesome folk who pay picture admissions." It was suggested that they leave Hollywood to "meet a few of us people who represent their audiences. . . . I simply cannot believe that any person can be deeply concerned with the state of the average man while sitting astride a polo pony." A newspaper editor in Youngstown, Ohio—hometown of the brothers Warner—recommended "a few months in some inland American town" to "see what Americans look like and how they act." According to an article on public relations in *Business Week,* the gap between business leaders and "the mass of people" made corporate PR necessary. It was a sign the film industry was as big and serious as it claimed to be.[30]

Victims of their own success, the men who made the movies needed "to get in touch again," to convince the public that their films could still speak to it. Hollywood humanized itself by injecting real "human beings" into movies; this was the industry's most basic public relations move, its institutional apology for the recent missteps. The "trend toward sweet and simple characters and 'down to earth' pictures" was "sweeping the film capital" just in time for MPGY, turning what was in part a strategy for keeping costs down into the virtue of an organized demonstration of Hollywood's insight into the lives of all the little people who really made the movies possible.[31]

If *naturalness* was the quality that stars were supposed to possess in the great year of unnatural public dissatisfaction with the movies, *humanness* might be seen as the correlative quality of its films. The adjective *human* was invoked with extraordinary frequency to describe and create a kind of identity among a range of movies, almost to the point of suggesting a fledgling genre within the genres in the way Rick Altman has described, if only one could imagine stepping out to see a *human* the way one might a *musical*. Numerous quiz pictures that were celebrated for their human, sincere, down-to-earth qualities appeared from all the studios, from lowly Monogram's *Barefoot Boy* to the much-lauded *Boys Town;* from RKO's old-fashioned family dramas, *Mother Carey's Chickens* and *Breaking the Ice,* to the contemporary family comedies *Safety in Numbers* (the Jones Family installment), *Sing You Sinners,* and *Rich Man, Poor Girl;* from films with established stars, such as *Three Loves Has Nancy* and *You Can't Take It with You,* to *Four Daughters* and *Girls' School,* which promised new players. These qualities characterized not only films starring popular adolescents—including the Deanna Durbin vehicle *That Certain Age; Stablemates,* with Mickey Rooney; and *Listen, Darling,* with Judy Garland and Freddie Bartholomew—but also those attending to the experiences of the middle-aged and elderly, such as *The Arkansas Traveler* and *The Young in Heart,* which caused a small flurry of manufactured excitement over the feature-film debut of stage actress Minnie Dupree at the age of sixty-five.[32]

The natural girl was especially adept at bringing the human element to the MPGY films. *Letter of Introduction* and *Youth Takes a Fling,* for example, starred Andrea Leeds, "Miss Humanity" of *The Goldwyn Follies* and, one might add, of 1938 in general. As the surrogate for the public in the latter film, Hazel advocates for movies that are believable, characters who act like "human beings," and stories that are "real." She could argue this position in part because Leeds herself was just about the most natural of the natural girls, an actress without "an inch of pose," whose appeal was linked to her transcendence of the usual things that separated stars from the rest of us. In *Letter of Introduction* Leeds played Kay Martin, an aspiring actress, but the story is above all a family drama; she comes to New York to meet her father, John

Mannering (Adolphe Menjou), a famous actor whose paternity she only recently discovered. Despite these unusual antecedents, Kay's distinguishing quality is ordinariness. In the opening scene a radio announcer broadcasts from a crowded street on New Year's Eve and looks for someone to tell him "what Mr. and Mrs. John Q. Public think." Like Oliver Merlin before him, he picks Leeds to speak on their behalf; she stands out from the crowd in her capacity to represent it. In the wake of *The Goldwyn Follies,* however, Universal had learned a thing or two about giving the public what it wanted. Kay is too human to talk with the announcer, and *Letter of Introduction* refused to go highbrow. It kept Edgar Bergen and Charlie McCarthy, as well as Leeds and Menjou from the *Follies,* but dropped ballet and opera. Rather than staging the motion picture debut of a soprano from the Met, it introduced Mortimer Snerd to film audiences.[33]

With Crawford's glamorous and hardheaded version of the "shopgirl's dream" on the wane, Leeds brought a different sensibility to the part of wistful shopgirl Helen Brown in *Youth Takes a Fling.* Helen works in the bridal department of a big store and dreams, fittingly, of marriage. In *Mannequin* (1937) Crawford's working-class Jessie Cassidy marries a shipping magnate (Spencer Tracy); in *Youth Takes a Fling* Helen prays for an aviator but then sets her sights on Joe Meadows (Joel McCrea), who delivers packages but dreams of running away to sea. She tries various tricks to ensnare him, making steak and apple pie, for one, to show off her homey talents, but her plans fail until seasickness unexpectedly intervenes, and Joe settles for the life of a land-bound husband. "Human and amusing," a "believable situation involving believable people," this boy-meets-girl story was treated as a "realistic . . . account of how two young people meet, court, and marry." The working woman's desire for marriage, and the working man's desire to avoid it, were thought to speak to the universal experience of falling in love: "what goes on between and around them is just what goes on between and around such a pair at that or any place now or any time." Not only were these "real folks on the screen," but they were "*you* on the screen! . . . living your own dreams . . . your private longings!" The conventionally happy ending of *Youth Takes a Fling* at least seemed rather conventional outside of movies, too, where more men marry than hop freighters to foreign ports. It approaches marriage as the most female of desires but also the most human of outcomes. If Leeds herself is not well known today, despite a string of major roles in the late 1930s, the reason may be that she went the way of the natural girl in 1940, leaving Hollywood as planned, to pursue the ordinary goal she shared with Helen Brown: to marry and raise a family.[34]

A film such as *Youth Takes a Fling* takes place in shared walk-up flats, not spacious penthouses, and focuses on the commonplace lives of department store workers rather than on the exploits of the industrious or idle rich who shop there (compare with Crawford's shopgirl in *The Women* [1939], who becomes a rich man's mistress, the kind of woman she is sick of serving at the perfume counter). *Youth Takes a Fling* offered audiences reality, Hollywood-style. That is, it was well suited to claims about its ordinary, human characters and qualities, even if the events in it may never have happened to an actual human being. Classical Hollywood films never abandoned "a kind of licensed zone of unreality," but they did not have to. The meaningful point of comparison for such simple comedy-dramas was not real life as such but rather the other films Hollywood had been churning out, which were newly seen as fantastically, flagrantly remote from the lives of most audience members, virtually unimaginable to them.[35]

THE HUMAN SIDE OF SCREWBALL

Another way of putting the last point: it was not at all lost on the industry that the rise of the Hardy series and other modest films about ordinary people coincided with the declining popularity of screwball comedy, one of the most notable of classical Hollywood cycles. The screwball era lasted from 1934 to 1942 (with the notable, glorious exception of Preston Sturges's films), when the war marched it out of favor. In 1938, however, at what turned out to be the midpoint, it was widely thought to be fading, a casualty in part of the problem that all genres, and the narrower cycles that took shape within them, faced: that they might, at least temporarily, be overdone, that repetition would override novelty. And as James Harvey has pointed out in a definitive study, these comedies were inspired by and paid tribute to the "styles and temperaments and skills" of the "most glamorous" stars at the height of their glamour. There was nothing "simple" or "everyday" about them.[36]

These comedies did sometimes unite lovers from across the class divide, as with the heiress and reporter romance in *It Happened One Night* (1934), which is usually considered a screwball prototype. Such characters and comedies in the 1930s have been called "egalitarian" and "democratic," as the upper classes—Ellie Andrews (Colbert) in *It Happened One Night*, for example—learn to appreciate other values and ways of living in the process of becoming less spoiled, more regular. But many other films in the cycle, including *My Man Godfrey* (1936), in which the forgotten-man butler is really just playing, and *Bringing Up Baby* and *Holiday* (both 1938), Hepburn's last two box-office failures before she left the movies for a time, focus on a fabulous upper-class milieu that is inextricable from their glamour. In *Holiday* Johnny Case (Cary Grant), a self-made, Harvard-educated financial wizard, may end up with the spunkier and more interesting of the upper-crust Seton sisters, but it is hard to see the improved union with Hepburn's Linda as a triumph of egalitarianism or plain-folk sensibilities. The movies' escapism literalized as escape, on a transatlantic ocean liner no less, rich characters who run off and devote themselves to a life of "fun," who make having fun an imperative almost as axiomatic as having to work—this film was indeed on holiday from the constraints under which most people operated.[37]

It was a sign of the screwball cycle's decline, and the studios' concerns about it, that the "Patrons Dictate" article put out to promote the ninety-four contest pictures announced that among the many comedies produced, there was "none of the dizzy type." This was simply untrue, an instance when audience preferences were thought to have shifted faster than production schedules, and promotion sought to wish away the error. Screwball comedies were well represented among the campaign films. They included *Three Loves Has Nancy* and *Vacation from Love* (both from MGM), *Four's a Crowd* (Warners), *You Can't Take It with You* (Columbia), *The Mad Miss Manton* and *The Affairs of Annabel* (both from RKO), *Hold That Co-ed* (Fox), and two United Artists films, *There Goes My Heart* (Hal Roach) and *The Cowboy and the Lady* (Samuel Goldwyn). Paramount released *Sing You Sinners,* a strange hybrid that contained some screwball elements, such as a cross-dressing musical number, amid a tangled blend of family drama, musical comedy, and horse-racing. *Carefree* (RKO) fell under the screwball rubric, too, although the eagerly anticipated reunion of Fred Astaire and Ginger Rogers after well over a year trumped any other generic associations. Few star teams in American film history delivered better on the industry's long-standing promise of entertainment, and the title *Carefree* not only reminds us of Astaire's graceful insouciance but also aligned the film quite nicely with the campaign's claim that movies provided a few distracting hours of "freedom from care."

An "'impossible' genre," musicals present a unique challenge to even the most flexible and forgiving ideas about cinema's relation to reality, the eagerly embraced illusion of it or oblique allusion to it. Spontaneous eruptions into song and dance more or less announce that the suspension of disbelief is irrelevant, perhaps detrimental, to the musical's pleasures. *Carefree* makes a case for the necessity and thrill of leaving reality behind. For the first and only time in their pairing, Astaire did not play a professional entertainer, which in previous musicals had integrated and legitimated the numbers, deriving them from the intrinsic properties of the role, as well as from the unique talents of the star. In *Carefree* the irrepressible Astaire instead played a psychoanalyst. Tony Flagg is a professional talker, not a dancer. Amanda Cooper (Rogers) becomes a patient at the behest of his friend Stephen Arden (Ralph Bellamy), who wants to marry her, but Amanda cannot make up her mind to do it. "We all try to escape reality," Tony advises Stephen before agreeing to help return Amanda to hers. To prove the point, Tony mentions that he had once wanted to be a dancer, but "psychoanalysis showed me I was wrong." The joke is on psychoanalysis, which *Carefree* was credited with developing as "a new font of humorous entertainment," but it is also on the luckless Bellamy, who remains best known for playing the solid, safe, and slightly dull second male lead in film after film. *Reality* in *Carefree* means marrying him, and it is a fate that one is sometimes tempted to think, in light of *The Awful Truth* (1937) and *His Girl Friday* (1940), screwball comedy evolved in part to prevent.[38]

Amanda is supposed to find her way into this reality by learning how to dream, but dreaming instead saves her from it. She dreams of dancing with Tony, in a much-praised slow-motion sequence that emphasizes the cinematic in a way that the Astaire-Rogers dances, which he insisted on filming primarily as full-body shots, with little cutting away, seldom did. The end of the dance and the dream seals the romantic implications with a passionate kiss, and the Rogers character is the first to realize her love for Astaire's, both elements that also set *Carefree* apart from their previous films. Less concerned with the niceties of psychoanalysis than with dissuading Amanda, he lectures her on the confusion and untrustworthiness of dreams: the "dream fantasy" often "makes things seem true to the dreamer when in reality they have no basis in fact." As we know it must, however, *Carefree* sides with the dream, with Astaire and Rogers, and with the musical's ability to create fantasies more powerful and attractive than any reality, to make fantasy become as deeply true as reality.[39]

Tony tells Stephen that psychoanalysis is "the one way we have of finding out what we really want and why we want it." But Tony does not help Amanda discover her wants so much as make her want certain things. Ever the unconventional practitioner, he hypnotizes her, first to make her want Stephen, and then, when Tony belatedly figures out his own desires, to redirect her affections back to him. In no other film is Rogers's putative lack of autonomy vis-à-vis Astaire more directly thematized; she is led, indeed, controlled, by him, even when nowhere near a dance floor. In the face of the actors' resistance to careers defined by their pairing—before *Carefree* Astaire made a musical with the decidedly unmusical Joan Fontaine, and Rogers starred in three nonmusical films, at a significant net loss to the studio—it is perhaps unsurprising that Amanda is made to want just what RKO did: another Rogers and Astaire picture. Public demand for their pictures was assumed, and audience responses to *Carefree*'s sneak preview seemed to bear this out. Preview comments revealed that viewers, who were very enthusiastic about the film, wanted their reunion. But Pomona was not the nation. *Carefree* was the first Astaire-Rogers film to lose money ($68,000), a result in part of the ever-growing production budget for their films, but except for *Roberta* (1935), it also grossed much less than their previous starring vehicles. Rural and small-town exhibitors writing in to the *Motion Picture Herald* disliked it very much. The pressing, seemingly unanswerable, question of "what we really want" from the movies would prompt RKO, less than two years later, to become the first major film company to rely on George Gallup's polling services to find out.[40]

More predictably, audiences did not want *Vacation from Love,* which lost a hefty $105,000 (almost one-third its production cost). In *Carefree,* when Tony refers to Amanda as "one of those dizzy, silly, maladjusted females" at the beginning of their acquaintance, it is so that she may overhear him and get angry; it is part of the mechanism by which the ultimate union of Astaire and Rogers is pleasurably postponed, thereby giving us a movie. *Vacation from Love* is the kind of forgotten (but prevalent), second-rate screwball comedy whose writing and pace are so off that the characters must periodically call each other "screwy" and "mad" just so we know what we are supposed to be watching. Bill Blair (Dennis O'Keefe) sees Patricia Lawson (Florence Rice) once and falls in love; he shows up at her society wedding and convinces her, at the altar, to abandon her fiancé. Bill and Pat wed before the night is over. Having narrowly averted one stodgy marriage, she wants to prevent another. They agree that they "are different" and "always" will be "different from all the others." They will "love, honor, obey, and always have fun!" It's the "'always have fun' part" that "makes it different." Fun is the great leveler in marriages, and theirs is only saved when they have such a good time trying to divorce that it rekindles their romance. "Bill, are we having fun?" Pat asks as they lie in a heap, having slid down a banister on their way out of the courthouse. "I'll say we are." By this point they do not seem so much amused as exhausted, drawing attention to a certain exhaustion of the cycle. The emphasis on being *different* and the relentless repetition of the word *fun* work like the insistence on how *screwy* Bill is; they serve to remind us of what is missing. These words, in other words, underscore how quickly such flimsy films and characters had come to feel like others of their kind, only worse, as well as how little fun it can be to watch people who are compulsively trying to have it.

In the other MPGY screwball comedies fun is usually tempered, or overridden altogether, by something less frivolous, as though the cycle were trying to repair itself. If these films are by no means screwball classics, they are also not so palpably the victims of repetition and exhaustion as the cycle faltered. Both *The Mad Miss Manton* and *There Goes My Heart* copied the heiress-and-reporter formula from *It Happened One Night,* but they also revolve around a kind of renunciation of screwball conventions. The slight, relatively inexpensive *Mad Miss Manton* (at $383,000, it cost only $50,000 more than *Vacation from Love*) was a moneymaker to the tune of $88,000, second among RKO's campaign offerings to the even cheaper and more opportune folksy family film, *Mother Carey's Chickens.* It threw in six or seven additional heiresses and an engaging if convoluted murder mystery, with some minor echoes of *The Thin Man,* another screwball prototype. On her way home from a costume ball, Melsa Manton (Barbara Stanwyck) finds a dead body that later goes missing, but her reputation for frivolous pranks undermines her credibility as a witness. She becomes an amateur sleuth, eager to prove that she is not the "silly" young heiress that reporter Peter Ames (Henry Fonda) has accused her of being. She and her friends set about keeping the police and newspapers on their toes. If crime-solving in the spirited *Thin Man* is another way to have fun, without (yet) having to advocate constantly, desperately, for doing so, in *The Mad Miss Manton* it is a cautionary antidote to fun's excesses. Melsa and the other debutantes are praised for their "public-spirited" efforts to solve the crime, compliments she comes to enjoy. She does not reform for love, although love eventually follows, but out of a kind of pride and civic-mindedness. The social integration of this once rather trivial young socialite involves more than the usual promise of marriage at the end.

The repudiation of screwball has a stronger thematic presence in *There Goes My Heart*. Hal Roach is much better known as the producer of Laurel and Hardy and "Our Gang" films, but he aspired to devote himself to A features and turned to screwball comedies in the late 1930s. He scored a hit with *Topper* (1937), a noisy proselytizer for riotous fun, in which wealthy, glamorous George and Marian Kerby (Cary Grant and Constance Bennett) love fun so much that they refuse to give it up even after they die. Roach's next screwball offerings sagged, in part because they pilfered so heavily from predecessors. The witless *Merrily We Live* (1938) is a *My Man Godfrey* rip-off, and *There Goes My Heart* begins with an heiress escaping from a yacht to elude a patriarchal tyrant, just as *It Happened One Night* had four years earlier. Ellie traded her yacht for a bus trip, and Peter Warne (Gable) had to drag her through the paces of how the other 99.9 percent lives. By contrast, Joan Butterfield (Virginia Bruce) goes straight to Manhattan and fulfills her heart's desire: keeping her identity a secret, she gets a job as a shopgirl in her very own Butterfield's department store, in yet another reversal of the Crawford trajectory. Before escaping the yacht, Joan's grandfather (Claude Gillingwater) calls her "spoiled and ungrateful" for bristling under his dictates, but quite unlike Ellie Andrews, Joan is not spoiled enough. One of "the richest heiresses in the world," she wants above all "to do something on my own, accomplish something in this world—drive a truck, sing in a nightclub." Her ambitions may not be lofty, but she does not want to be "an idle ninny." *Fun* in the sense of the irresponsible, silly pleasures that screwball comedies so often stood for is of no interest to her; instead, she petitions repeatedly for the "freedom" to take care of herself and live more like "a normal person."[41]

Joan is thrilled to share a studio apartment with coworker Peggy O'Brien (Patsy Kelly) and to learn all about Murphy beds and selling kitchenware and how to finagle electricity when you don't have quarters for the meter. There is really nothing for reporter Bill Spencer (Fredric March, in a reprise of his role in *Nothing Sacred* [1937]) to do. After Joan has disappeared, Bill is assigned to find her. In another self-referential gesture to the cycle he resents the assignment: "The girl is daffy; everybody knows it." But she's not daffy, and she doesn't need reforming. Whereas *It Happened One Night* unfolds as an education of Ellie by Peter in such things as donut dunking and piggybacking—when properly performed, the pastimes of "a real human"—Joan is already there. She is regular, a "swell girl," qualities Bill needs to acknowledge rather than inculcate. She is already "satisfied with," in fact, longs for, "the kind of a home [he] can give her," a broken-down beach shack. His Hollywood prejudices are the obstacle to their union—if she's crazy rich, she must be screwball—rather than her character. Neither reviewers nor ads identified *There Goes My Heart* and *The Mad Miss Manton* with the *human*, with the kind of real people—"*you* on the screen"—that audiences were presumed to want, which is perhaps another way of saying that the daffiest thing about Joan Butterfield is her ambition to walk away from millions and be a working stiff. But that she already possesses an appreciation for the simple working life, and requires only an education in the mechanics of it, serves as a reminder of how powerful the movies' desire for the *human* was and how supple its uses.[42]

Three Loves Has Nancy, described in one trade paper as being "in the wacky vein of the nut comedy school," probably did not inspire anyone to identify real people within it either, despite the best efforts of Janet Gaynor and the film to pitch her character, Nancy Briggs, in just that light. In this film a snooty rich man must learn to appreciate the "homespun philosophy" of another down-to-earth woman. As in *Youth Takes a Fling,* where Joe's nickname is "Kansas" and Helen also migrated from the heartland, the film privileges small-town characters and values, which have a home even in New York, the usual haven of screwball's elites. Nancy is a sensible, folksy, middle-class southerner who follows her missing fiancé to the big city. She was a type that Gaynor had long played, and the actress's sensibilities were in tune with the new priorities of 1938. In 1931 *Photoplay* had identified her as a notable exception to the current turn toward glamour among female stars; as an aspiring actress in *A Star Is Born* (1937), she impersonates glamour girls Garbo, West, and Hepburn in an attempt to attract the attention of industry bigwigs at a cocktail party, which is comical in part because those stars are so wildly inappropriate to the star Gaynor was. Indeed, in that film the producer Oliver Niles (Menjou) grooms her for stardom precisely because he anticipates that public tastes are going to be taking a turn toward the "natural."[43]

Injected into the world of wealthy Manhattan bachelors, Nancy sees right through it and them. Her one acquaintance there is Malcolm Niles (Robert Montgomery), a successful writer of trivial fiction. He dislikes her intensely. To Malcolm's dismay, his friend and publisher, Robert Hanson (Tone), takes a fancy to Nancy and hires her as his cook, a position that enables her to dispense southern food, as well as southern wisdom. Finding her to be "the first genuine person that's ever come into my life," Robert falls for her, followed, grudgingly, by Malcolm, who takes longer to appreciate Nancy because he's been, as she puts it, "so busy putting those phony characters in those books of yours, you wouldn't know a real person if you met one." "I'm real," she insists. "Not something that came out of a silly book." It is odd to witness a character with such a palpably artificial southern accent, in a film from a cycle associated far less with realism than with escapist frivolity, protest so earnestly on behalf of her own reality. Again, the *real* here functions comparatively, in contrast not only with Malcolm's characters but with the playboy writer who creates them. If no one in *Three Loves Has Nancy* comes off as real, we are to understand that the film and the earnest Nancy, unlike Malcolm, know what "a real person" *looks like,* and in 1938 such a person looks a lot like she does, with her feisty common sense, modest background, and small-town ways.

Goldwyn's *The Cowboy and the Lady* was perhaps the least successful of these comedies. It struggled throughout to manage the integration of the *human* and screwball, as B. R. Crisler suggested in his *New York Times* review: "the picture still seems to be in need of a final revision to bring it either more nearly into conformity or more ludicrously into non-conformity, with life as it is lived outside of movie studios." *The Cowboy and the Lady* tries quietly to accomplish what *The Goldwyn Follies* promiscuously failed to do: to produce a film that might have something to appeal to everyone—urban and rural, rich and poor, ladies and cowboys. But also like the *Follies,* it was a troubled production and became Goldwyn's third failure in a row. Many reviews were favorable, however, and its box-office chances were thought to be very good given the popularity of Cooper, who had at last returned to the West from stints in Asia *(The Adventures of Marco Polo)* and Europe (*Bluebeard's Eighth Wife* [both 1938]). Cooper played Stretch Willoughby, and Merle Oberon, another Goldwyn star, was Mary Smith, a humble name for an exalted young woman. Mary's father (Henry Kolker) is a wealthy judge and possible nominee for president. He tries to insulate Mary from the world, but she doesn't want to be a lady. He is thwarted by fun-loving Uncle Hannibal (Harry Davenport), who others suspect is "crazy," in case his spontaneous jitterbugging in the living room doesn't make that clear. Mary is sent down to Palm Beach to avoid a scandal. She protests her exile with the by-now-predictable lament: they are not "living like normal human beings." Mary knows what she wants, like Joan Butterfield, but if Mary is also naturally disposed toward the "human," she needs help from Gary Cooper to find out just what that involves.[44]

Normalcy arrives first in the form of Katie (Kelly again) and Elly (Mabel Todd), her family's Palm Beach maids. They think Mary is kind of a "cold fish" but feel "sorry for" her, so she pretends to be a maid and goes along on their date with some cowboys from a traveling rodeo. Mary never had so much "fun" in her life, but her date, serious Stretch, is almost immune to fun. This is a virtue, not a defect. He wants to marry her and take her back to Montana. After some dithering, Mary realizes that she loves him, too, and they elope. Her father is furious. She agrees to return to Palm Beach to play hostess at a dinner for the party's elite, at which the nomination will be decided. Stretch follows her there, to discover her sitting at the foot of the table instead of waiting on it. At this point *The Cowboy and the Lady* is suddenly interrupted by a Capra film, and one wonders whether Robert Riskin, one of a dozen writers who worked on the script, contributed this scene. Stretch is invited to join the formal dinner party by Hannibal, who informs him that politicians are always eager to talk with "the man on the street." As Mr. Deeds, Cooper at least waited for the New York wits to insult him before administering a lecture and a punch, and it took an encounter with a desperate farmer to transform the reluctant millionaire into a philanthropist. Stretch just goes on the attack. He is something of a misanthrope, but this does not prevent him from speaking up for "the people," even though he declines to speak as them. They ask him what he thinks of Judge Smith as a nominee. "You know you don't give a hang what I think," Stretch informs the surprised audience of stuffed shirts. Judge Smith ought to stop "looking down his nose at people," and they should all "go out and find out what [the people] think and feel, and what their needs are and what you can do to help 'em." Apropos of nothing, *The Cowboy and the Lady* identifies itself with the peoples' opinions and needs, but these are left vague, for it is sufficient here to be simply on their side. In contrast both with *Mr. Deeds* and even *The Goldwyn Follies* and its entertainment imperatives, there are no needs in this film, aside from Stretch's emotional ones, that are not being met.

Even Cooper's bankable earnestness cannot save this scene or the film. Stretch is mad at Mary, not the politicians, who say only enough to be caricatures, having black ties rather than opinions. But Stretch believes that the politicians and their wives are rude; the film delivers, as the *Hollywood Reporter* noted approvingly, "a lesson in manners." What riles him is that they all lack "the decency" to treat him "like a human being." To be treated like "a human being" means not being treated like "the man on the street," the representative of something not only other than the individual he is but anathema to the individual he is, which is, strictly speaking, closer to a man on the ranch. His appeal is a version of Nancy's claim to be "real": recognize *me*. It also insists on an acknowledgment of what we all have in common, as distinct from the shared but separate interests that may be thought to distinguish the folks in cowboy boots (or men on the street) from the gentility in formal dress. Only people who transcend such parochialism can live like "normal human beings."[45]

The Cowboy and the Lady does bring together lovers from different classes, dissolving the political divide in the process. Like Stretch, the film cares about human beings and what it takes to be treated like one and to live like one. The chastised judge deals with Stretch's appeal by giving up politics and lighting out for the territories with Hannibal and Mary. The ostensibly democratic union that takes place is also just a human one. Stretch returns to find Mary already in Montana—the Smiths are not so chastised as to forgo flying. She is out of her evening gown and into an apron in the boardinghouse's kitchen. The hostess is learning to become the (unpaid) servant she had pretended to be, and *The Cowboy and the Lady* ends on a decidedly domestic note.

Many of the MPGY screwball comedies conclude in this way, not simply by creating the couple, and thus gesturing toward a marriage that takes place in the literally unforeseeable future, but by having created the marriage and sometimes the home. That is, these screwball comedies are not simply romantic but are ultimately domestic, and the home is not the setting for much of the madness, as with the Bullock mansion in *My Man Godfrey,* but the goal of turning from it. *My Man Godfrey* ends with a wedding, but only when Irene Bullock (Carole Lombard) fast-talks a bewildered and passive Godfrey (William Powell) into the ceremony. In MPGY films, couples are unmistakably committed. *Carefree* ends with Astaire and Rogers walking together down the aisle, once Bellamy has been expelled for good; *Four's a Crowd* indulges in some humorous confusion about who will finally marry whom but is wedded to the idea of a wedding, with two couples tying the knot. *There Goes My Heart* concludes with a marriage performed by silent film star Harry Langdon as a creepy preacher. It takes place in the very beach house where Bill and Joan will modestly, which is to say humanly, live.

Their privacy is underscored by the exclusion of the camera from the interior of the house as the ceremony takes place.

The Cowboy and the Lady and *Sing You Sinners* include strangely similar scenes, played for comic and sentimental effect, involving a phantom house, the future site of a longed-for family. Stretch's phantom house has a frame, and he walks through it pretending that he and Mary already live there together. It has no walls, and so a group of incredulous cowboys watch with amusement as he navigates unseen furniture and plays the adoring husband to an invisible devoted wife. In *Sing You Sinners* the house of David Beebe (Fred MacMurray) and his longtime fiancée, Martha Randall (Ellen Drew), is wholly imaginary. He brings her to the empty lot he would like to buy and build on when they can finally marry, and there is rather more pathos than comedy in their hopeful plans regarding the configuration of rooms and furniture. Through phantom houses these films manifest a down-to-earth passion for domesticity among these robust male leads. As a way of representing and emphasizing what does not exist within these films, these elaborate pantomimes of a deferred domestic life operate as figures for the elusiveness of that thing called "the real" in the movies.

These MPGY comedies split the difference between the zaniness of a screwball cycle temporarily on the wane and the modest pursuit of the ordinary at the heart of the family films that were the rage in 1938. MPGY was a propitious time to have modified the extremes of the cycle; after all, if the goal of the campaign was to persuade people that the film industry was not only a "big" but a "serious business," and not at all "the creation and the field of endeavor of zanies," it made sense to downplay or tame the zaniness of such films and gravitate toward the sober new order of things. *Sing You Sinners* prompted speculation that Paramount would develop it into another family series, but this story about a small-town family, the musical Beebe brothers—Joe (Crosby), David, and Mike (Donald O'Connor)—and their mother (Elizabeth Patterson), was scarcely of the Hardy Family school. David works in a garage and has postponed marriage because he is worried about supporting two families; Joe is good-natured but too shiftless to hold a job. All regular enough. But the brothers also perform together as well-paid nightclub entertainers, which provides the opportunity for some lively and sometimes zany musical numbers. For reasons not explained, they dislike entertaining and only work at it when their mother makes them. After some false starts Joe moves to Los Angeles and gets a racehorse, younger brother Mike acts as jockey, the brothers foil a plot to fix the

big race, which their horse wins, and David and Joe vanquish the gang-
sters who kidnap Mike in retribution. The film ends with the brothers
performing together again, after their mother has threatened to abandon the family if they refuse. The singing, loving, fighting Beebes were
billed as "the Gol-Darndest Family in the U.S.A." but also described as
"an average American family," with the film represented as "a human
story of a family." To refer to this incredible family and plot as *average* and *human* illustrates how routine these categories had become
for thinking about films and how flexible, at times even absurd, their
application might be, as though to treat any family of modest means
in a small-town setting allowed the studios to embrace that hallowed
something called *the family* and take the implicit promise of normalcy
to the bank.[46]

YOU CAN'T TAKE IT WITH YOU

The title "gol-darndest family in the U.S.A." belonged more properly to
the extended clan of *You Can't Take It with You,* Columbia's MPGY
blockbuster. Based on a Pulitzer Prize–winning play by Moss Hart and
George S. Kaufman, *You Can't Take It with You* was one of the most
acclaimed films of the year, perhaps the likeliest candidate to convince
the public it was motion pictures' greatest. Both a screwball comedy
and a Capra, a kind of generic signature in its own right, it appeared on
many ten-best lists and won Academy Awards for best picture and best
director. The film's success may well have put screwball comedy back
on track. It took the cycle's evolution in 1938 to its logical extreme:
You Can't Take It with You is a domestic as well as a romantic comedy, organized around a family capacious enough to include anyone
who embraces its eccentric lifestyle; its center is the family home, whose
demolition is threatened; it was embraced as one of the most human
movies of the campaign.

You Can't Take It with You could scarcely have been received otherwise. Capra was the most popular and critically acclaimed director of
the 1930s, and the famed "Capra touch" was a uniquely "down-to-
earth quality," a human touch. Above all it described a relationship to
people, both characters and actors. He insisted that actors, even extras,
come across as "flesh and blood human beings living a story." Quirky,
distinctive business individualized and humanized characters while providing audiences with "a pleasing and convincing image of themselves,"
"their own lives . . . and dreams." Piggybacker and hitchhiker Peter

Warne exemplifies the qualities of the "real human" that he praises so highly; if he serves as "an archetype of middle-class normality who restores order and conventionality" in *It Happened One Night*, it is because this film, and the Capra oeuvre in general, expanded our understanding of what normality and conventionality might entail.[47]

You Can't Take It with You takes the revision of screwball comedy a step further than other MPGY films; the eccentricity that is one of the hallmarks of the cycle—the behavior and values that set screwballs apart from the forces working against them—becomes the new normal. Dizziness is not simply compatible with but the vehicle for the fundamentally human. In *Vacation from Love* the protagonists insist on how different, different, different they are from ordinary people, while the project of *You Can't Take It with You* is to make ordinary people different. It was in many ways the perfect film for a campaign that rejected the idea of a mass audience but needed to attract as many people as possible to theaters. Honoring the differences that make us all unique, the film is committed to a radical individualism that embraces them as something we all have in common.

You Can't Take It with You bears a family resemblance to the films that make up the Capra "trilogy": *Mr. Deeds Goes to Town*, *Mr. Smith Goes to Washington* (1939), and *Meet John Doe* (1941). Along with several actors in common (Jean Arthur, James Stewart, Edward Arnold), they are all movies with a message of sorts, sharing a trajectory in which idealism, sincerity, and sentiment triumph over cynicism, and the forces of good transcend the forces of greed. But in *You Can't Take It with You* there is no plucky young man from the provinces who battles corruption, as well as his own demons, before getting the girl. Instead, Martin "Grandpa" Vanderhof (Lionel Barrymore) "could have been a rich man" but turned his back on business thirty years ago because he "wasn't having any fun." He harbors a posse of individualists committed to his ideals, which do not include allegiances to the people, the disenfranchised, the "John Does," nor to democratic principles, beyond a commitment to the freedom to do as you please. The Vanderhof home is a parodic extreme of the idea that a man's house is his castle, the tangible, brick-and-mortar symbol of a deeper spiritual freedom.

The eccentricity that sets the quirky individualist in screwball comedies apart from others is here the glue that binds the family together. The range of their interests is underscored by the breadth and distinctiveness of an excellent ensemble cast. Grandpa's daughter, Penny (Byington), writes plays and paints; his son-in-law, Paul (Hinds), makes firecrackers in the basement; granddaughter Essie (Ann Miller) dances and makes candy; her husband, Ed (Dub Taylor), plays the xylophone and operates a printing press; Grandpa collects stamps, attends graduation exercises, plays the harmonica, and fosters the eccentricities of others. They cohabit with a few unrelated free spirits who have been persuaded to pursue their crooked genius there: Mr. DePinna (Halliwell Hobbes) delivered ice nine years ago and never left, and he spends much of the film dressed in a toga; Mr. Poppins (Donald Meek) is a timid rabbit of a man who designs mechanical timid rabbits. Granddaughter Alice (Arthur) is the most conventional family member—it is while working as a secretary that she becomes engaged to the owner's son, Tony Kirby (Stewart)—but when the couple takes an impromptu dance lesson in Central Park from some freakishly precocious children, we know that Alice is in the family fold and Tony is a kindred soul, too.

The outliers are Tony's upper-crust parents. The original play lacked a certain tension, and so the film expanded the minor role of the generic uptight businessman-father into financial tycoon Anthony Kirby (Arnold), a voracious "symbol of capitalism at its worst," whose conversion to the Vanderhof way is its triumph. *You Can't Take It with You* opens in the forbidding skyscraper canyon of Wall Street, where Kirby is in the process of creating "the largest individual monopoly in the world," in munitions, the biggest deal of his career. The necessary political support has been lined up; all he needs is to buy twelve blocks that surround a competitor's factory for his plant. The only obstacle, it turns out, is Grandpa Vanderhof. Grandpa's Manhattan is a cozy village. He promises his worried neighbors and friends, renters all, that he will not sell his house; if the entire parcel cannot be acquired, no one will have to move. "You can't take it with you," the film teaches us, but it privileges another axiom, too: "you can't force a man to sell his home." The film disparages superfluous wealth but demonstrates a hearty appreciation for the necessities that anchor such freedoms as the Vanderhof clan enjoys.[48]

Indeed, although *You Can't Take It with You* has tended to be seen, then and now, as endorsing "the blessings of poverty" and treating "idleness . . . as a kind of higher wisdom," the anarchic home harbors a bustling hive of entrepreneurs rather than slothful nonconformists. Grandpa is an "expert" stamp collector paid to appraise collections; Paul and Mr. DePinna sell firecrackers for "ten cents a string"; Essie dances while filling orders for her homemade candy, which Ed delivers along with ads he prints for the fireworks. One of the industrious

Mr. Poppins's inventions plays the tune "Whistle While You Work," and the pet raven is admonished to "go back to work" when it slacks off. Even the dance lesson in Central Park, which strives for something of the casual pleasure of the "Man on the Flying Trapeze" scene from *It Happened One Night,* is not a spontaneous eruption of communal good spirits but the kids' way to earn money, and it costs Tony a dime. In *Holiday* Johnny's plan to "find out why [he is] working" means not working at all. Tony, who dislikes finance as much as Johnny does, quits too, but his dream is to devote himself to chemistry. The fun ethic of *You Can't Take It with You* is a backdoor work ethic, an invitation to pleasurable labor, and its rewards are material, as well as spiritual. The alternative to Kirby's munitions monopoly is not unproductive individuality run amuck but candy and fireworks businesses.[49]

The point is not to do nothing but to do what you love. Kirby doesn't. He suffers from an unsettled stomach and a bankrupt soul. The man who would control the country's access to weapons in a world on the brink of war needs to be saved more than he needs to be stopped. Both *Mr. Smith Goes to Washington* and *Meet John Doe* illustrate the crushing effects of monopolies so powerful they are never fully vanquished. There was no monopoly in the original *You Can't Take It with You,* and in the film it is primarily a sign of values gone awry. Tony's arsenal of objections to it includes an unsuppressed yawn during a business meeting and the ironic inquiry about whether his father has "forgotten the slingshot market." The whole thing is a bore.

Capra takes monopoly seriously, but not as an economic or political threat. One of his favorite themes as a filmmaker was resistance to mass everything; in his words Capra sought to amplify "the rebellious cry of the individual against being trampled to an ort by massiveness—mass production, mass thought, mass education, mass politics, mass wealth, mass conformity." His comment helps us to understand not only the ethical value assigned to the Vanderhof home and its artisanal practices but the problem with monopoly as such. It is just too big, too far out of human scale, a point reinforced by Arnold's distinctive corpulence, as well as by the early shot of Kirby in the lobby of his building, intent on finalizing the big deal. The extreme low-angle shot reveals a man, at his ostensible moment of triumph, dwarfed by the monumental scope and space of his endeavors. Monopoly is a symptom of the massiveness that besets the individual from all sides, which is brought home by the requirement that the intimate seat of Vanderhof originality be sacrificed to his project.[50]

Monopoly can be vanquished in *You Can't Take It with You* because business is just another "hobby," as Kirby calls it during an uncomfortable meeting with his prospective in-laws. They must help him substitute something more congenial; Kirby must learn, that is, what hobbies really are. The defense against the massiveness and impersonality of monopoly is symbolized by the little harmonica. Grandpa whips his out in jail, where everyone is taken following the fireworks explosion at the house, an accident caused by Kirby's henchmen. The men's cell is huge—it seems to get bigger and more crowded as the scene progresses—drawing attention to the dozens of random and disconnected strangers who share it with the Vanderhof/Kirby contingent. A few prisoners stand out by virtue of their race, but overall the scene distinguishes between the individuals we have met and this crowd, a roster of Forgotten Men from Central Casting. The crowd behaves like one: they do a group double take, threatening yet amusing, when Kirby is identified as the famed "banker," and they spring into immediate mass action when he throws aside a barely smoked cigar. The one man to refrain from the cigar scramble, while wordlessly marveling at the spectacle, is rewarded as much for his individuality as his restraint by Tony, who gives him cigarettes.

Both Grandpa and Kirby find the fracas distasteful, but only the latter is contemptuous of these "scum." Grandpa angrily inquires what makes him "such a superior human being." Because Kirby lacks "friends," he is "a failure as a man," "as a father," and "as a human being." Kirby tells him to "get a pulpit," but Grandpa prefers the harmonica. The way to make friends, to be fully human, is to entertain and to be entertained. "Never a dull moment," Grandpa happily remarks, not once but twice from his perch in the cell. Unlike the cigar they will shortly fight over, the harmonica on which Grandpa spontaneously plays "Polly Wolly Doodle" unites these men in singing and dancing and humanizes them, without the necessity of individualizing them. In an instant, for an instant, the handy folk instrument makes folk of the crowd (see figure 10). In the end the harmonica will humanize Kirby too, when he recalls his childhood passion for it and joins Grandpa in a duet of the same song. Folk culture is the common ground on which middle- and upper-class movie eccentrics can meet.

You Can't Take It with You has to work hard to bring Kirby down to human scale. But in something of a break with Hollywood protocols, the humanity of two working-class black characters is assumed. Rheba (Lillian Yarbo) is intelligent and capable and monitors the Vanderhof

FIGURE 10. Popular culture makes folks of the masses in *You Can't Take It with You.*

zaniness with good-humored, somewhat detached affection as the family's servant. We meet her in the film's most dynamic shot, when the camera cuts from the closing doors of an elevator, by means of which Grandpa liberates Mr. Poppins from meaningless office work, to the opening doors of a kitchen cabinet at the Vanderhofs, through which we see Rheba's face. She is our introduction to an alternative way of life that she neither represents fully nor repudiates; that is, Rheba seems to enjoy the family and her work, but being a servant is her job rather than her vocation or identity. This differentiates her from the others in the house, as well as from the stereotyped black servants of classical Hollywood film, whether the sassy, slow, or subservient variety. It may be tempting to see her simply as the undervalued labor on which the others' flighty lifestyle depends, but to do so is both to ignore the film's high regard for her quiet normalcy and cheerful organizing influence and to miss the entrepreneurial ethic chez Vanderhof. It also discounts how different this film's treatment of such a character is from virtually all mainstream films of the era.

Her sweetheart, Donald (Eddie Anderson), is more stereotypically comic, a bit hen-pecked by Rheba, unemployed, and joking about relief.

But he also works side by side, unremarkably, with the other men in the workshop. And Rheba and Donald are included in some key group shots of the extended Vanderhof family, as involved, at times literally integrated, members of it. They also appear in some of the film's publicity photos along with the rest of the principal cast. Capra received at least seven letters thanking him for casting Anderson and Yarbo and for creating better parts for black actors. It may have seemed less important that Donald was part caricature than that both characters were individuated from each other and, like the others in the Vanderhof household, from the others in the Vanderhof household. Rheba may be a bit "bland" in comparison with her employers and Donald, but this quality sets her apart, too. It is, in a sense, her eccentricity.[51]

Even snooty Mrs. Kirby (Mary Forbes) has a hobby—spiritualism. Penny scoffs at this, which draws a reproach from Paul: "Now, Penny, you mustn't criticize other peoples' hobbies. You've got one or two of your own, you know." Paul's criticism of criticism is not in the original play, and it speaks on behalf of the same values as another notable MPGY patriarch, the Average Movie-Goer. Paul rejects criticism, while the Movie-Goer acknowledges its inevitability by way of disabling it: "We're all different." And our differences set us free: "A dull world it would be if we weren't." Grandpa's quest for "never a dull moment" drove him back down the elevator thirty years ago, and he rescues Mr. Poppins from dullness at the adding machine. The worst horror that Mrs. Kirby at first imagines is that Alice is "probably from some dull middle-class family." Capra himself wrote that "the cardinal sin" in filmmaking "is Dullness." The insistence on pleasurable differences in tastes in the institutional ads becomes, with the film's exhortation against dullness, the duty, the moral imperative, to cultivate and indulge them. Hollywood perpetually worried that sermons in films were synonymous with *dull* and hence with *unprofitable*, but *You Can't Take It with You* embraces the intrinsic entertainment value of differences among individuals who are as delightfully individualized as possible, pitching itself as an all-star cinematic antidote to boredom.[52]

Many reviewers observed that the play had been content to feature a "madcap family" whose "enjoyment of life" required neither explanation nor justification. The film, on the other hand, turned these delightful eccentrics, especially Grandpa, into philosophers with a point to make about enjoyment. Most reviewers welcomed the changes and found the film as good as and usually better than the play. One effect of downplaying the "madness" that had already fallen out of screen fashion was to make the characters "far more likable, far more human." Capra and Riskin, the film's screenwriter, "humanize everything," according to one reviewer. Another was to improve upon the movie eccentrics' merely "adorable" predecessors by making them "profoundly wise." Following the pattern set by *Mr. Deeds Goes to Town*, after Capra famously decided his films had to "*say* something," *You Can't Take It with You* offered audiences a "profound lesson in life and learning." Most critics applauded the effort and the way the film made ideas palatable. After all, "the serious thoughts . . . are coated with the sugar of fun"; it provided "a message with laughter." One viewer wrote to Capra that "seldom have I ever known a production that so carefully preserved its moral without having any effect on its entertainment value." There was a tendency to marvel at Capra's ability to pull off the elusive combination of ideas and fun, of message and entertainment, but in *You Can't Take It with You* the synthesis was total, the point of the film. The moral about the primacy of enjoyment had to be expressed by demonstrating its commitment to entertainment value at every point.[53]

The "something" that *You Can't Take It with You* stood for was the basic human right to enjoyment, elevated to an obligation, and it is only by exercising this right that we become human. The film did not simply represent the delights of "escape and wish-fulfillment" as well as any movie of its time; it promoted them explicitly, energetically, as higher goods, available to anyone. From the industry's perspective, it was hard during MPGY to improve on an entertaining sermon about escapist pleasure; *You Can't Take It with You* was like an institutional ad come to life. "Do As You Please" might be a creed to which "few intelligent persons would subscribe," but it was also seductive.[54]

Critics on the left, however, were less thrilled than other reviewers. *You Can't Take It with You* added insult to injury, because the films of Capra and Riskin had already "proved" what "left film criticism" had long argued, that "real reaction to real things is not only artistically necessary but surefire boxoffice." They had revealed and cultivated a popular taste for social significance that might point Hollywood in a new direction, but *You Can't Take It with You* merely exploited the discovery of "gold in them thar soapboxes." The film added a speech in which Grandpa urges Penny, apropos of nothing, to write a play about "ism-mania": "Communism, fascism, voodooism . . . When things go a little bad nowadays, you go out and get yourself an 'ism,'" which means, "'Think the way I do or I'll bomb the daylights out of you.'" Among other things, critics on the left objected to the conflation of communism and fascism and regretted the speech as "nauseating" fodder for the Dies Committee, but politics as such is again beside the point. The speech constitutes another "rebellious cry" against massiveness—in this case mass political movements. Thus the alternative is not democracy but another "ism"—"Americanism"—which is represented by exemplary individuals and free-thinkers: Washington, Jefferson, Lincoln, Edison. "When things got tough for those boys, they didn't run around looking for 'isms.'" Apparently, "the house came down" at the Radio City Music Hall in response to this speech. The "upper-middle-class" audience offered "even greater applause" to a comic exchange, from the play, with a tax collector. Grandpa claims not to "believe in" the income tax and so refuses to pay it. "Not with my money," he says, the very words Barrymore would utter years later, as Mr. Potter in *It's a Wonderful Life* (1946), to urge the building and loan to foreclose on delinquent homeowners. In Grandpa's mouth it is a benign, if cranky, extension of the attractive principle about not doing things you don't want to do rather than a sign of greed or a failure of citizenship, populism even the well-to-do could get behind.[55]

The one thing missing from Capra's list of masses busy trampling us to orts was, of course, mass culture. Capra knew well the toll it could take on those who produced it. He also "rebelled against the regimentation that makes robots of most of us" as the very active president of the Screen Directors Guild, which fought to get directors more control over their films in what he called "the mass-production system" of Hollywood filmmaking. Capra's activities in this line were part of the publicity for *You Can't Take It with You,* a real-life example of the principles the film expounded but also evidence that collective action and individual freedom are not always, intrinsically, opposed. Capra notoriously launched himself against the forces conspiring against the individual with his own "rebellious cry" of "one man, one film," taking credit for his films' vision and artistry at the expense of talented collaborators, as well as the studio under whose constraints he achieved his greatest success. Critical of the studio system and the practices that reinforced its methods of production, Capra put himself forward and was accepted more than any other filmmaker as the maverick who bucked their bad effects, the "motion picture director who does as he pleases." The humanity *You Can't Take It with You* displayed was not only the actors or characters: "that human quality which pervades the film from beginning to end is Capra." Thus it was also, "from first to last, stamped with one man's individuality." Just as its characters do, Capra and *You Can't Take It with You* make mass production go away. The film's faith in the concrete economic value of eccentricity is something that Capra's idiosyncratic and wildly successful filmmaking was in a position not only to inculcate but to exemplify. Its success might be measured by the reflection that it was the film that turned "the now-familiar *Capraesque* formula into a commodity."[56]

FOUR DAUGHTERS

Even more than Columbia's all-star extravaganza, *Four Daughters* exemplified the values most in demand by the fall of 1938, which made it one of the most celebrated films of the campaign. Based on a short story by sentimental film favorite Fannie Hurst, it is a modest paean to small-town family life and featured a talented cast lacking only in name recognition. At $564,000, roughly one-third the cost of *You Can't Take It with You*, *Four Daughters* was typical of Warners' more conservative fiscal policy for the fall, but the story of the musical Lemp sisters, and the feminine fluttering of hearts that occurs after an attractive stranger comes to live with them, was an oft-noted anomaly for the grittiest of Hollywood's top studios. That the film won such widespread acclaim, and its estimated profits more than doubled that of any other Warners campaign film, was a tribute to its resonance with the tastes of the time and the studio's shrewd understanding of the fantastic exploitation possibilities of simplicity, sincerity, and real human characters.

Four Daughters was more natural than most films. It costarred three actual sisters, Warners contract players Lola (Thea Lemp), Rosemary (Kay Lemp), and Priscilla Lane (Ann Lemp), as three of the daughters. A fourth Lane sister, New Yorker Leota, was apparently considered, but the studio declined to be quite that sentimental about family ties and cast contract player Gale Page as Emma, the oldest sister. The characters could remind you of the people you knew, because you did not know most of the actors well from previous films. Lola Lane had been in films since 1929, but Rosemary and Priscilla arrived in Hollywood in 1937 as singers with the Fred Waring Band. They launched their film careers in Warners' *Varsity Show* (1937). Page did not make her first film until 1938. These were still new faces, and so *Four Daughters* offered exactly the fresh personalities the industry was looking for, in a story designed to showcase them.

This was only the beginning of the film's new talent. When Errol Flynn peremptorily declined to participate, the romantic lead was assigned to Jeffrey Lynn, who had played a few minor roles previously. As Felix Dietz, the unknown, boyish Lynn preserved the modesty of the film's scale and tone, its signature accomplishment, in a way the rakish Flynn could not have done. But *Four Daughters* is best remembered today for the screen debut of John Garfield (who had already established himself on the New York stage) as the surly outsider, Mickey Borden. While producer Hal Wallis worried about the lack of a "name cast," the film and its publicity insisted on turning novelty into a virtue and *Four Daughters* into an exercise in name-building and star-making—with the public's help.[57]

The film is a story of courtship and marriage, of how daughters and sisters become wives. Ernest Talbot (Dick Foran) is Emma's earnest suitor, but she does not love him. Thea becomes engaged to Ben Crowley (Frank McHugh), a wealthy businessman. Then Felix comes to Briarwood, joining the faculty of the music college where patriarch Adam Lemp (Claude Rains) also teaches. Felix moves in with the family, and the sisters fall in love. He loves buoyant Ann, and she accepts his proposal with the understanding that marriage won't change anything, either their easygoing relationship or connection to the family. Thea marries Ben, and Kay moves to Philadelphia to pursue a singing scholarship. Emma grieves. When Ann realizes Emma's unhappiness, she leaves Felix at the altar and marries his friend Mickey, as selfish as she is self-sacrificing, and they move to New York. In the meantime Ernest's calm handling of the elopement crisis persuades Emma that she really loves him, not Felix, after all. During a visit home, Mickey realizes how little he fits into the world that means so much to Ann. He purposefully crashes a car and dies, freeing her to marry Felix and allowing the family to reunite.

Following the credits, *Four Daughters* opens with a shot of a white picket fence, a tree in blossom, and a colonial house. After much upheaval, a similar shot concludes the film, an indication of the durability of this family, that change is cyclical and spring always comes again. Flowers are everywhere in the film. They serve frequently as transitions between scenes, and Ernest is a florist; among other bouquets, he delivers the delicate orchids to Thea that throw the household into a tizzy with the first of the romance plots. Later Ben, at a loss for conversation with the family, strikes upon the happy observation that the daughters are "a rosebud garden of girls." The proliferation of flowers symbolizes these blooming young women, budding stars that Warners is cultivating.

In the first scene the camera moves slowly through the blossoms before entering the house through open French doors. The family is playing music together. After a close-up of Adam and an establishing shot of the musicians, Ann, Thea, and Emma are introduced one by one, through separate pan and zoom shots, each of which begins with another sister at the edge of the frame, so that although attention eventually focuses on the individual, the shots also emphasize each sister's relation to the family. The shot of Kay shows Ann behind her, and the camera pulls out to include the other sisters as well. The film repeatedly showcases sisterly relations. There are several tight shots of the four of them, and they are also frequently shown as spectators of another's actions, as when Emma, Kay, and Ann together watch Thea leave for her first date. And readying Thea for it is a production that involves the community: the stockings of one, the slip of another, the scarf of a third, a ritual that is repeated. Kay even "relax[es] for" Thea. It is the unbreakable bonds of sisterhood and family that the film embraces, visually and thematically. After Thea becomes engaged to Ben, Ann is horrified at the possibility that she would marry him, not because Thea doesn't love him—Ann barely listens when her sister rejects love as "over-rated, old-fashioned" and talks about her social ambitions—but because she cannot believe that her sister could love someone more than she loves them. Ann and Emma pledge, half-seriously, not to marry away from it.

The Lemp family makes music together recreationally, for its own pleasure, the kind of homegrown entertainment that commercial amusements such as the cinema helped to erode. But the young Lemps are not as stuffy as the weighty classical performance that opens the film might suggest. Kay peeks at the copy of *True Romance* hidden under her music. The young women's tastes run to the popular in music as well; they can't resist bursting into lively swing, to the chagrin of their purist father. If the sisters' tastes lean toward the contemporary, there is still ample room for old-fashioned, small-town ways. They like their music to swing, but swinging on gates is highly prized, too. Felix and Ann first meet when she joins him on the front gate, and at the end they are back at it to effect their reconciliation. Gate-swinging also provides the film with its Capraesque comic ending; an elderly, scowling neighbor secretly, joyously, takes a few turns after the couple is finished. Gate-swinging stands for home, the small town, romance, and youth. It is even the subject of flirtatious conversations about best practices, as though *Four Daughters* were so moved by its own simplicity that the film feels compelled to call attention to it. It is gate-swinging, more than swing music, that sets the tempo and provides an organizing trope. Back and forth, Felix and Ann get together, break up, get together again. Like the blossoms on the tree above the gate, swinging is a sign of change and constancy. The swinger is in motion but remains comfortably in place, suspended between alternatives that require no choice. The family can play classical music, and the girls break into swing; the film and the sisters, comfortable with the ways of modernity and the small town, can have it both ways.

Gate-swinging takes place at the threshold of the home; although marriages are plentiful, and the film follows the three daughters who become wives, it is also about how the four remain sisters. Ann violates the vow she made to Emma, but there are unforeseen benefits. When mercenary Thea mistakenly believes that Ben was badly injured in the accident that kills Mickey, she berates herself for being a bad wife and realizes how much she cares. She married, it turns out, for love as well as money. Emma had always wanted "a knight in shining armor" until she saw how "quiet, capable, [and] dignified" Ernest was during the elopement crisis, and he becomes the family's secondary caretaker, a male version of the hardworking Aunt Etta (May Robson). What Thea and Emma discover is not romantic passion but deep-seated affection; one might say that each loves her man like a sister. Kay, who sings rather than courts, is the only family member absent from the Christmas reunion, which suggests that marriage is less a bar to sisterhood than a career, although she joins the family after a fashion. Kay enters the home via a radio broadcast of her performance of Mendelssohn's "On Wings of Song," a cozy marriage of classical music and popular culture.

The family union and reunion is possible because of the genuine outsider in its midst. Mickey is the alternative that *Four Daughters* cannot accommodate and finally expels. He both welcomes and resents his misfortunes and is determined to make others suffer with him. Whereas Ben, as Thea's guest, approaches the dinner table with a satisfied "There's nothing like a good home-cooked dinner," Mickey enters the house and sneers: "It's homes like these that are the backbone of the nation. Where's the spinning wheel?" Cynicism and contempt for all things domestic have just walked in the door, bringing rudeness along for the ride. Ann questions Mickey about his philosophy. She listens to him complain about his tough life and "the Fates, the destinies," who are always "up there, working overtime against me." Ann is sympathetic about his hardships but dismisses his attitude toward them with a candid "Of course, you know, you've been very silly." To her credit, and to the surprise of anyone familiar with the individualist ethos of classical Hollywood film, after announcing her own creed—"that a man decides his own destiny" and anything is possible with "enough courage" and "enough ambition"—she acknowledges the silliness of that position too, with the help of just one smirk from her interlocutor. Mickey requires a middle ground; if people don't always make their own destiny, then Ann will make Mickey's. She takes him on as a project, which involves, circa 1938, getting him "to liv[e] like a human being," to become more like them.

Flowerpots, chintz curtains, and creases in his pants won't do it. Ann can only humanize Mickey by making him fall in love with her. Loving Ann is as close as he comes to being a gate-swinger; she is the one thing that moves him out of his orbit of contempt and self-pity. Ann helps Mickey cheat the Fates just once, when she abandons Felix and marries him. The marriage brings him "closer to [happiness] than I've ever been before"—always only almost. It brings Ann as close to unhappiness as she is capable of feeling, which has less to do with the misalliance than with the separation from her family. New York City is a radical change, although we never see the busy streets or any other exterior shot to identify it. Rather, the city is important for its interiors. There are only three interior settings in the whole film. Two are in New York and appear briefly: the Bordens' apartment, which is surprisingly decent given their putative poverty, and a restaurant where they eat with some musician friends. The city is not really a crowded, dirty, alienating alternative to Briarwood, something that could so easily be shown; it is simply not home. The third interior, of course, is the Lemp house, a tribute to Warners' economy, as well as the family's self-sufficiency—even the aborted marriage was to have taken place there, as though home is a place you never have to leave.

And you can go home again, as Ann does at Christmas. It is on this trip that Mickey realizes there is more to his separation from the Lemp family than his contempt for it. Shortly after their arrival, Ernest seizes Emma and kisses her under the mistletoe. Ben gives his wife a smooch, too, and is scolded for his trouble. The camera pulls back to make more room, and Ann obligingly drags her father into the frame. It pulls back farther until Mickey comes into view in the far left foreground, in what becomes an over-the-shoulder shot (see figure 11). In choosing

FIGURE 11. In *Four Daughters* Mickey (John Garfield) does not belong in the Lemp family or in the family film.

her father over her husband, Ann renders Mickey a spectator of all this familial affection, but unlike the sisters, who take turns companionably watching each other, his gaze renders him apart from, not a part of. The film cuts to a close-up of Mickey, who smiles uneasily at a joke Adam makes. At this point Felix's voice thrusts Mickey's face from the frame. Not to be outdone, as at home with the Lemps as ever, Felix pulls the camera back to the mistletoe, where he has commanded Aunt Etta to appear. The eight of them, laughing, fill the frame; there is no room in this family for Mickey, even if there were anyone left for him to kiss. The camera cuts to another close-up of him, no smile this time, as he takes the measure of his alienation, which he now seems to understand is, in fact, exclusion.

Their rejection of Mickey leads to his death. We know it's a suicide because after watching the windshield wipers move back and forth, like the arc of the swinging gate, he turns them off and speeds up on a snowy road. It is also evident from the bleakness inside the car, so utterly unlike the rest of the film: the music grim and urgent; the claustrophobic low-angle shot of Mickey through the steering wheel as he lights a last cigarette; the shadows on his face; the strangely ecstatic smile.

Killing himself enables Mickey to reject this family. It makes exclusion exclusively his again.

Mickey could not really be humanized, which is to say he could not be assimilated into the middle-class family that he desires as much as disdains. The Lemp home is the backbone not only of the nation but of the family film. In keeping with his insistence on sleeping on "the other side of the railroad tracks" in Briarwood, Mickey seems to be commuting in from another movie altogether, one with different generic and formal conventions, and from another decade. Most notably, the style of the suicide scene, not to mention the intrusion of anything as wholly remote from the warm domestic embrace we have received as a suicide, aligns these elements of *Four Daughters* with what would later come to be called *film noir*.

The kind of film that cynical, urban Mickey more properly belongs to is one far more in keeping with the narrative and stylistic tradition of Warner Bros. than the family comedy-drama. In addition to expanding the appeal of what is essentially a film for women, the part of Mickey served as a vehicle for delivering Garfield as a promising and distinctive new talent to audiences. Mickey was the prototype for future Garfield roles as the angry, isolated "city boy," including further appearances with Priscilla Lane in *Daughters Courageous* and *Dust Be My Destiny* (both 1939). In *Four Daughters*, when the musicians propose heading to South America, one of them remarks that it's "a topical country." Another corrects him: "Tropical. 'Topical' means right now, up-to-date." Here is a nod and wink to the real Warners, the studio that built its reputation, and the careers of actors such as Garfield, on topical films that captured something of the texture of contemporary life and problems. Mickey doesn't go to South America, but he remains an exotic within the film, his sardonic commentary on the conventions of the family drama providing a fitting Warners antidote to its sentimental excesses.[58]

Mickey may have infiltrated the family film, but according to reviewers he did not derail it. They were quick to point out that "it has many gay and light-hearted moments" despite the surprising element of tragedy, and the film's "purpose . . . is to lift up rather than depress." The difference between his "sour, fatalistic outlook on life" and everything else was widely noted at the time, but the disconnect was scarcely remarked as a flaw. Garfield stood out in the lavishness of the praise he received, amid performances that overall were thought highly distinguished. Like Mickey with Ann, he wrested the film away from the other actors. Indeed, the review of *Four Daughters* conducted by the Production Code Administration inexplicably assigned it to the "Social Problem" category, as though succumbing to Mickey's account of his circumstances and the force of Garfield's performance.[59]

A rare critic who did not care much for *Four Daughters* still considered Garfield to be "an actor of substance and considerable integrity. His sharp, clipped speech is something new for the screen, his personality, a strange, unique thing to come across in a world of glamour boys," as befitted the trend of the time. Reviewers would struggle with the language to define his appeal. When Garfield was called "an actor of the natural school," it was not in the sense that Loy, Henie, the "unaffected and natural" Priscilla Lane, or any of the other so-touted stars were considered natural. Neither strange nor unique, they were thought to possess a "just folks" normalcy that made audiences comfortable, and their naturalness described a quality of personality rather than of technique. By contrast, Garfield's performance in *Four Daughters* was highly self-conscious and "introverted," "slow-paced and psychologically profound," to the point where he seemed, to one critic, "detached" as an actor from the rest of a film in which relationships are paramount. Much has since been made of Garfield's work with the Group Theatre, a pioneer institution in method acting. The idea of the "natural school" pointed to training and technical proficiency. Out of the sentimental, nostalgic world of the family film, at the moment of its greatest appeal, came a transformative performance style that was dedicated to creating vivid, psychologically complex characters. Garfield's remarkable performance was just as "strange and out of place" in a film like *Four Daughters* as Mickey Borden was in the home of the Lemps.[60]

And it was also remote from the scheme of things in the fall of 1938. *Four Daughters* was usually seen as a triumph for the family film and the new reality of cozy middle-class homes. But in his hardship, the "self-conscious, cynical, reckless and fatalistic" Mickey, as well as the actor who portrayed him, injected reality of another kind. "In this medium of sweetness and light which we call the cinema, we are rarely treated to a person so heartbreakingly close to reality." Mickey was hardly less contrived in his working-class misery than any of the other characters in their fundamental complacency; what made him seem real was his insistence on "punching little holes in the fantasy" of Hollywood wish-fulfillment and happy endings. He expects nothing from his marriage to Ann but a partner in his tough luck. It was Mickey's relation to an unrealistic medium as such, as well as to the family cycle—his

position not only as a character but as a cynical and sharp-eyed spectator of the action—that enabled him to represent the possibilities of a
more realistic filmmaking.[61]

What all of this amounted too, of course, was a very *human* film, a
term applied with predictable and particular abandon to *Four Daughters*. Over and over it was celebrated as "a human, heart-warming
story," a "very human story," "a most human comedy drama," with
characters that have "the universal human touch." There was no reason
to get by on just one *human* when two would do: "It's a believable,
human movie, loaded with human touches." Calling *Four Daughters* "rich in homey, human entertainment essentials," one delighted
small-town reviewer/exhibitor elevated the *homey* and the *human*—
these terms were often treated as coextensive—to cinematic necessities.
To produce something truly *human* was to bring forth from fiction a
deeper truth, beyond but not without entertainment value. Thus *Four
Daughters* was not simply a movie but "a sympathetic and believable
human document," "a simple, human document of universal appeal."
As "a resounding answer to pleas for less artificiality and more reality in the movies," it reminded reviewers of how far Hollywood films
were thought to have wandered from the realm of their audiences' lives.
"Hollywood has been giving 'escapist' themes for so long now that a
film with a story as simple and true to life as 'Four Daughters' . . . is
almost a sensation." Mickey's sacrificial suicide did not disturb the reviewers any more than it did Felix and Ann. One reviewer's praise for
the film came across as impatient contempt for the film industry, making it sound as though the Lemps and their satellites had simply taken
matters into their own hands: "The characters outrage Hollywood tradition by speaking the speech of recognizable human beings in recognizable situations."[62]

No one was more eager to embrace this remarkable human achievement and bold repudiation of business as usual than the company that
made it. A special advertisement in the form of an open letter from
Jack Warner ran in big city newspapers across the country. Only the
studio's vice president in charge of production could announce and interpret such a momentous event. Like the institutional advertising for
MPGY, it was visually plain and full of text, as Warners likewise tried
to distinguish the ad from typical movie ballyhoo, without giving up
the language of superlatives on which film promotion depended. *Four
Daughters* offered "something" so "remarkable," so "truly unique,"
it "should be seen, must be seen, will be seen by every man, woman

and child in this great city." It not only represented the culmination of Warners' efforts but brought glory to the industry as a whole: "'FOUR DAUGHTERS' [is] a picture destined to fulfill every promise the motion picture industry has ever made to the public; a picture that in its humanity and greatness will prove forever unforgettable." He lingered over "three young players"—Priscilla Lane, Garfield, and Lynn—and predicted their "glorious" future, because the public would warmly embrace them: "We believe that you, after seeing them, will make them stars by your acclaim." He purported to be "prouder" of this film than of more ambitious achievements: *Anthony Adverse* (1936), *The Adventures of Robin Hood,* and the unconventional *Story of Louis Pasteur* (1936) and *Life of Emile Zola* (1937). What did *Four Daughters* offer that popular historical spectacles and prestige biopics did not? "Thrilling sincerity" and "heart-warming simplicity." Pasteur labored to serve humanity; *Four Daughters* exemplified it. If sincerity seems less thrilling than, say, the siege of the castle at the end of *The Adventures of Robin Hood,* or the San Francisco earthquake in *The Sisters,* another Warners MPGY melodrama, the pairing of such terms was ubiquitous in ads for films with a large dose of human appeal. The language of thrills sought to persuade moviegoers that films with virtually no action could excite the emotions and thus deliver heart palpitations of a different but just as satisfying sort.[63]

Warner signed the letter "with all sincerity," and he did seem thrilled, but at least one Chicago reviewer was less moved: "Hollywood's obvious amazement . . . over the fact that the film turns out to be delightful instead of tedious, strikes us as a little ingenuous. In spite of the success of the Judge Hardy pictures . . . the studio has been in a perfect dither of astonishment . . . which makes it plain that nothing surprises Hollywood so much as simplicity and nothing startles it so much as the discovery that there are bright pictures to be made without recourse to the customary sophistication, hokum or out-and-out melodrama." Or rather, the Hollywood executive saw the advantage of presenting himself to the public as a figure for it, as though he, too, were a charmed and excited viewer of the film, and just as delightfully amazed by what the industry could accomplish. Warner pointed out that his "business is making pictures, not advertising them," but he based his appeal on the fact that he had "seen" *Four Daughters,* not that he had created it.[64]

Jack Warner's letter to the public was in keeping with the rest of the promotional strategy for *Four Daughters,* which was thought novel enough to merit discussion in the trade press. There were three distinct campaigns, an approach that addressed the selling problems and opportunities presented by a "classy" film about small-town life with no real star power. The first, a "dignified" prestige campaign, targeted "discriminating audiences in cities of a million and over." The second, "a modified 'class' campaign," was "designed for smaller cities and for general clientele in the big cities," while another catered to small towns and houses "where straight movie copy is the only proven way of selling a picture." Warner's letter was part of the first, unorthodox campaign, whose other ads included only one illustration, a small drawing of four young women's faces in profile, gazing upward, exalted either by their part in this exceptional film or enraptured as the feminine audience for it. There was also a follow-up letter from Warner, "You have seen 'Four Daughters,'" highlighting the degree to which producer and public agreed on the merits of the film; his predictions had all come true. It ended with another tribute to the public relations benefits of the film—"One critic said 'Four Daughters' is a credit to Warner Bros. and the motion picture industry"—and then trumped it: "The greatest credit, however, must go to you, the movie-going public, whose never-failing response to our finer efforts provides us with desire and incentive to make ever greater ones." Thus Warner reminded readers that the public is ultimately responsible for the production of distinguished films, even if it only receives informal credit.[65]

The second campaign was less abstract and did not indulge in the same sort of solicitations of public understanding and cooperation. It was a more conventional effort to sell the film and the stars rather than the studio or the industry. The ads included plugs for Warners' three stars-in-the-making, with photographs of Priscilla Lane, Garfield, and Lynn. There was lots more about "thrills" too. If this treatment could be thought "classy," it was only in comparison with the third campaign, whose ads exploited the romantic angle—"KAY wanted love . . . mad dangerous love! THEA wanted love and riches at any price! EMMA wanted love for the glory of loving!"—and the sisters' competition for the same man. "Girls yesterday, women today . . . because they fell in love!" This *Four Daughters* was all but unrecognizable as the film of distinction that had made Jack Warner so proud.[66]

Although the campaigns were designed with the differences between urban and small-town audiences and classes of theaters in mind, the advertising booklet instructed that campaigns could be combined. Exhibitors did just that. An ad from the Paramount in Gulfport, Mississippi, for example, moved between sensationalism and dignity. The bold headline, "We WARN YOU! Woman-Wise Fannie Hurst Bares the most Intimate Secrets of the Feminine Soul," was followed by references to "Human Emotion" and "brilliant inspired Portrayals," ending with an urgent yet flowery warning of another sort: "To See it is to Love it. To Miss it is to Regret it all your Life." Sid Holland of the Elkhart Amusement Company divided his signed ad in two; the right side earnestly advised readers of the film's quality, "the touch of inspiration [that] makes it live with a sincerity, a humanity, a warmth," ending with: "I cannot truthfully say that 'FOUR DAUGHTERS' is the biggest, most lavish, most expensive picture of the year. I CAN truthfully say that no picture will give you more enjoyment." On the left he exploited the "Girls Yesterday! Women Today" romance: "Kay Loved Beauty. Emma Loved Glamour. Thea Loved Wealth. Ann Loved Life. Then They All Fell in Love with The Same Man!" The three ad campaigns accommodated different desires and expectations, and exhibitors combined them because these differences obtained within as well as between theaters and communities. There was no single *Four Daughters* because there was no unified audience. But as different as people are, they could still fall in love with the same film.[67]

And thus the film offered, according to one ad, "a story as great as all humanity, its appeal as universal!" The charm of the *human* was that it could be made to speak vaguely to what we all have in common, to something essential, something beyond the vagaries of taste that informed three ad campaigns. It was the closest thing the industry could imagine to a film of mass appeal in the absence of a mass audience. Making such a film was evidence of Warners' humanity; the studio harbored sweet and cheerful Priscilla Lane, as well as bitter, cynical Garfield, whose Mickey himself bears witness and succumbs to the Lemps' and the film's charm. Loving *Four Daughters* was evidence of our humanity. This film was "bound to strike a responsive and appreciative chord in the hearts of any audience no matter how widely tastes and preferences may differ." Filling films with human beings might fill theater seats with them too.[68]

BOYS TOWN

If a pleasant, well-made family drama such as *Four Daughters* could be treated as a public relations boon for a troubled industry, *Boys Town* was in an even stronger position to convert the faithless. An "uncommon credit on Hollywood," it tells the story of selfless Father Edward

Flanagan (Spencer Tracy), a Catholic priest who in 1917 opened a home for boys in Omaha and devoted his life to proving that kindness and care, not reformatories and prisons, were the best way to deal with disadvantaged boys, "regardless of race, creed or color." Its claim on the *real* was literal and urgent; in contrast to the usual disclaimer about the fictiveness of people and events represented, the foreword insists: "There is such a place as Boys Town," and "There is such a man as Father Flanagan." And this film, too, as we have come to expect, was both celebrated and sold for "its earnest, compelling, deeply emotional 'humanness.'" The real Boys Town was a "unique" and "great experiment" in creating "good American citizens" out of potential delinquents and in winning public support for that project. *Boys Town* was an experiment as well, whose outcome was likewise not at all foreordained. At a time of presumed demand for real stories about real people, this film could claim to deliver the goods, but to the extent that the public's desire for reality was understood as the wish to see its own lives and problems represented, in the gentle, soft-focus fashion of *Four Daughters,* the story of its protagonist and his unorthodox lifework ran something of a risk. As a social-problem drama about an actual preacher, the serious *Boys Town* offered a more direct challenge to the assumption that audiences wanted entertainment, not preachment, than the wacky *You Can't Take It with You* ever could. *Boys Town* might establish whether widespread public support existed or could be generated for movies that delivered serious messages on behalf of legitimate social goals.[69]

Boys Town is related to a cycle of films that were treating the problem of crime and juvenile delinquency from a sociological angle. It begins grimly, in prison. Father Flanagan listens to a prisoner's death-row confession and harsh, moving indictment of "the State," whose indifference and incompetence turned "a lonely, starving kid" into a murderer. "One friend when I'm twelve years old, and I don't stand here like this." Other films in the cycle show how criminals are made, dramatizing the process and the outcome of such dead-end lives, and some, such as MPGY's B film *Juvenile Court,* reveal how they are unmade. *Boys Town* emphasizes how criminals might never be formed at all. Father Flanagan's struggle to care for the boys and prevent delinquency is the film's dramatic center, a substitute for the sensationalism that gave crime films so much of their appeal. *Boys Town* was also notably devoid of romance, a "man meets boy meets boy meets boy . . ." story without a couple, with scarcely even a woman, let alone anyone as buxom as

Juvenile Court's reform-minded Rita Hayworth. Tracy is "father" to hundreds of boys, but this film family is an immaculate conception. A sexless priest in a sexless film: thus is glamour wrung out of an MGM product, and unlike Tracy's first priestly turn in *San Francisco* (1936), there are no Clark Gable and Jeanette MacDonald to put it back.

Father Flanagan's philosophy is simple: "There's no such thing in the world as a bad boy." As creeds go, this was as telling for a 1930s film as was the insistence on enjoyment in *You Can't Take It with You*. There were plenty of people who thought not only that bad boys really did exist but that the movies, and crime films in particular, played a significant role in the production of them. Henry James Forman's *Our Movie Made Children* (1933) was a popular and heavy-handed summary of the Payne Fund Studies, a notable social science research project that sought to ascertain the effect of movies on American youth. The book's title made clear the irresistible influence Forman thought they exerted. "Motion pictures are a school," and its lessons were not salutary. "The road to delinquency . . . is heavily dotted with movie addicts, and obviously, it needs no crusaders or preachers or reformers to come to this conclusion." For Forman the movie habit was a deleterious *addiction*. The "constant repetition" of scenes of crime and violence "must sooner or later wear paths in young brains in the least susceptible or suggestible," regardless of any "Crime Does Not Pay" moral the movies hustled in toward the end.[70]

The movie preacher of *Boys Town* reaches a different conclusion. After a fight between Mo Kahn (Sidney Miller) and Whitey Marsh (Mickey Rooney), a disagreeable tough whose stubborn resistance to Boys Town tests Father Flanagan's theory, the boys have to "watch" a western with their backs to the screen. The punishment's effectiveness is demonstrated by the excitement with which the news of a movie is greeted, their disappointment at the condition of attendance, and the friendship that develops straightaway. The compulsion to attend movies produces nothing more serious than the desire for more movies, which are a benign and useful disciplinary mechanism for producing better boys, wielded by a priest no less. Although the content of movies like westerns might be thought to promote antisocial violence as a way to resolve conflict, *Boys Town* proposes another way. The first children we see are involved in a lively street fight; they seem very bad indeed before Father Flanagan opens the first home. *Boys Town*'s own commitment to a better breed of boy is evident in its handling of the next fights. We do not see the one between Whitey and Mo; it occurs behind a closed door and apparently consists of a single punch. Punishment is exacted. Later the film teaches boys how fights should take place; Whitey and Freddie Fuller (Frankie Thomas) take their irresolvable disagreements into the ring, where they box strictly by Hoyle's Rules. The movie violence for which Hollywood was frequently scolded is productively channeled into disciplined, competitive sport, a now licit form of entertainment.

I have suggested that the public relations aspirations of MPGY were unrelated to matters of self-regulation and censorship; the industry was much less interested in aspiring to goodness than in making good films that people wanted to see. With its timely humanness and lack of glamour, allied with such unimpeachable virtue, *Boys Town* could achieve both goals. Although the film models a process of "cleaning up" the movies, however, it is skeptical of the organized pressure groups that drove that effort. While more gently represented, the church hierarchy is shown to be as neglectful as the state. Father Flanagan receives permission from the bishop to proceed with his "unorthodox" plan but no help of any kind. Sociology is not theology. Rather, his project depends on winning "public support." Without that, his affluent friend, Dave Morris (Henry Hull), will not lend him money to expand the home into a "town for the boys" on more than two hundred acres. It is good to have God on your side but more important to win over the press, which is not "friendly" to his project.

Father Flanagan calls on the unsympathetic newspaper publisher John Hargraves (Jonathan Hale), who objects to his "tacit criticism of things as they are." The priest is "flying in the face of the very best of public opinion." Here Hargraves gives himself away. Public opinion does not come in grades like meat; the "best" is simply the thinking of an elite, unrepresentative segment of it. To persuade him, Father Flanagan reminds him that he sometimes counters the "best of public opinion," too, as a publisher: "You lead public opinion." But toward the end of the film, when Whitey is mistakenly blamed for a bank robbery and the existence of Boys Town threatened, Hargraves refuses to "forg[e]t [his] duty as a newspaperman," which means pandering to the "women's clubs" that are gunning for it based on rumor, rather than keeping the public informed of facts. He "owns the most powerful string of newspapers in the Middle West," yet the publisher seems oddly disempowered, capitulating to noisy pressure groups rather as the movies did. The miracle of *Boys Town* was to criticize the influence and limitations of their orthodoxy, while establishing itself as a film that won over such groups as well as the moviegoing public.[71]

Hardheaded Hargraves thinks that "'no such thing as a bad boy'" is "just a catch phrase, sentimental nonsense." Father Flanagan tries to work the sentimental angle anyway to gain his endorsement. He points out that when Hargraves was "eleven or twelve" and "got into trouble," he had parents to put "their arms around [him]" and "talk things over with." A robust hashing-out of problems was the signature of the Andy Hardy series; during the inevitable crisis Andy seeks out his father to "talk something over with [him], man to man." The impact of such parental guidance on the development of boys is proved, so far as cinema goes, in the difference between Rooney as Andy Hardy and Rooney as Whitey Marsh. But the conservative publisher—unlike Louis B. Mayer, the conservative studio head who so favored the Hardy films—is immune to the tacit reference to MGM's most valuable brand. Hargraves does not think that the idea of "a town for boys, governed by boys" is "worth a shot," but the hallmark of another treasured MGM asset sways him. Father Flanagan's manner, or lack of manneredness, rather than his arguments carries the day. "Your sincerity *is* worth a shot," Hargraves concedes, a tribute to Tracy qua priest. Sincerity was Tracy's signature quality as an actor. He projected a kind of honest earnestness and integrity, and his roles increasingly reflected this. Joan Bennett's comment is characteristic of the way colleagues and many reviewers spoke of Tracy: she "never had the feeling he was acting." He was among the most natural of stars.[72]

It is fitting that Rooney as Whitey figures as the most important internal threat to Boys Town, after he is mistaken for a bank robber. His exaggerated performance, first as the cocky tough and later as the weepy penitent, contrasts starkly with Tracy's restraint. By the film's release, his style was described in terms such as "Rooney rampant" and his "mugging" frequently remarked, although the actor also continued to register as an archetype of male adolescence. Like Mickey in *Four Daughters,* Whitey is a hard-luck case, but Garfield's performance was about psychological realism, whereas Rooney's is all gesture. Garfield's intensity moderated the sentimental excesses of the family film and infused it with something more like the Warners house style, while Rooney's mannerisms highlight performance over part and keep *Boys Town* from an excess of reality, tempering the social-problem elements with floods of tears. Whitey reforms in the end; Rooney's technique stays the same. His sobbing confession that he loves Boys Town but had to warn his brother, one of the robbers, before saving it, dissolves whatever might have been sensationalistic about the scene in which the priest and the other boys capture the gang into such unabashed sentimentality that no red-blooded boy would ever think of emulating it (see figure 12).[73]

A hammy actor is not necessarily a bad actor, and he is certainly not a bad boy. Sentiment is not nonsense. Whitey's reward is that he is finally elected the mayor of Boys Town by his peers. He lost when he ran on the "Don't Be a Sucker" ticket, bribed other candidates, and treated the election as an empty spectacle. Now that cynicism has yielded to sentiment, Whitey wins by acclamation. He proves his fitness for office because he did not seek it, and he cries a lot at the election. *Boys Town,* and the ending in particular, attests to the merging of two tendencies at MGM in the late 1930s and 1940s: screenwriter and future studio head Dore Schary's attraction to democracy in action, and Mayer's unbridled sentiment.

The film tries to live up to the democratic principles by which the town is self-governed as much as it does to the studio's sentimental ideals, but results are mixed. On the one hand, Boys Town, like *Boys Town,* is what happens when Catholics and Jews work together. The ecumenical spirit is pervasive even though Dave is never explicitly identified as Jewish. Yet he is a pawnbroker with inflections that, if not necessarily Semitic, don't seem Nebraskan. The character was described as Jewish everywhere in reviews and commentary that mentioned Hull's performance, which attracted much praise. It is as though the film can't demonstrate its own broad-mindedness unless it marks Dave in this way, so that it may accept and honor him regardless, oddly challenging and reinforcing stereotypes at the same time.

The film also highlights Father Flanagan's commitment to caring for all boys "regardless of race, creed or color." Whitey's most serious affront to the ideals of Boys Town is his anti-Semitism. He insults Mo enthusiastically and often; even his first overture of friendship is to offer Mo the job of "finance commissioner" for helping him to become mayor, a joke Mo doesn't get. The central lesson someone named *Whitey* must learn is tolerance. The film demonstrates this most forcefully in a montage of close-ups of the boys uttering different prayers over lunch. Mo, in a *yarmulke,* offers one in Hebrew, and a boy who might be Native American says nothing at all. Whitey asks: "What's the matter? Can't you all learn the same words?" They don't need to at Boys Town, he is informed. "You say the kind of grace you want to say." "Everybody worships as they please, thinks the way they want to think." This is rather different from the lesson in *You Can't Take*

FIGURE 12. Spencer Tracy's restraint contrasts with Mickey Rooney's hyperactivity in *Boys Town*.

It with You about individual freedom. Religious belief is not just one kooky taste among others, and Mo's right to pray as he likes is taken more seriously than Mrs. Kirby's right to like spiritualism. "We have to respect each other if we're going to like each other, and . . . we have to like each other if we're going to get along," Father Flanagan instructs Whitey after the fight with Mo. We have to respect each other to get along because we're all different, but there is no "thanks be." Difference here is not a fetishized antidote to dullness but an acknowledged source of conflict, a problem to be grappled with. *Boys Town* labors to show that respect for difference is as much about obligations to the community as the right of individuals to think and do what they please. And these lessons are actual lessons, part of Whitey's and our introduction to the Boys Town regime. *Boys Town*'s courage lay in delivering its preachment as preachment, which is not always woven into the fabric of the entertainment.

There are no lectures on racial tolerance. An irate article in the *Pittsburgh Courier*, an African American weekly, mentioned that *Boys Town* was supposed to have significant parts for boys of the race but did not, for which the author blamed the "Jews who control the indus-try." Instead there is blackface. It is not the Jew who blacks up; in this film Jewish boys can and will be Jewish boys. Mo surreptitiously black-ens Whitey when the latter comes into the barbershop for a haircut and massage. The rest of the boys find this hysterical a few minutes later at roll call. Whitey may have been asking for it: when he saw a statue of a boy with outstretched arms, he launched into "Mammy." The enter-tainment value of blacks in Hollywood was something of a creed. Racial difference is all about making and having fun; it provides a comic break in the monotony of uniformed boys at attention, a momentary glimpse at how tiresome life on this island of moral perfection might sometimes be. You can disrespect difference when it's just Mickey Rooney putting on a show, when it's not really different.[74]

If *Boys Town* does not entirely practice what it preaches, it may be because the film must demonstrate how well preachment and solid entertainment can go together. *San Francisco* had brought them into conversation a few years earlier; Mary Blake (MacDonald), a night-club singer and preacher's daughter, gets a bit too serious for her boss, Blackie Norton (Gable), who gets enough of that sort of thing from Father Tim (Tracy). Blackie stops her: "If you're going to preach, Mary, please sing. That's what I believe in." By the end of the film, chastised by the earthquake, Blackie realizes that there is no percentage in god-lessness and joins Mary and the rest of the city in "Battle Hymn of the Republic." Preaching and singing are united in a splendid production number; song makes preachment palatable. Preaching is far more in-tegral to *Boys Town,* and the point is that a Hollywood film can talk at you but still perform for you, doing what it is supposed to do best. Tracy's self-effacement advertises the film's humble emulation of the values of the real Boys Town and its self-sacrificing founder, as do the relative modesty of its budget and what we might call its spectacular lack of glamour. Tracy's lauded, "sincere portrayal" of Father Flana-gan, for which he won his second Academy Award in a row, and *Boys Town*'s "honesty, sincerity, and the fervor of its message" bespeak the film's quiet faith in its own good works. But not too quiet. Rooney's over-the-top self-dramatization draws attention to its commitment to entertainment, the endless, almost pathological desire to please, which was perhaps the keynote of this actor's egregious style.[75]

As *Variety* put it, after noting that *Boys Town* was rewarded with spontaneous applause at the preview, it "is at once delightfully and sig-nificantly about something important, in civic and private life." It was, in other words, significantly significant, not a trivial gesture toward importance but a genuine "social service," "excellent in social values," "a real contribution to American ideals of service to humanity." And such significance was also delightful, to critics as well as audiences. Indeed, *Boys Town* delighted critics in part because of what it said about the possibilities for an enlightened screen. It served as "a fresh demonstration that the screen can turn out shows which are worth seeing as well as entertaining." The experiment paid off, insofar as viewers would be "fired by its message" but also "absorbed by the story." No wonder Louella Parsons wrote, "I am proud of being in motion pictures after seeing 'Boystown' [sic]," despite only barely being in motion pictures. It made one wish one were.[76]

It is one thing for movies to be "clean" or unobjectionable; it is quite another for them to perform a useful public service. *Boys Town* is as savvy as Father Flanagan becomes about the importance of getting public opinion on your side: that's how you stay in business. It creates public support for a film that would seem to put the good of Boys Town ahead of *Boys Town*, or at least to blur the difference between mutually reinforcing benefits, the making of good boys and good films. *Time* speculated that *Boys Town* "may well turn out to be the answer" to Father Flanagan's plan, at the end of the film, to raise money to enlarge Boys Town again. Such publicity for so worthy a cause, generated by Hollywood's most extravagant studio, would benefit the home as well. *Boxoffice*'s prediction was more accurate: *Boys Town* "will dip deep into the hearts of theatre patrons of all ages and classes and should dip comparably deep into their purses to roll up the profitable grosses so splendid a feature merits." The particular gamble that was *Boys Town* paid off in spades for MGM—$2,112,000 in profits, its best showing of the year, on production costs of $772,000—but not for the real Father Flanagan. He thought the publicity would increase donations, but contributions were reported to have gone down in the wake of the film's release, and the number of boys who sought aid increased. It was theorized that Boys Town did not seem to the public to require benefactors any longer: what movie star does? This was another little industry embarrassment but not a disaster. The film generated so much good will, not to mention a sequel in 1941, and it was charitably unpunished for the incalculable effects of publicity, from which the industry itself also suffered at times. *Boys Town* enjoyed a worthy reputation as a film that "should send audiences back to their homes, happy that there is such a thing as a picture theatre and thanking circumstances that permitted them to have enough money to partake of its entertainment." If nothing else, *Boys Town* makes you grateful that you can afford movies like *Boys Town*.[77]

MARIE ANTOINETTE

Into an environment that celebrated the *human* at the expense, one might say, of most everything Hollywood had come to stand for, that found salvation for a chastened industry in plain stories about plain people, MGM also released its prestige superspecial *Marie Antoinette*. If *Boys Town* represented a newer, less ostentatious direction for Hollywood's most extravagant studio, *Marie Antoinette* was a bejeweled artifact from a more profligate time. In the works for five years, with a production cost of almost $3 million and one of those casts of thousands, it starred Norma Shearer in her first role since the ill-fated *Romeo and Juliet*. According to Tino Balio, it was MGM's "most lavish extravaganza of the decade," planned before producer Irving Thalberg's death, an imperial tribute to his wife and his own filmmaking prowess. Shearer's marriage to Thalberg had solidified her position as "queen of Metro," but by the film's release she no longer reigned supreme, except perhaps by studio fiat. Fellow MGM star and natural girl Myrna Loy, who appeared in eleven films to Shearer's two between 1936 and 1938, wore the crown of "Queen of the Movies" following the newspaper poll of December 1937. In Hollywood, monarchy was democratically elected by a powerful authority, the "consumer" who was really "king."[78]

And movie queens, like actual queens, could be deposed. *Marie Antoinette* may once have looked like a sure bet, with stars, spectacle, and glamour to spare, but in the wake of an ambivalent reception following the July premiere in Los Angeles, it emerged as one of the year's riskiest productions in a time fraught with risk. MGM was still the most successful of the studios by virtue of its star power and the *ne plus ultra* quality of its films. By the fall of 1938, however, the queen and the film about her seemed to symbolize everything the film industry was busily defining itself against to placate a public whose dissatisfaction had taken on historic proportions. An article in *Screen & Radio Weekly* warned: "The Revolution Has Come to Hollywood, and the Glamour Kings and Queens Are Marching to the Guillotine." Big names were no longer sufficient to attract moviegoers to a film: "Since the revolution," the old movie royalty were just "public figures who face a recall vote every time they appear on the screen." And sometimes before then,

as Shearer was in a position to know. "The public took over the casting" of *Gone with the Wind,* amid a blaze of publicity, and she was
the one among the many stars announced for the role of Scarlett to be
definitively rejected by it. Whereas "the public" "insisted on" Gable,
reports claimed it just as unequivocally did not want Shearer. Parsons
mentioned the "avalanche of letters" she had received to protest her
casting, and Hopper thanked "all you fans for writing in your frank
opinions," which prevented Shearer from making "one of the greatest
mistakes of her life."[79]

Marie Antoinette is not simply another example of George Custen's
astute description of the Hollywood biopic as a genre in which "the star
system speak[s] about itself," "animating its own values" of celebrity,
personality, and prestige through "a parallel world of stars." It is an
artful allegory of the dangers facing the system, highlighting the fragil-
ity of Hollywood's own aristocracy and claim to serve the public. It ges-
tured to the new order of things, in which the raw power of the public
could no longer be ignored, and heralded the advent of something like
democratic practices that were frighteningly out of control. If an angry
French people could eliminate its unpopular queen, an angry moviegoing public might likewise bring down a movie about her.[80]

This Marie Antoinette would not dare, as her unfortunate predecessor had legendarily done, exhort the hungry hordes to "eat cake." What
other films in other years might have done as a matter of course to craft
a more agreeable heroine took on special significance in the context
of the industry's public relations problems. The robust campaign for
Marie Antoinette within the larger MPGY drive would make of the unpopular queen a sympathetic woman, transforming her from a symbol
of indifference to the public into a figure for it. The film makes a case to
the public for leniency, understanding, and ultimately affection. Queens
are people too.

The keynote of a sumptuous costume drama about the French Court
was, of course, glamour, but such a film might nonetheless indulge a
taste for the *human* at the same time, an outcome portended by the
film's source material. It was based on Stefan Zweig's 1932 biography,
Marie Antoinette: The Portrait of an Average Woman. It was the tragedy of "this insignificant Habsburg princess" to have greatness thrust
upon her, he wrote in the introduction. Like stars, some queens are
made, not born. She was "not exceptionally able nor yet exceptionally foolish; neither fire nor ice; devoid of any vigorous wish to do
good and of the remotest inclination to do evil; the average woman of

yesterday, today, and tomorrow," who would be "elevated to the rank of a star performer" in the "stupendous drama of the opening phases of the French Revolution." Marie Antoinette, historical icon, possessed universal qualities; she was less a queen of her time than a woman for all time.[81]

Marie Antoinette's ordinariness is emphasized from the start. In a cold Austrian palace the chattering archduchess learns that she is to be married. She knows and cares nothing of politics and is swept away by the prospect of a romantic alliance. More the giddy American schoolgirl than an aristocrat sensible of her obligations, Marie Antoinette bubbles: "Is he attractive? Do you think he'll like me?" Her no-nonsense mother (Alma Kruger) understands the irrelevance of such questions to Franco-Austrian relations and informs her daughter that she will be the next queen of France. Squealing with delight, and still wanting to know if the dauphin is "handsome," Marie Antoinette is seduced by the prospect of a glamorous career. "I shall be Queen of France," she dreamily murmurs.

The empress warns her gushing daughter that she "must learn to be worthy of [her] destiny," and the story of *Marie Antoinette* is how a rather silly young woman becomes a mature and intelligent ruler. Her transgressions—extravagance, triviality, promiscuity—stem not from bad intentions but high spirits and the failings of others. She is the victim of a loveless, unconsummated marriage, despite her patient efforts to be an exemplary wife and to produce an heir, and of the bitter jealousy of Madame du Barry (Gladys George), who actually has sex with her Louis (John Barrymore) but can never be queen. Finally, the dauphine "depose[s] that milliner" and establishes her presence at court, which leads to a montage of assorted entertainments, each a bit more scandalous than the last. After she loses a diamond necklace on a bet, an emissary from her mother arrives to condemn her behavior. Count de Mercey (Henry Stephenson) warns her against "this extravagance, this mad pursuit of pleasure, which can end only in—" She interrupts: "But not in boredom." If Marie Antoinette was "Terrified of Being Bored," the filmmakers were rather more fearful of the audience's ennui than of hers. One problem was that her frivolous activities are about the most pleasurable parts of the film and are certainly more upbeat than what follows. Conference notes on an early draft of the script, from Thalberg and others, expressed concern that "a reforming queen is so much less interesting than a hectic one." Marie Antoinette the scold, who talked about the peoples' misery and pressed Louis (Robert Morley) into action, was dropped, although the reformed, penitent queen remained. Her "sense of queenship," of "the abnegation of the individual to the principle of royalty," was emphasized at Thalberg's insistence to prevent the ending from being "unbearably harrowing."[82]

She does indeed learn to be a queen, but only by first becoming a woman, thus reversing the trajectory of her royal predecessor in *Queen Christina* (1933). Christina (Garbo) discovers womanly desire, for John Gilbert's Antonio as well as for beautiful things, which prompts her to abdicate the throne. She becomes one of us. To be sympathetic, the extravagant dauphine must learn self-denial, to want less not more, or rather, to want something for which there is no material equivalent. She is like us in her desire for love but also painfully excluded from what we are free to enjoy. This is what Count Axel de Fersen (Tyrone Power) from Sweden (on loan from Fox) teaches her. They first meet at the gambling house where she loses her necklace. He knows who she is, but she coyly pretends to be the "star" of the *opera comique,* and he insults her by treating her as "a little actress." His indifference angers but attracts her. When Marie Antoinette apologizes and then kisses him, he replies that the generous words come from the dauphine, but her lips are those of a "soubrette." With Fersen's help she learns to stop acting the wrong part, or any part at all. The dauphine cannot be common, like everybody else, but she must learn to be natural, that is, like herself (see figure 13).[83]

He convinces her that she possesses a truly noble nature, but it has been disserved by the artificial and extravagant conditions into which circumstances have planted it. Fersen is in a position to make these judgments because he has loved Marie Antoinette from afar for years: her former governess went to work for his family, and that gossipy employee raised him on a steady diet of archduchess anecdotes. He reveals all this at their next meeting, just after the king has told her that he will annul her marriage and send her back to Austria. He dies before acting on his threat but not before Marie Antoinette, believing she will soon be free, has innocently fallen in love. Fersen understands her conspicuous behavior and forgives it because he knows human nature. She "made pleasure a shield against loneliness and slander," because she is "so eager to be loved." If the "dream of love" goes unrealized, he tells her, anyone, "even the highest," will try to fill the void with "noise, fame, excitement, and pleasure." Marie Antoinette has been acting naturally all along. Her behavior, the cheap artifices of a soubrette, is no longer

FIGURE 13. Queens are people too. *Marie Antoinette* publicity still, Margaret Herrick Library, Academy of Motion Picture Arts and Sciences.

understood as common; needing what others need, unable to get it, simply makes her human.

A little too human at times, according to George Richelavi, a technical adviser on the film. He objected to the "little intimacies such as touching people's hands or body" that Shearer, as queen, indulged in. "Her present behavior as a normal human being" was acceptable as a Hollywood archduchess and princess, and Richelavi could understand the appeal of such "a very human touch," but it was his job to press for the real distinction between queens and everyone else. Thalberg pressed for it too. He had wanted Fersen to try to persuade Marie Antoinette to give up the throne for him. Fersen would scorn the corruption of the court, and she would counter with her intention to improve it, to be a worthy queen. In that version the queen magnificently trumps the woman. In the film it is Fersen who reminds her of her duty. Now that she understands her behavior in terms of what she shares with others, she wants what others want: "happiness. Even a queen wants that. More than anything in the world." She asserts her human right to love and is indifferent to her position, becoming what one MGM executive called, in a letter to Loew's president, Nicholas Schenck, "a queen every shop girl will understand and love." She does not want to be "applauded and adored and obeyed," a desire the people will soon immoderately gratify. Their derision may cost Marie Antoinette her head, but not even their love would satisfy her: "I cannot wear my crown upon my heart." Although Fersen first educated her about the "dream of love" as a universal desire, he now urges upon this longing woman the incompatible obligations of a queen, whose "happiness" comes from "the love of your people." They must part. She chooses public duties over private rights. The queen trumps the woman, but the woman put up a fight.[84]

Her resolve is evident in the next scene, the accouchement. Louis's impotence is miraculously resolved by his coronation, as though sexual desire itself responds to the obligations of monarchy. The scene occurs in a virtual theater where aristocrats lounge and chat, awaiting the performance of her duty to produce a son. The camera eventually arrives at no less a figure of public-spiritedness than Benjamin Franklin, who is on hand to condemn the "barbarous" French custom of turning the private experience of childbirth into a public spectacle. The Austrian emissary explains that "a French monarch belongs to the public." So did stars, but they had first to be created by the public, not dynastic succession, as Franklin's presence reminds us. Marie Antoinette's privacy is immaterial because, unlike a star, her personhood is irrelevant; she represents political continuity, not individual distinction. She chooses France over Fersen as she quietly gives birth to her public duty.

This scene is a turning point in the film. The camera cuts abruptly from a shot of the proud but overwhelmed Louis holding his son, within the familiar discursive space of the superspecial costume drama, to social-realist shots of peasants toiling in the fields. They are reminiscent of another revolutionary moment, achieving "a kind of Russian montage sensibility." A steely voice-over by Joseph Schildkraut, as the nefarious Duke d'Orléans, intones the suffering of the people. The voice-over does not seem to express the peasants' thoughts so much as furnish them; they pause in their labors, as though to listen to the diegetic rumblings of discontent, manufactured by an ambitious aristocrat, that produce the angry urge to rebel.[85]

It is time for the plot development called the French Revolution, and it functions as little more than a transition from one moment in Marie Antoinette's life to another. From the fields the camera cuts to

the queen's carriage; a few peasants hurl rocks and insults, a rare moment of violence in a film that disavows shots of crazed masses around
the guillotine. Her children want to know why the people are "angry
with you." "They're unhappy," she tells them. There are "things they
don't understand, and things they don't forget." Such is the film's commentary on the causes of the Revolution. Her days of recklessness and
extravagance are over. With Fersen's help she has changed from a fatu-
ous and irresponsible dauphine to a mature queen and devoted mother,
but the people don't care. Their hostility is fueled by Orléans and others. Having learned a valuable lesson about recklessness and jewelry,
she refuses to buy an expensive necklace that is offered to her when
"people [are] starving." It is purchased in her name to discredit her, and
the plot works. As tensions mount, Louis regretfully dissolves the as-
sembly, which is "here by the will of the people," as one angry member
proclaims, but only because his ministers advised him to do it. The king
didn't mean to be antidemocratic. The monarchs are manipulated and
deceived by their mutual enemies, like the people. The king and queen
are guilty of something more like bad public relations than bad will;
they are just misunderstood.[86]

What the people do not understand, but *Marie Antoinette* insists on,
is that the royals they rebel against are very much like them. The queen
tells her husband that they are just "little people with a terribly big
task." Swept up in the tide of history, they are fundamentally unsuited
for the roles they must play. Louis XVI is not without talent outside
the political arena. "What an excellent smith [he] would have made,"
and he would have been "far happier." We know that she would have
been happier with Fersen. The film makes the case that on some level
the Revolution is the result of miscasting (a theme whose development
is the best excuse for the hopelessly wooden performance of Power).
In the end the majesties prove worthier of their destinies than such
unpromising beginnings indicated, but they never should have played
those parts in the first place. Hence the poignancy of the family dinner
in prison after the king has been voted to the guillotine. There is an
awkward moment, when the dauphin commands the jailers to bring a
chair for the king, but such innocent bad taste is smoothed over by his
tactful and sympathetic father. The royals share a simple onion soup
like the peasants they should have been, enjoying an intimacy that has
evaded them for most of the film. The last supper privileges family normalcy over royal prerogative and honors Louis as a loving husband
and father.

Marie Antoinette has already undergone the same transformation; queenship is enhanced rather than diminished by becoming more of a woman, a wife, and a mother. By the time she rides to the scaffold in a drab muslin shift, her hair carelessly shorn, aged and seemingly without makeup, all physical markers of the queen and star are gone. During the last meeting with Fersen she looks more like his mother than his sweetheart. The queen of France accepts her fate, but the onetime Queen of Metro was more defiant. It was her idea to superimpose a close-up of the young archduchess on the queen's haggard face as she awaits the guillotine, which reminds us of her once vital humanity and ensures that the "last image in the film" of Shearer was not "a sad unflattering one." But MGM might have come up with the shot on its own. Marie Antoinette was billed in publicity as "the movie queen of her day," who set the fashions, had acting ambitions, and "dreamed of being everything that the popular star [Shearer] represented." The queen is dead; long live the Queen.[87]

Stars and the films that showcase them also "belong to the public," and their fate, too, rests upon its whims. After its general release, *Marie Antoinette* was treated by most critics as a triumph, for the studio and for Shearer and even, again, for "the moving picture art." It was widely admired for its pageantry and lavishness and, apart from Power, the acting. The MGM publicity machinery worked overtime to call attention to the new standards the film had set for what *Photoplay* called "luxurious authenticity," measured in the number of costumes (1,250), wigs (5,000), real human hairs used in them (750 million), and extras (some 5,500). Along with these details, and the fabulous cost, publicity trumpeted the studio's commitment to historical research. A museum was even installed at the Astor Theatre in New York to show off what had been "ransacked" from "the furthermost reaches of the far flung M-G-M empire." Despite the well-publicized pursuit of a certain kind of material accuracy, one currency of the biopic in its heyday, some naysayers drew attention to the film's thinness as actual history, objecting to the license taken with the romance and the Revolution, as well as the sympathy generated for a monarchy that was by and large "a stupid lot." These critics were inclined to lament the decision to ignore the "great drama" of the French Revolution and treat it "as incidental color for a royal tragedy" and "a setting for [the queen's] loves." Hollywood loyalists praised it precisely on these grounds, the ones the film itself had pushed, that it offered the very *human* story of Marie Antoinette, the woman. The film was "richly human in thrilling drama, daring intrigue and tender romance," and Shearer gave an "absorbingly-human interpretation of a woman's sometimes carefree, oftimes [sic] desperate seeking for happiness." *Marie Antoinette* evoked a deeper realism that did not "merely scratch . . . the surface of history" but was beyond history: the characters possessed "vitality and realism as people motivated by desires, hates, loves and ambitions, no different from those of today."[88]

Such reviews took their cue in part from the publicity, which marketed the film as an artifact that spoke powerfully to and about the present. As much as the publicity for *Marie Antoinette* trumpeted the heroic efforts to recreate the texture and temper of the French Court, the studio wanted to ward off the impression of slavish devotion to remote historical particularity, in case the film might be seen more as an academic exercise, a cinematic version of the museum created for it, than living entertainment. History in the ads was often raised by way of the naughty queen's "scarlet history." Even within the context of a public relations campaign that made a virtue of the restraint Marie Antoinette had shown too late, the exploitation possibilities of the "Royal Bad-Girl" whose behavior left others "too shocked for words!" were irresistible. The publicity also urged that "the greatness of 'Marie Antoinette' lies in its humanness. Here are no cold, stuffy historical manikins giving lackluster imitations of past personages." If we already "know the scarlet history" and "the story of [the] glamorous queen," "now the screen gives us . . . 'MARIE ANTOINETTE' the woman." And this woman was a version of women everywhere, as noted in an article published in Shearer's name:

> Marie Antoinette was a very human person. Her virtues and faults were not different from those of any modern woman. . . . Marie Antoinette was outspokenly fresh and impatient of ceremony. She never could hide her feelings. Hating her royal robes and ornaments, she exclaimed when freed from them, "Thank heaven I'm out of harness!" That sounds most 1938! . . .
>
> Director W. S. Van Dyke II and I tried our best to work the little and perhaps relatively unimportant but definitely humanizing things about Marie Antoinette into the picture.
>
> Her sheer joy of living for one thing. . . . She made mistakes, of course. . . . But her mistakes were so entirely human that it is impossible to hold them against her.

The French queen was a natural girl at heart, neither a figure from the past nor simply timeless but relentlessly up-to-date. A queen may have no peers, but this one was "human" because so recognizably one of us. Unlike the peasants, we understand her.[89]

But do we? Loew's had initially planned to road-show the film at increased prices; however, returns from its initial engagement at the Carthay Circle in Los Angeles were disappointing. Numerous memos circulated regarding its poor showing vis-à-vis other big films that had played there at the same prices. In its third week the take was off about 25 percent from such films as *The Great Ziegfeld* (1936) and *The Good Earth* (1937). The decision not to road-show *Marie Antoinette* became an important part of an advertising strategy that promoted a fortuitous sense of noblesse oblige. The Campaign Book announced to exhibitors that MGM had cancelled road-show plans "as its sincere contribution and gesture of enthusiastic cooperation with the united industry drive," manufacturing a public relations opportunity out of business misfortune. Following the company's advice, theater ads across the country announced that "While New York and Los Angeles Pay $2.00 for this Mighty Hit—You See It, By Special Arrangement, at our REGULAR POPULAR PRICES!" There was no special arrangement, of course, only the anxious realization that the populace prefers its prices popular, and that a potentially unpopular film about a notoriously reviled queen had better accommodate them. The prices were not popular enough, however, and the film lost $797,000.[90]

Fears that *Marie Antoinette* was "too heavy or tragic for popular consumption" eventually led to some twenty minutes of cuts for the domestic market. Comments overheard at the Carthay Circle suggest that some patrons did have reservations about a film that could only end with "the depressing thud of the guillotine," but it may have been doomed on other grounds. Vivian Sobchack has noted that historical films necessarily imitate the magnificence they portray and give rise to a form of publicity that insists on the parallels between epic expenditures—of money, talent, effort—and epic events. *Marie Antoinette*'s publicity invited a more stinging parallel to the film's own historical moment. To bill *Marie Antoinette* in terms of "shameless escapade and extravagance—while a nation hovered on the brink of destruction! Dazzling pageantry—filmed at [a] cost of millions!" was to highlight the connection between the profligacy of pre-Revolution France, MGM, and the film. During the recession a hugely expensive movie about a recklessly extravagant queen—out of touch, until too late, with her time—equated indifferent and foolish rulers with indifferent and foolish filmmakers. It was not the reviewer for the *Nation* but Hedda Hopper who observed that "'Marie Antoinette' won't bankrupt M.-G.-M., as the former queen did [France]," but "the time for such a picture is out of joint" given "our fast shifting problems of today. Had Irving Thalberg lived, I'm certain he would never have made it." MGM's very own Louis was to blame.[91]

Marie Antoinette "returns us to a bygone day when 'colossal' was a new word on the tongues of movie magnates," and as such it "commands your respect and attention," wrote one reviewer who found herself somewhat unmoved by the film. MPGY sought to generate respect and attention, too, but it wanted something more: to rekindle loyalty and affection. MGM's story of the unfortunate queen is about how difficult it is to restore such feelings once lost, and this film was not the ideal vehicle for doing so. "The public's tastes have changed. . . . People aren't impressed with 'gigantic, colossal' spectacles any more. Who cares if it took three years to make a picture at a cost of $1,000,000 or more? Who cares if there are 100 or 10,000 people in the cast? That is no criterion of a good picture." *Marie Antoinette* was something of a museum piece after all, a relic of the spectacle era, a problem perhaps less because it was extravagantly out of touch with its historical moment than because its extravagances were unprofitably out of touch with the desires of consumers.[92]

The same might be said of MGM's *The Great Waltz,* another MPGY historical film that lost $724,000, on a production budget of $2,260,000. This one really was Mayer's fault. Set in Vienna, *The Great Waltz* narrates the "spirit" of the life of composer Johann Strauss II (Fernand Gravet), the nineteenth century's "Waltz King," concentrating on his musical achievements, as well as his domestic troubles with his wife, Poldi (Luise Rainer, in the two-time Academy Award winner's rush to Hollywood oblivion), and his opera-singer mistress, Carla Donner (Miliza Korjus in her American film debut). Unlike "the mincing measure of the minuet," as a title card from *A Tale of Two Cities* (1935) dismissed the formal, joyless dance of the French Court that we see again in *Marie Antoinette,* the robust waltz was a dance of the people, popular first with peasants and introduced to society through public dance halls. The people had moved on, but Mayer saw no reason they could not be brought back. He loved the waltz and hoped the film would do for it what MPGY strived to do for films. His efforts included a "bring back the waltz" campaign with a nationwide waltzing contest to promote the film.[93]

The Great Waltz was a bit like *The Goldwyn Follies,* only with waltzing instead of ballet. It stages the waltz as something that magically summons people to it, as though meeting a preexisting demand. In the beginning Strauss's orchestra plays to an empty café, but soon the windows are thrown open and people stop in their tracks. Crowds storm the café and effortlessly dance in rhythm; the applause at this novelty is thunderous. The camera cuts from this scene to a formal party and a fussy minuet; it only takes Donner to sing one of the waltzes, with full coloratura treatment, for a dubious aristocracy to be won over too. Yet efforts to portray the waltz as up-to-date only make it seem out of step. The film tries to align the waltz with forward thinking; it is identified with revolutionary politics, for example, but this is a revolution that culminates in a new emperor. The foreword ties it into other social and cultural changes, but to announce that "in Vienna in 1844 'nice people' neither danced the waltz . . . nor kissed their wives in public . . . nor listened to new ideas" makes the obliteration of such orthodoxies seem laughably recherché instead (ellipses in original).

While MGM was trying to persuade the public that there was a place for the waltz in the modern world, and Strauss was packing extras into the Viennese cafés of a hundred years before, Darryl Zanuck over at Fox was packing real people into theaters for another MPGY film, *Alexander's Ragtime Band,* a lively musical tribute to Irving Berlin. As Alexander, Power was cast more or less as what he was, a twentieth-century American entertainer, to better effect. Early in the film, after playing in a classical music concert that bores him, he declines to accompany a couple of attractive young socialites to a party, even as one laments: "I've saved all my waltzes for you." Instead, he hurries off to a Barbary Coast café, and amid such "class apostasy" modern popular music is born, with ragtime inspiring the same spontaneous excitement as the Strauss waltz it replaces. And even with a notably weak story, *Alexander's Ragtime Band* was an enormous hit and generated much more enthusiasm than *The Great Waltz.* Movies may like to fantasize about a warm public response for what they have to sell, but ultimately it is the public that decides what to buy.[94]

The manager of the Fox in Tucson knew this. He took out an ad to complain when attendance was poor at local screenings of *The Great Waltz* in November. "Why Make Fine Pictures?" berated the public for not "believ[ing] it was worth seeing" and tried to build attendance on the final night. It was all well and good to advertise its "simple, down-to-earth elements" and call it "essentially a mass attraction," but the film's distinctive and stylish (read arty) direction by Hollywood newcomer Julien Duvivier, European themes and stars, and, lest we forget, Viennese waltzing did not make good on that promise. Many of the rural and small-town exhibitors who wrote to the *Motion Picture Herald* about both *The Great Waltz* and *Marie Antoinette* admired the pictures, and most preferred not to play them. Such films attracted "people who seldom go to the movies" but not those who usually do; they were "not for the masses." The mass/class distinction mattered for them, and it was not one that a womanly queen or a waltz-loving immigrant mogul could wish away. *Fortune* wrote about MGM's declining reputation in August 1939, with pictures that were "failing to make their customary splash in the trade." The prime examples were *Marie Antoinette* and *The Great Waltz,* "expensive superspecials . . . presented to an American public that has not even yet shown any inclination to return to Metro their negative costs." These films represented the antithesis of what audiences of the moment were thought to want, and their striking failure contributed to a change in the studio's image as much as the Andy Hardy successes did.[95]

THAT'S ENTERTAINMENT

The films discussed in the last four sections were conceived and received as something quite special, even bordering, in the best tradition of Hollywood hyperbole, on unique and unprecedented. At the same time their goals were also cast in fashionably modest terms. As with so many other films in and out of MPGY, shaping and shaped by a consensus about the public's most recent entertainment whims, each sought to communicate a fundamental human quality that would bring audiences pleasurably into contact with themselves. The *human* was flexible enough to accommodate many different types of films and characters, from priests to queens, and from dizzy grandpas to small-town daughters. It made room for individual particularity, or fetishized it in the case of *You Can't Take It with You,* while insisting on what we all have in common, the feelings and values that we share. Recognition humanizes Kirby, Whitey, and Marie Antoinette; even if humanity cannot save the latter, it makes her a better queen. Falling outside the scope of the human, Mickey Borden kills himself when cynical detachment gives way to a deeper, intractable exclusion.

These films were identified as reflecting credit on the industry as a whole during MPGY for one or more reasons: for artistry or a conspicuous lack of artistry, for reverberant social messages, for being so completely in touch with the tastes of the time. Each functioned, in other words, as an ambassador for the industry and the sweeping promises it had made to the public, and I have lingered over them in part because they were such privileged texts within the larger public relations framework. But less exceptional films stood out as ambassadors, too, often inadvertently and unfortunately so. If every film manifests in some way the industry's priorities, several MPGY films brought the public awkwardly face-to-face with them. The roster included four films about Hollywood, as well as others that represented movies and moviegoing and reflected on their social role. In depicting studios and theaters, in showing the movies as sites of labor, play, and recreation, these films also performed a version of the work of the institutional ads, although their treatments often challenged the claims the industry made about itself in print. When it came to selling "the movies" within films that actually represented them, the industry frequently failed to turn its own medium to advantage.

One cluster of films did tout the benevolent social function of the movies, primarily from outside the films' diegesis. Like the G-Men films of the mid-1930s, which evolved to circumvent the MPPDA's ban on gangster films, the four MPGY "racket" films shifted attention from criminal activity to law enforcement, from the excitement of watching underworld empires built to the redemptive, less thrilling pleasure of watching social order restored. The racket films, which ranged from Bs *(Smashing the Rackets* and *Crime Takes a Holiday)* to programmers *(Racket Busters* and *I Am the Law)*, were based on Thomas Dewey's successful prosecution of organized-crime figures in New York. Released in a blaze of reciprocal publicity, as the district attorney and gubernatorial candidate made headlines nationwide throughout the summer and fall, these films revolved around ambitious prosecutors who used Dewey's methods to achieve equally spectacular results. Like Dewey, they urged the importance of public cooperation in cleaning up the rackets. The real problem is "not criminal brains nor greed, not lax law enforcement—but *public indifference,"* as the foreword to *Smashing the Rackets* puts it. The racket films' basic theme is that from intimidated workers and businessmen to blasé consumers and ineffectual community leaders, the public is complicit in its victimization by racketeers, and even the most resourceful prosecutor can only triumph when civic conscience overrides apathy and fear.[96]

The prosecutors' successful efforts to enlighten that conscience are mirrored in the racket films' own dynamics of persuasion. The films put themselves forward as a vital public service, an "army of film Deweys" that broadcast the dangers of inaction and the obligations of citizens to resist. As some of the ads for *Racket Busters* put it: "DO YOU KNOW . . . that every person in every town in all America pays tribute to racketeers? . . . that *you* and *you* and *you* are needed in the fighting army of racket busters!" "See it, America, and FIGHT BACK!" An indifferent public could become an informed, engaged, and vigilant audience. Special screenings underscored this message. For example, twelve hundred boy scouts experienced the "profound moral lesson" of *Racket Busters* in Milwaukee, a city "free of criminal rackets," a Scout executive hastened to observe, "because of that vigilance which the film teaches as necessary." An exhibitor in Elkhart, Indiana, invited prominent citizens to preview *I Am the Law* and ran their endorsements. Elkhart's freedom from such problems was likewise noted: "Let us keep it that way. Don't fail to see the picture." Civic leaders denied the pervasiveness of the rackets, so far as their own communities were concerned, but championed the roll of cinematic education in keeping crime at bay. A writer for the *Detroit Free Press* thought that the studios "owe[d] a huge debt of gratitude" to Dewey but acknowledged the debt as mutual: thanks to the films, "the Great American Public is being wised up to how the hoodlums operate."[97]

The "Dewey cycle" lionized the real-life racket buster while making the films look good, too. It faded soon after this concentrated burst, however, which coincided with the untimely news that charges of a "racket in film labor" had been brought to the National Labor Relations Board. Willie Bioff, the movies' own gangster and the power behind "one of the most vicious company union rackets in this country," was accused of accepting a $100,000 bribe from Joe Schenck of Fox, part of a series of payments from the majors to avert labor strikes and thwart collective bargaining. The Bioff scandal gave a new inflection to the remark of prosecutor Hugh Allison (Walter Abel) in *Racket Busters:* "the public takes [the rackets] as much for granted as it does its radio or its moving pictures." The industry wanted the public to appreciate movies again, not to wake up and start fighting them. But the racket films didn't need Bioff to disappear, for the same reason that the cycle goes virtually unmentioned in studies of the gangster film. This preachy quartet failed to reproduce the vitality that made earlier gangster films such dynamic forces in American culture. They were repetitive in many particulars, as well as in their general contours; there was no way for an "army of film Deweys" not to look regimented. Breen suggested that Columbia abandon *I Am the Law* because it was so similar to *Smashing the Rackets*. When Warners was sued for plagiarism over *Racket*

Busters, a lawyer determined that all of the racket stories submitted between 1936 and 1938 were pretty much alike and noted the film's similarity to the studio's own *Marked Woman* (1937). If anything, Warners had only plagiarized from itself. Whatever their impact on crime-busting, the racket films highlighted the standardization of a product squeezed by both financial and moral pressures. At a time when the specialness of movies was so urgently touted, the racket films' notable lack of specialness—not identical but still the same, just sometimes not as good—called particular attention to the formula behind the films.[98]

I Am the Law stood out in one way. The only one to represent the movies, it implicates them directly in the rackets. John Lindsay (Robinson) turns special prosecutor after discovering the pervasive influence of rackets in his city. He learns about it at a movie theater, not in the form of a newsreel designed to educate the public about the threat racketeers pose, like the one featured in the opening scene of *Bullets or Ballots* (1936), or a racket film such as the one we watch, but as the result of a violent attack on the theater. John is sent by his wife, Jerry (Barbara O'Neil), to *Snow White* so that she can pack for a trip they never take. As he hands the usher his ticket, patrons rush from the building (see figure 14). The scene cuts to the office of a newspaper editor, where John demands action. There we meet the first of the frightened businessmen who make his future job so hard. The exhibitor recently joined the Theater Owners Protective Association and has since been harassed by its competitor, the equally corrupt Theater Owners Mutual Aid Association. He won't protest because a stink bomb in his theater is preferable to "dynamite" in his home. The editor is uninterested in the story; such things happen all the time. John is indignant: "There was a panic in the theater. People might have been hurt, maybe killed." At the suggestion of the editor, John goes straight to a meeting of the Citizens Committee to protest, and by the time he leaves, he is in charge of investigating the rackets. The trip cancelled, John consumed by his new job, Jerry can only lament: "If only I hadn't sent you out that day to see *Snow White.*"[99]

In *I Am the Law* the rackets are indeed pervasive. The public does not combat them at the theater; nor does it go there to experience "relaxation" and "freedom from care," as the campaign ads urged. The theater is, rather, a place where moviegoers might be "hurt," even "killed," and sending a person to one of the most acclaimed films of the decade is something to regret. At least one man was alert to the problem the scene posed. Joseph Breen was adamant about getting rid of it. He

FIGURE 14. In *I Am the Law* theaters are places where people might be hurt, even killed.

wrote to Harry Cohn in April: "We recommend, under the general head of industry good and welfare, that you do not plant the suggestion that there is any racketeering in the theater business. The 'stink bomb' business is not acceptable, and all the talk about racketeering and panics in theaters, should be omitted—for obvious purposes." He repeated the warning a few weeks later, adding, "It is certain that theater exhibitors everywhere will not welcome any such suggestion from their screens. It would appear to be bad psychology, and worse business, to throw out such a suggestion, by way of a picture on the screen, to groups assembled in theaters." The wrangling over this scene continued into July. Breen's points about stink bombs and panics directly addressed the relationship of film content to industry public relations, emphasizing the way that the representation of the moviegoing experience in *I Am the Law* might negatively shape perceptions of the movies and theaters and impact them both: bad psychology, worse business. Breen's failure to persuade Cohn not to badmouth the movies indicates the limits of his power to protect the industry from itself. When it came to such "general" matters of "industry good and welfare," the PCA could fuss and advise but not mandate changes. What may have been truly unadvisable from the standpoint of smart business practices and public relations, especially on the brink of a conspicuous PR campaign, was technically permissible under the Code.[100]

Whatever the reasons for Cohn's intransigence, he was hardly the only mogul under whom unflattering representations of the industry flourished, in general and during MPGY. Hollywood's impulse toward self-referentiality is not hard to understand. Many films, from backstage musicals and revues to biopics of actors and musicians, express the conviction that watching people act as entertainers is intrinsically entertaining. Public fascination with Hollywood was crafted to the point that the studios became the synecdoche for an industry whose actual seats of power were in New York. Stars were as vibrant as the gangster and as iconic as the cowboy, and it would have been almost remiss of the film companies not to have looked to themselves for material. Of the four MPGY films about Hollywood, only *Keep Smiling* offers a mainly sympathetic account that punctures the stereotypes with a few hard truths about the movie business. *Boy Meets Girl, The Affairs of Annabel,* and *Fugitives for a Night* offer scathing commentaries on the industry that was elsewhere celebrating itself to counteract all of the negative commentary generated about it recently. Their tone tends toward the satiric, and they treat the industry as an object of contempt. Moreover, at a time when Hollywood was striving to meet the perceived public demand for pictures about plain folks, the MPGY films tended to insist on Hollywood denizens as a breed apart, in the process reinforcing the very images of the industry that the campaign wanted to discourage. Such films may have demonstrated Hollywood's ability to laugh at itself, but they also betrayed a wonderful obtuseness. They assumed not only that audience outsiders would get the jokes but that the line between satiric and realistic treatment of an enterprise famous for its fabulous excesses would be obvious to them.

Boy Meets Girl was by far the most prestigious of the four Hollywood films. Based on the successful Broadway farce by Bella and Samuel Spewack, who also wrote the script, the film was brought in for under $600,000, even though Warners spent $100,000 for the rights. The play had been warmly received as a contribution to the "tradition among the wits, satirists, and intellectuals of the land that motion pictures are written, manufactured, and exploited in a manner that approaches lunacy . . . and that any sane person who observes this marvel closely will be stricken with a hysteria of uncontrollable laughter." With the film version, the legitimate theater's ferocious mockery of Hollywood became Hollywood's desperate lampoon of itself.[101]

The film begins with overhead and street-level shots of the bustling studio: this is the real thing, Warners "on location" in its own demesne.

Bobby Law (James Cagney) and J.C. Benson (Pat O'Brien) are fast-talking screenwriters whose antics drive producer C.F. Friday (Bellamy) to distraction. Unlike Warners, which shrewdly, stubbornly, weathered the Depression without declaring bankruptcy, Royal Pictures is in receivership, and C.F. needs a hit or he will lose his job. However uninterested most 1930s films were in the problem of unemployment, its specter looms large over every MPGY film about Hollywood; the corollary to an industry perpetually in crisis was the career crisis—the anxious producer, star, or director who has "lost it."

As "the only college-bred man" among the executives, C.F. wants "to do something fine, something dignified, something worthwhile," "a big picture," "with sweep, with scope, stark, gripping, but with plenty of comedy and a little hokum." He happily embraces Benson and Law's idea for a "Cowboy and the Baby" picture, with a little romance thrown in for the old "boy meets girl" angle. It will pair fading cowboy star Larry Toms (Dick Foran) and the as yet unborn baby of Susie Seabrook (Marie Wilson), a ditzy commissary waitress. Susie's baby, Happy, is a huge hit: "A star is born!" C.F. and studio head B.K. (Pierre Watkin) are thrilled. But Larry wants to marry Susie; he can only protect his sagging career by controlling Happy's. The writers need Happy, too. Benson and Law reunite Susie and a British extra, Rodney Bowman (Bruce Lester); the two fall in love, but they decide to head to England, where Happy will grow up "normal." Benson and Law's hysterical mantra—"Boy meets girl; boy loses girl; boy gets girl!"—does them in as boys lose baby. The film's title, the most basic cliché of Hollywood narrative, pokes fun at the triteness of the romantic imperative that the film itself necessarily stages.

Boy Meets Girl shows Hollywood film production to be the least serious, effectual, and significant of enterprises (see figure 15). The character of C.F. combines the assumed ignorance of the movie executive with the pretensions of the pseudo highbrow, whose commitment to dignity and significance is belied by the alacrity with which he jumps, along with his boss, on the cowboy-meets-baby bandwagon. The kind of foolish Hollywood faddist who consumes only raw carrots and milk for lunch, C.F. is even more out of touch than Oliver Merlin of *The Goldwyn Follies*. Until Warners saw his salary demands, it had wanted to cast Menjou, who had by then become the producers' favorite image of the producer—dapper, refined, and intelligent. The earnestly goofy Bellamy brought to the part a native foolishness quite unlike the figure Menjou cuts. Merlin takes measures to rebuild his declining reputation,

FIGURE 15. The studio as insane asylum. *Boy Meets Girl* publicity still, Margaret Herrick Library, Academy of Motion Picture Arts and Sciences.

but *Boy Meets Girl* is played strictly for laughs. C. F.'s cluelessness is treated not as a problem to be solved but as part of the basic equation of filmmaking.[102]

The seamlessness of the classical Hollywood style has been read as an ideological project that erases the labor through which films are constructed, another way in which the world of cinema naturalizes itself, separating moviegoers from the real world and its discomfiting demands. As a movie about the making of those films, *Boy Meets Girl* portrays the studio as a place of perpetual play, by which I mean not that work is depicted as fun, the way it is in *You Can't Take It with You,* but as unnecessary; there is no labor to efface. C. F.'s job is hard to distinguish from other peoples' luxurious relaxation: he cannot be disturbed when "in conference" with a masseur and a manicurist. We hear Benson and Law before we meet them; or rather, we hear a record in their office that plays the sound of typewriters banging away, which frees them to create havoc on the sets. They don't ever do any actual typing because screenwriting is a form of free association, 100 percent inspiration and no perspiration, a matter of talking and moving so fast that the audience for their spontaneous pitch is mesmerized into enthusiasm. Indeed, Cagney and O'Brien spoke so quickly that Hal Wallis wrote several memos to complain. He acknowledged the necessity of "tempo, and speed," but their lines could not be heard, a problem the finished film did not entirely overcome. But the point of the writers' performance is that what they say doesn't matter. Success is a matter of spinning out nonsense faster than dim-witted people like producers can think. The sound of typing represents the writing process and product perfectly. Audiences may want dialogue to make sense, but satirizing the screwball gibberish out of which movies are made results in the screwball gibberish that materializes onscreen.[103]

These people do not work for a living, but they are surely paid. At a moment when the outrageous individuals of *You Can't Take It with You* were busy establishing, to great acclaim, that sufficiency is next to godliness, *Boy Meets Girl* makes a big deal of exorbitant Hollywood salaries. We learn that C. F. is "a $50,000-a-year man" when he chastises a mere extra for his unsolicited advice on costumes, and Benson and Law earn more than that. The cowboy can't get over "the idea of writers getting $1,500 a week for acting like hoodlums." After more than an hour of their crazy, exhausting behavior, C. F. attempts to chastise Benson and Law: "Do you realize that you're making more than the president of the United States?" The interjection of quasi seriousness, which draws attention to screenwriters' high salaries, amid their ongoing, real-life efforts to unionize, reflects at least as badly on the industry that pays dearly for such twaddle as it does on the writers who con rich rewards out of it.

Law corrects Larry: "We're not writers, we're hacks." Law is a proto–Joe Gillis (William Holden) of *Sunset Boulevard* (1950), contemptuous of Hollywood, verging on self-loathing. Screenwriters were on average the best educated and by reputation the least satisfied of studio talent. As the novelist James Farrell put it, the writer's "real means of production is his soul," and writing for the dream factory could only result in alienation, the sound of typing. The writer's "material is thrown into the hopper of movie making," where it was frequently reworked by several additional hands and then given to yet others to interpret, who "grind it into pieces." The successful writer traded creative autonomy for extravagant weekly wages. Benson is frank and unambivalent about the bargain: "I like pictures. I'm knee-deep in debt," his loyalty bought by the financial requirements of a beautiful, expensive wife, who remains offscreen. Law is discontented because he wants to write a novel in Vermont, a place where he can "touch life" and "feel life" and write about "life in the raw. . . . There is no boy, there is no girl. These are people, real people," not the phonies who populate Hollywood and its films. Like C. F., he claims to want to make something significant, and if we take his frustrated ambition a little more seriously, it is because he knows that significance and cowboy-and-baby movies are incompatible. But hacks are as much slaves to the system as their bosses are. When his contract is extended by a year, Law forgets about Vermont and real people, another sham intellectual. There are only boys and girls and babies. When Peggy (Penny Singleton), the manicurist, was invited to "be the audience," and asked whether she would like to see one of Larry's pictures "again with a new title," she issued an unequivocal: "I would not!" But the film concludes with Benson and Law spinning the same plot all over again for some other cowboy and some other baby. The novelty becomes the blueprint becomes the cycle, or rather, it fails to become anything but the same picture under another name.[104]

The characters in Boy Meets Girl solicit and disregard the opinion of its surrogate for the public, but its publicity machinery plugged the film as exceedingly attentive to public preferences. The pressbook was full of articles on the public's role in creating Warners' newest star, not Baby Happy but his mother. Wilson was chosen as the waitress "because the nation's movie fans wanted her. They bombarded the studio with letters and telegrams." Another promotional article claimed that "big-salaried actresses like Joan Blondell and Marion Davies" had been considered for Susie, but Wilson's success as a "dumb blonde" in B films was bringing in "the third greatest amount of fan mail on the lot. And when the moviegoing public takes a player to its collective heart, something has to be done about it. Accordingly, with the public laying down a barrage of letters to the Warner front office, and with everybody in Hollywood, from office boys to stars yelling that Marie was the gal, the execs went into a final huddle." The public had its way. The stories were printed in newspaper reviews and articles about Boy Meets Girl, and they were also picked up by gossip columnists such as Jimmie Fidler and Sidney Skolsky, who circulated many spoon-fed anecdotes about the actress's reported ditziness, bringing the screwball world of this Hollywood film into the discursive environment that received it. There was a dumb studio angle as well: Warners did not know what a good thing it had in Wilson until the public expressed itself on the subject. The huddling, dithering executives are always the last to get it.[105]

The boisterous energy and frantic pace of a film whose protagonists could talk their way into and out of anything failed to mesmerize audiences the way Benson and Law did C.F. The film designed to look like a send-up of industry self-absorption became instead an example of it. By all reports film folk thought very well of the film, and the trade press was laudatory. The *Hollywood Motion Picture Review* was an exception: "Patrons outside of Hollywood will not understand the dialogue, double-meaning phrases, gags or puns on the various studios, stars, etc. The locale is laid in a movie studio and the action portrays writers, actors and executives as silly, ridiculous and fit subjects for an insane asylum." Rather than finding all this great fun, the *Review* considered it not only doomed to fail at the box office but "a detriment to the motion picture industry." The *Review* did not trouble to hide its satisfaction a few months later, when its contrarian opinion was borne out in red ink. *Boy Meets Girl* "seems to be coming in for the worst public reception of any picture released this season. Exhibitor comment from the field types it as a mess, a box-office flop, and smells so badly that many theatremen are being compelled to refund patrons their money." Paul Harrison used *Boy Meets Girl* as an example of the failure of the Hollywood preview system, which suffered from too many "yes men" and not enough real people. "When 'Boy Meets Girl' was previewed here a few months ago, the hand-picked, Hollywood-wise audience whooped and applauded. Magazine, radio and newspaper critics were generous in awarding bells, booms and bull's-eyes," and all the trade papers but the *Review* "went overboard." Despite the atmosphere of excited self-congratulation, "the picture has been dying, painfully, ever since."[106]

Small-town and rural exhibitors detested *Boy Meets Girl*. No other MPGY film received such uniformly negative comments in the *Herald*. Indeed, the film seems to go out of its way to earn the enmity of such exhibitors' patrons. It belittles the cravenness and stupidity of the kind of western star that played well in those situations, as well as the audiences who like him—Larry is "the idol of illiterates." When a scandal about the identity of Happy's father threatens to break, C.F. wonders about the reaction "this is going to bring from the sticks, uh, from the provinces," a joke for the benefit of urban and industry sophisticates at the expense of all those real people in Vermont. The film had its critics among more cosmopolitan types as well. One Fifth Avenue resident went so far as to telegraph his outrage to Warners. He called it an "absolute insult [to] my intelligence" and demanded a refund, or he would "boycott Warner films indefinitely." Total revenues for *Boy Meets Girl* were $654,000, which exceeded production costs by a very meager

$63,000. It is estimated to have lost $195,000, the largest amount of any Warners MPGY film. In the wake not only of its failure, but the actual indignation that greeted it, *Boy Meets Girl* served as a monument to the reasons MPGY had been launched in the first place.[107]

The other MPGY Hollywood pictures were all B films and were released with much less fanfare than, and hence nothing like the disgrace of, *Boy Meets Girl*. *The Affairs of Annabel* is a more successful farce, in part because it is so much less ambitious. Lanny Morgan (Jack Oakie) is a feckless publicity agent at Wonder Pictures. The opening shot of a movie poster includes the studio's motto, a gag barely cold from *Hollywood Hotel* (1937): "If it's a good picture—IT'S A WONDER." This act of theft sets the tone for a send-up of everyone involved in filmmaking. It pokes particular fun at the outrageous promotional efforts of publicity men and producers, as well as the willingness of a $5,000-a-week star, Annabel Allison (Lucille Ball), to suffer their torments to boost her career. In the process it also reveals, as *Boy Meets Girl* did, the abject lengths to which the film industry would go in the attempt to attract and entertain audiences, even at the expense of the dignity they were trying so hard to acquire.

Annabel's last picture did not do well, and she needs a hit. "We've got to get the public to like you again," studio head Howard Webb (Bradley Page) tells her. The solution to Annabel's problem is not to make a good picture but to generate the right publicity. Her new film tells an old story: she is a poor maid; one of the guests is a multimillionaire; they fall in love, and it ends happily. Lanny hatches a publicity scheme whereby she will work as a real maid to prepare for the part, which goes fine so long as he sneaks into the house to do her work. But then a couple of kidnappers come to stay. How to get Annabel out of there? Call a story conference (another massage), and let your "high-priced" writers script a solution. They are useless, however, as is the Russian director, Vladimir Dukov (Fritz Feld), who has been on salary for six months without making a picture. He demands something with "a little realism," but the real bullets that fly from the house when he tries to "direct" her escape are "too much realism" for him. In the end Lanny and Annabel vanquish the kidnappers on their own, and the international press coverage results in "the greatest publicity" of her career. "More important than that," Lanny tells her, "the public loves you again." But the film industry never met a resource it did not find a way to squander. Having acquired all this free publicity, the New York office decides to change the title of the film from "The Maid and the

Man" to "The Diamond Smuggler" and to rewrite the story to fit the title. *The Affairs of Annabel* ends with Lanny at it again. Annabel is taken in for questioning when police discover some diamonds on her, planted there to secure a new round of headlines.

The Affairs of Annabel purports to understand the importance of public opinion to the well-being of the industry and the careers of its stars. Annabel's face is on the cover of *Photoplay,* which crops up constantly in the film, another reminder of the promotional machinery that is always at work. But the public does not simply need to be aware of or interested in Annabel; rather, it must "love" her. Lanny's techniques, on the other hand, subscribe to the Hollywood adage, proved so untrue during 1938, that there is no such thing as bad publicity, demonstrated in the film by the equivalent value assigned to catching a criminal and being a criminal. While MPGY sought to reorient an industry traditionally assumed to be invested in publicity at all costs—despite the various scandals and missteps—toward a heightened consciousness of its image before the public, the film enacts as well as narrates the converse. Like *Boy Meets Girl, The Affairs of Annabel* trades on the short-term commercial goal of amusing the public, while disregarding its own putative concern with the representation it offers and the potential effects on public affection.

The Affairs of Annabel and *Boy Meets Girl* were released within two weeks of each other, a one-two punch. The trade press was as enthusiastic about *The Affairs of Annabel* on the grounds of sheer entertainment value as it was about *Boy Meets Girl,* and while some reviewers applauded the films for demonstrating Hollywood's ability to "poke . . . a lot of hilarious fun at itself," and to "join in—nay, to lead—a laugh at its own expense," this was not the kind of leadership that the film industry was trying to establish. Hollywood's perennial problem was that it got no respect. However often Hays and others reiterated its economic importance as the third- or fourth- or tenth-largest industry in the nation, it faced the challenge of distinguishing between the seeming frivolity of its products and selling methods and the seriousness of the business that stood, sometimes cowered, behind them. The goal of MPGY was not just to get the public to love the film industry like a favorite star but to persuade it to embrace the making of commercial entertainment as a significant, stable, and indispensable enterprise.[108]

The Affairs of Annabel and *Boy Meets Girl* detract remarkably from this goal. Part of the pleasure of the former was that it contained "a wealth of that nonsensical detail which has caused many people to form the opinion that Hollywood and its denizens are the silliest things on earth." Screwball comedy had just about exhausted audiences with absurd and eccentric characters whose mad pursuits had nothing to do with their lives. *The Affairs of Annabel* and *Boy Meets Girl* suggested such characters were not merely products but reflections of a screwy and out-of-touch industry. It was as though they sought to prove that the movies were indeed "the creation and the field of endeavor of zanies." The films were satires, but the trade press recognized that the ground of satire is the real. And indeed, for an industry that had for so long reflexively shunned reality, which is here something people in Vermont experience and directors in Hollywood run away from, satire may function as a superior way of telling the truth. "Every foot of it is pointed satire on the foibles of the motion picture industry," the *Hollywood Reporter* wrote of *The Affairs of Annabel,* "and it pulls no punches." To "pull no punches" is to tell it like it is. Another article noted that Lanny's crazy publicity schemes were "not beyond the bounds of Hollywood press agent reasoning or imagination." Hollywood was not just a field ripe for satire, but in some sense it was already a satire of itself. Thus Harrison concluded that "there's too much Hollywood" in *Boy Meets Girl,* not, as one might think, entirely too little.[109]

RKO released a second Hollywood film as part of MPGY; the small profit it made on *The Affairs of Annabel* ($21,000) was mostly lost on *Fugitives for a Night* ($15,000). Like *The Mad Miss Manton, Fugitives for a Night* is a blend of comedy and mystery, but it deals with the ugly, unglamorous side of Hollywood, in a sharp screenplay by Dalton Trumbo, and it cost even less than *The Affairs of Annabel* ($106,000 vs. $183,000). Matt Ryan (Frank Albertson) is a would-be actor who has found work only as a "stooge." The existence of such a person is in and of itself a blot on the reputation of the industry: part "bodyguard," part "nurse," part "tutor," the stooge is paid to make the star for whom he works look good, even at the expense of his own dignity. He is the ultimate studio "nobody," berated by producers and stars and scorned by everyone else.

Fugitives for a Night explicitly raises the question: "What kind of business is this?" The answer is that it's a "hard" one, full of cold and calculating people, and the cause of murderous rages, as well as angry jokes. Matt arranges for a group of young women to mob the studio's most important star, John Nelson (Allan Lane), but is fired when they turn out to be unattractive. He is immediately hired by Dennis Poole (Bradley Page), whose career is in crisis after two flops. Dennis is the exception to the film's representation of stars, executives, and even stooges as egotistical and often mean, concerned only with their own advancement. He is genuinely decent, the opposite of the petty, malicious Nelson, and treats Matt with kindness and respect. Unfortunately, such virtue in Hollywood is too good to be true. Dennis is also a murderer. He kills Maurice Tenwright (Russell Hicks), a nasty producer whom he blamed for his decline. There are, of course, any number of people who would want such a man dead, but the detective knew who had done it: "Have you seen Poole's last two pictures?" Dying at the box office is a self-evident motive for murder. Matt and the film are disinclined to judge Dennis harshly though. As he puts it, without irony: "Whether he did it or not, he's the nicest guy I ever worked for." In the end Matt and his new girlfriend, publicity writer Ann Wray (Eleanor Lynn), decide to quit the thankless, dehumanizing movie business. They buy a lunch wagon, whose owner is thrilled to get enough money to return to Oklahoma City. He is as sick of serving movie people as Matt and Ann are of being movie people, which does not bode well for the couple's new career choice either.

Of the MPGY Hollywood films, only Fox's *Keep Smiling* presented Hollywood as neither completely crazy nor toxic. It conveys a few tough realities of the business while also retaining some pleasant fantasies. *Keep Smiling* was a vehicle for Jane Withers, Fox's other child star and a significant box-office presence in 1938. She was an ungainly girl, with a persona that was knowing and naughty but by this point basically nice—in other words, an altogether more imaginable child than that miniature vessel of dimpled perfection, sweet Shirley Temple. In *Keep Smiling* Jane Rand (Withers) leaves boarding school for Hollywood to live with her only relative, Uncle John (Henry Wilcoxon), a famous director whom she barely knows. She arrives just as his effects, including an Oscar, are being auctioned. His career has foundered on alcoholism, the emblem of Hollywood self-destruction. John did not even "realize he was slipping," and now no one will hire him, because "in this business, when you're through, you're . . . through." Defeatism is not Jane's way, and she approaches Jerome Lawson, the head of Globe Pictures, to plead her uncle's case. Lawson is a sympathetic, indeed, paternal figure, a quality attributable in part to the casting of Jed Prouty, patriarch of the Jones Family. There is nothing of the raw food faddist or idiot savant about him. Lawson is a competent and responsible businessman who speaks truth to Jane. "It takes a lot of money to make a moving picture." Her uncle has held up productions in the past, and an unreliable director leads to losses. "I can't take chances with the studio's money like that." *Keep Smiling* keeps quiet about the spiritual price of success, the drumbeat of *A Star Is Born,* another film about alcoholic talent, in favor of the concrete economics of running a studio. This is a rare moment when the industry is really treated as a serious business, its decisions based on sound fiscal policy rather than the happy inspiration of quirky "geniuses." A child can understand this logic.

Filmmaking is still a gamble; the good producer just knows how to manage risk. Lawson "take[s] a chance" on Jane, casting her in a film over the director's objections: "Sure, she's unknown and has no training. But that's the way stars are found," at least in the Hollywood film. Lawson proves more sentimental than his calculations would otherwise suggest. He takes pity on John and casts him as an extra. When the film's director alienates everyone, including the budding child star, Lawson now has an asset, Jane, that must be protected, so he makes John the director. The studio manages to be both rational and sentimental, a competent business enterprise and a surrogate family that enables the formation of real families; with the revival of his career, John can marry his former secretary and care for his niece. Jane doesn't need to flee to England for a "normal" life because there is nothing wrong with Hollywood that a canny child cannot make right. There is, however, one grim casualty that exceeds the happy resolution. Jane's help came too late for an old actor, Mr. Travers (Pedro de Cordoba), who collapses just as he is offered a stock contract with the studio. Too long out of work, he basically starves to death at the threshold of success. His death is a chance for Jane to shed the child star's salutary tears, which illustrate the film's compassion for one of the industry's own. But by representing the human costs in terms that evoke the most brutal material reality of the Depression, the actor's death serves as a reminder that hard times make the movies a hard business after all.

A little child shall lead them: this was a story Hollywood could well tell about itself, with Temple, Rooney (just turned eighteen), and Withers three of the top-ten box-office stars in 1938, and Durbin generating big profits at Universal. It was a theme of many Temple films. *Little Miss Broadway* is a kind of companion film to *Keep Smiling,* in which it falls to the child who saved Fox to preserve a different species of entertainment and entertainer. Betsy Shea (Temple) is adopted by the owner of the Hotel Variety, which houses a community of odd, out-of-work vaudevillians. Sarah Wendling (Edna May Oliver), the building's owner, wants to close the hotel because of the noise and déclassé environment.

Her nephew, Roger (George Murphy), takes Sarah to court; he wants to buy the hotel with money she controls and to spend $50,000 on a show that will put the performers back to work. The issue on which the case hinges, according to the judge (Claude Gillingwater), is whether the idea for a vaudeville show is good business; as Zanuck phrased it in a script conference, Roger must prove it is "a sound investment." The proof is to be found in the entertainment value of the performances Betsy, along with Roger, give. Their numbers satisfy the judge, and even the skeptical Sarah, that there is no better profit-generator than a Temple, but the impulse to thematize and even reengineer her popularity, to prove it beyond a reasonable doubt, brings doubt into play. Zanuck was already worried about what to do with Temple after her previous picture, *Rebecca of Sunnybrook Farm* (1938), and *Little Miss Broadway* did nothing to resolve his concerns. Exhibitors remarked the inevitable, that Shirley was fast approaching her expiration date. Surrounding her with older, even ancient, vaudevillians could not hide that she was growing up. The doomed wish of *Little Miss Broadway* is that Temple remain Little Miss Cinema, that Fox's own "sound investment" not yield diminishing returns.[110]

In *Little Miss Broadway* the child star saves vaudeville by way of making a case for her film career. Other MPGY films blame motion pictures for the collapse of theatrical traditions and talent and even entertainment as such. In *Letter of Introduction* John Mannering reluctantly leaves the movies to appear on Broadway with his daughter in *Return to Paradise*. Despite his previous success on the stage and his family's illustrious theatrical history, he cannot make it through opening night. "Ten years of those cursed pictures have done something to me," he says in the dressing room. Drunk and forgetting his lines, he commits suicide after the curtain is brought down on his failed performance, or rather, he is virtually pushed into traffic by the hostile comments of audience members on the street outside the theater. "Carrying a play in New York" is hard work, real work, and the movies have unfitted him for it. In *Secrets of an Actress* Fay Carter eventually succeeds on Broadway after declining to join a road company. "There is no road anymore," she explains, only "a double feature movie, a newsreel, a travelogue, and trying to get in on a bank night." Her roommate, Marian (Isabel Jeans), later warns her against going: "If the dust storms don't get you, the double features will." Double-feature programs, like the one *Secrets of an Actress* was designed to play on, are both the reason "the road" is gone and why you wouldn't want to head off on it anyway. The film companies liked to sound off about double features, blaming exhibitors and the public that complained and yet insisted on them anyway, never the production system that made them profitable and necessary. This film taps into the dissatisfaction while meeting the demand, making an emphatic and embarrassingly justifiable case against itself.

Theaters represented enormous real estate investments, as well as the nexus of film, industry, and consumer. MPGY films subjected exhibition to the same scorn they lavished on other aspects of the movie business. As with double features, the major companies bemoaned bank and dish nights, even as many of their theaters participated in them. These giveaways were the butt of jokes in *Mr. Chump* and *Mr. Doodle Kicks Off,* as well as *Secrets of an Actress,* the kind of B movies most likely to be helped along at the theater with them. In *The Gladiator,* another B, Hugo Kipp (Joe E. Brown) bumps into a woman who drops her purse as she rushes into a theater. Her urgency has nothing to do with the picture; it's "Cash Nite" with a $1,500 prize. Good-hearted Hugo has no interest in the movie either; he buys a ticket so that he can return her bag. The theater is packed, and Hugo wins the prize in a scene that underscores the risks of giveaways such as bank night, not to mention $250,000 movie quiz contests. The camera pans across the faces of audience members, who range from dismayed to disgusted at having lost. One angrily complains that "it's always a guy like that" who wins. Movies are not something you attend to be entertained—wrestling and football serve that purpose in *The Gladiator* (wrestler Mountain Man Dean got second billing to Brown). You go to the movies to win money and then are deeply resentful when you don't. Although praised in the trades as one of Brown's best efforts, *The Gladiator* was not the sort of film to tip the balance back in favor of the entertainment on the screen.[111]

At least one industry insider worried enough about the impact of movies that belittled the industry to write to Breen about it. Goldwyn complained about *Boy Meets Girl* and asked him to intervene. Breen responded that his office had "no authority" to rule that a picture found acceptable based on the Code was unacceptable on "other grounds— the grounds, for instance, of general industry good and welfare." The man who issued multiple warnings about panic and racketeering in the theater in *I Am the Law* had nothing to say to Warners. He did, however, take note of some other films. From "the standpoint of general industry policy," he urged RKO "to avoid anything that might reflect unfavorably" on the industry in *The Affairs of Annabel.* He did not address the wisdom of satirizing it; rather, he pointed to "the character-ization of your leading woman. . . . We recommend not playing her too tough, particularly in the opening sequence in the jail," to which one of Lanny's publicity stunts has sentenced her. *Fugitives for a Night* elicited a broader warning: "the nature of the story, the general flavor, and the background, in their general treatment of the motion picture industry and its personnel, reflects [sic] very unfavorably on the industry as a whole." Regarding *Too Hot to Handle,* an action film about newsreel reporters with more courage than integrity, Breen was concerned about "the indication, throughout this script, that newsreel cameramen are in the habit of faking shots, which are later palmed off on their New York offices, and later put into circulation as authentic news scenes. It seems to us that this suggestion may react unfavorably on our newsreel companies, and on the theatre-going public generally." Breen, it seems, objected when the morality of the industry and its people was called into question, after the fashion of the PCA's handling of sex and crime. He did not intervene over threats to its reputation based on disparaging treatment of peoples' intelligence or the industry's seriousness of pur-pose or the quality of its films. There was no penalty for making the film industry look ridiculous. That was harmless entertainment.[112]

The MPGY Hollywood films raised questions about just how harm-less these representations were. *Keep Smiling* was praised in the trade press as "the most complete insight into motion picture studio opera-tions yet given the general public," a point that could only exacerbate what *Variety* regretted as its signal flaw: "Another exposé of Hollywood drunkenness . . . this Withers starrer doesn't help the picture business reclaim a lily-white reputation at a time when it needs good will. The story can't help but pound home to Hollywood that it's about time the picture business stopped rapping itself in its own costly product. As if the columnists and radio chatterers aren't doing enough harm." *Fugi-tives for a Night* generated similar concerns: "Here again is a picture which tips inside stuff and picture industry behavior that does no one any good. Other industries don't seem to indulge in publicizing their most undesirable side, even for gain." The act of doing what no other legitimate industry ever would—turning out products that make a point of showing it in its worst light—could not but hurt Hollywood's repu-tation. In a letter to Hays, John Hamrick, the owner of an affiliated theater chain headquartered in Seattle, applauded the campaign but complained that films such as *Boy Meets Girl* and *The Affairs of Anna-bel* counteracted its good effects. There was little point in the industry's "seeking a dignified place" when these movies "belittle us in the eyes of the public." The industry declared itself with the American people in their current dislike of the movies while also trying to cure them of it. It spent a million dollars to convince the public to love and respect the industry and its films and even more than that on reasons not to do any such thing.[113]

Only one film depicted the movies in an unequivocally enthusiastic light. The pro-movie dialogue in *Safety in Numbers* may well have been purposefully added for its public relations value, so unintegrated is it with the rest of the film. The Jones family is discussing whether it is ever right for a couple to elope when parents disapprove of the marriage. Suddenly Herbert, the husband of Bonnie, one of the Jones children, interrupts: "I forgot all about it! . . . I've got tickets for the Bijou!" The script continues:

> The problems of love and marriage instantly forgotten, all the Joneses, except Jack [the son who is contemplating an elopement, unbeknownst to the family], whirl.
>
> GROUP (simultaneously) The Bijou!
>
> Hot Dog!
>
> Why, how nice, Herbert!
>
> I haven't seen a show since Bonnie's last birthday!
>
> Come on, everybody!
>
> My coat's upstairs! Etc.
>
> And with the exception of Jack and Toni [his sweetheart], they all hurry out, Bonnie and Herbert last. In the doorway Bonnie stops to kiss him.
>
> BONNIE It was grand of you to think of that, dear!

How easy to show that the movies help us to forget our problems, make our wives happy, and become the hero of the family. How easy to convey the idea of the theater as a beloved local institution—nothing said *neighborhood* like *Bijou*—in a small-town family film, without recourse to costly ads and long-winded arguments. How easy to boost the industry in just a few lines rather than devoting a whole film to putting it down.[114]

At a time when the industry was supposedly so public relations–minded, it is a little surprising that more favorable mentions were not incorporated into films, especially into ones like the Jones Family series, whose episodic nature lent themselves to digressions of this kind.

Would it have killed the Hardy family to enjoy a movie together? The MPGY films had no trouble representing abiding loyalty to college sports in a number of pictures, including *The Gladiator, Hold That Co-ed, Mr. Doodle Kicks Off,* and *Touchdown, Army!* (all football), *Campus Confessions* (basketball), and *Brother Rat* (baseball). The film industry was in an advantageous position to use its own medium to reinforce the messages it sought to convey by other means during the campaign. But most of the stories Hollywood chose to tell about itself in the MPGY films militated against its self-proclaimed goals. Perhaps individual companies knew they were selling out the larger good, as *Variety*'s comments and Breen's ignored advice suggest, but thought the short-term gain worth it. Perhaps they did not believe that movie messages were taken seriously, the advice and badgering of the PCA notwithstanding. Or perhaps these films express the idea that the most important message a movie could communicate to audiences was an obsession above all with entertaining it, for which no sacrifice of reputation or dignity was too great, and anything might be forgiven.

THE FOURTH ESTATE

Not everyone shared Hollywood's willingness to have a laugh at its own expense. Following a preview of *There Goes My Heart* at Grauman's Chinese, an angry chiropractor threatened "drastic action" because of the film's implication that members of his profession could receive training at correspondence schools. The director of the American Optometric Association's Department of Public Relations objected to another MPGY comedy, *Brother Rat,* for depicting girls who wear glasses "in an unfavorable light." He warned of the potential dangerous effects on "thousands of girls needing eye care." These are examples of the way that movies could irritate and offend as much as they amused (and of how amusing other peoples' irritation could be), without launching the industry into paroxysms of damage control. The letter writers spoke on behalf of small constituencies to say the least, and their pleas on behalf of the seriousness of their profession fared no better than Goldwyn's. They did not need an MPGY to take Hollywood seriously, finding an affront to their businesses in even the most innocuous representations of them, a sensitivity to which the film industry remained largely immune.[115]

Not all of Hollywood's targets were so easily ignored. The occasional letter from an irate chiropractor, left to languish in PCA files, was nothing compared to the very public complaints of newspapers regarding Hollywood's unfair treatment of the press in films. The newspaper business was itself in transition. The 1930s brought widespread failures and mergers of individual papers; the struggles of even major chains such as Hearst and Scripps-Howard were widely reported during 1938. Radio had become an ever more important source of news. Its ad revenues were growing, hence the grateful note that many MPGY editorials took of the movies' confidence in newspaper advertising as the best method of bringing its message to the public. Meanwhile, the influence of the newspaper as an organ of public opinion was thought to be eroding. In particular, liberal critics gleefully pointed to the reelection of Roosevelt in 1936, despite the opposition of a reported 85 percent of the nation's newspapers, as evidence of their "waning power." Spokespersons for the newspaper found themselves in the unfortunate position of having to deny that "the public is losing its interest in the press" and to make a case for their relevance. Like the movies, the newspaper business had problems as an industry and an institution, but it was more alert to the ways that unfavorable representations in the movies might exacerbate its ill fortunes. In 1915 the U.S. Supreme Court had declared that movies were not a part of the "press," nor one of the "organs of public opinion," thereby paving the way for government censorship, but the press did not confuse legal rights with social effects. Newspapers reciprocated the film industry's faith in their medium's capacity to influence public opinion and demonstrated an eagerness to manage public relations problems of their own.[116]

Just as Hollywood griped about hostile press coverage, the newspapers were themselves angry at the movies in 1938. Exhibitors turned increasingly to advertising films as a way to deal with ailing box offices. The trend, which newspapers viewed as a direct assault on their bottom line, did not help relations between the industries. Frank Knox and Paul Bellamy, publishers of the *Chicago Daily News* and the *Cleveland Plain Dealer,* respectively, met with Will Hays in April. Hays soon went on record in opposition to theatrical advertising. At the American Newspaper Publishers Association convention, Knox announced that Hays had also taken steps to address "numerous complaints" about the depiction of their business in the movies. To smooth relations, Knox was pleased to report, the producers "promised to stop portraying newspapermen in an unfavorable and 'untrue' light."[117]

This information was likely of more interest to newspaper publishers and staff than to their readership, but the film industry's promise "to reform its traditional screen portrayal of the drinking, dashing and slightly irresponsible newspaper reporter that makes newspaper men and their employers 'look ridiculous' in the eyes of the public," and "to portray newspaper offices more nearly true to life," was reported in many articles. It even became the subject of enthusiastic editorials: "Considerable change has come over the newspaper business in late years, but, even so, it was never the rowdy, drunken, reckless, careless thing that the movies make of it. . . . Newspapers are managed efficiently by sober executives, assisted by responsible writing men and skilled craftsmen." But newspapers that welcomed news of Hollywood's cooperation could not have been pleased with the results, so far as MPGY films were concerned. A December editorial in the *Austin (MN) Daily Herald* found cause yet again to protest that Hollywood (and radio) depicted the newspaper office as "either a nuthouse or recreation room with a halo of romance" and the typical reporter as "the next thing to an idiot," or else "thrilling" and "heroic." The editor countered that the newspaper business "is a serious avocation, carried on in just as serious a fashion as is any other industry." In other words, Hollywood films continued to put newspapers in the same position in which the film industry had found itself in 1938—having to defend their seriousness and service to the public.[118]

The MPGY newspaper reporters pretty much run the gamut laid out in the *Daily Herald*'s editorial, from thrilling hero to idiot. However mundane or serious newspaper work may actually have been, reporting lent itself to the glamour treatment because of the potential for excitement and adventure. When Universal undertook to negotiate Durbin's awkward age in *That Certain Age,* it chose a dashing foreign correspondent as her first movie crush. Vincent Bullitt (Melvyn Douglas) works for her father's chain of newspapers, but there are no newsrooms or reporting, only a mansion in Connecticut, where he is resting after having taken a bullet in Spain. The dangers of reporting in a world at war are as nothing to the perils of teenage love, especially when the image of Universal's most valuable star was at stake. But Bullitt's fantastic career leaves romance safely in the realm of fantasy. The correspondent's reputation comes away clean because Durbin's must; her first, much-publicized onscreen kiss turns out to be an anticlimactic peck on the cheek.

The other side of excitement was instability. In *The Sisters,* a melodrama set at the turn of the twentieth century, man-of-the-world Frank Medlin (Errol Flynn) sweeps Louise Elliott (Bette Davis) off her small-town feet and takes her to San Francisco. Like Bobby Law in *Boy Meets Girl,* he has ambitions to be a novelist, to produce something important about the nation's "growing pains" in the manner of Dreiser, and the fact that reporters don't make $1,500 a week encourages him in this venture. But he is one of the hard-drinking types that the movies were no longer representing. "Irresponsible and restless," with nothing really to say, he abandons both work and wife to become a man of the world again. In the end he wanders back to her because Warners put it up to a vote during previews, and audiences preferred unmotivated reform to the logic of character. Once again, Ian Hunter didn't get the girl.[119]

The "idiots" were reserved for a couple of B pictures, comedy-mysteries that featured reporters who do not cover the news so much as stumble over it. In *The Missing Guest* a goofy reporter, actually called "Scoop" Hanlon (Paul Kelly), is sent by his editor to spend the night in a haunted house. The human-interest angle becomes an actual murder story, and in the process of trying to keep the scoop for himself, he solves the crime. In *Time Out for Murder* Barney Calahan (Michael Whalen) is another bumbling reporter, with a photographer sidekick who likes to throw hot flashbulbs at people. With the help of Margie Ross (Gloria Stuart), a much brighter woman who works for a collection agency and wants fifteen dollars out of Barney, they lurch toward the murderer's identity. Henry Fonda is not an idiot in *The Mad Miss Manton;* he's just a fool in love who uses the newspaper to work through his personal obsession with the socialite, while incidentally reporting on a murder. The crime-solving columnists of *Personal Secretary* are not idiots either, but the newspaper business is depicted as a dirty, frivolous sideshow. A publisher wants his astrology columnist to steal material from a popular gossip columnist at a rival paper so that he can publish the items first. She thinks the plan is contemptible and attempts to lecture her boss: "Isn't there such a thing as ethics in this newspaper business?" He replies, "Oh, please, let's dispense with trivialities." The unscrupulousness of publisher and press established, she gets to work.

Four's a Crowd is a screwball comedy about the newspaper business *and* public relations, the only MPGY film to treat a "phase of human activity not previously dealt with in detail on the screen." Even those who liked it often found the plot not worth trying to recount; for its many critics it marked another "tolling" of the screwball cycle's "death-knell." It reunited Flynn, Olivia de Havilland, and Patrick Knowles, along with Michael Curtiz, from *The Adventures of Robin*

Hood, Warners' most successful film of the year (*Four's a Crowd's* pressbook promised exhibitors " 'Robin Hood' stars for Robin Hood business"). Perennial career woman Rosalind Russell rounded out the screwball foursome. Pat Buckley (Knowles) is the uninterested publisher of a newspaper that is about to fold. He knows and cares little about the business. Jean Christy (Russell) is the tough reporter who convinces Pat to save the paper by rehiring the former managing editor, Bob Lansford (Flynn). Bob left journalism to become "public relations counsel," the term Edward Bernays coined to lend dignity to his burgeoning profession. Bob is no Robin Hood, and neither are his clients. His job is to convince "hated capitalist[s]" to polish their reputations by becoming "beloved philanthropist[s]" and "public benefactor[s]," willingly giving back to the poor for selfish reasons a portion of what they have taken. Bob's barber (Herman Bing) is not impressed by the work of public relations. "I call it bamboozling the peoples. And I am the peoples." The newspaper bamboozles them too. It is failing in part because Pat's "policy . . . has always been to be polite to important people." After Pat hires Bob with full editorial authority, having neglected to read his contract, the paper reverses course. It becomes gratuitously rude to important people. Bob uses the paper to make enemies, for the purpose of turning newly hated capitalists into clients. The paper "is published for the people," which is all well and good, except that "few of them can think, but most of them can feel." Appeals to reason are wasted on it. The newspaper is not a necessary agent of democracy, an organ of public opinion, but rather like the Hollywood film, it traffics in emotions, at its worst sensationalizing whatever it touches.[120]

The film calls the whole public relations endeavor into question but in the end redeems it, because only a reformed Bob can marry Jean. The paper has made heartless millionaire John P. Dillingwell (Walter Connolly) "the most hated man in America." He hires Bob to change that. The plan is for John to build a polio clinic under a (temporarily) false name. Outraged by Bob's double-dealing and in ostensible defense of journalistic integrity, but really motivated by jealousy over his relationship with John's granddaughter, Lorri (de Havilland), Jean plans to publish that John is behind the gift. Bob asks her to "kill this story," because it will kill the clinic. He knows that Jean thinks of him "as a sort of racketeer," but she is wrong. Bob is genuinely sincere in his desire to help "unlucky poor devils." He is not in public relations for himself or for his clients but for the "people who can't take care of themselves." Wearing "bright and shiny Sir Lancelot armor," Bob is Robin Hood after all, the ends justifying the crooked means. Moreover, John has changed, too; he now wants to fund the clinic for social, not selfish, reasons. The point of public relations is not finally to change what the public thinks—to substitute good reputations for bad—but to perform good works for their own sake: to get the clinic. It makes the client become as virtuous as everyone is supposed to think him.

Warners didn't need audience previews to know that the ending of a romantic comedy required a change of heart. It is private relationships that count in classical Hollywood, not what the barber calls this business of "public relationships." *Four's a Crowd*'s insistence on Bob's good intentions depends on our not understanding his speech as one more ploy, his final sale, the greatest manipulation of all. The implausible good will behind all of Bob's misdeeds is the film's way of bamboozling us.

Nothing in the film salvages the reputation of the newspaper business. The press remains a vehicle for the crude manipulation of a gullible public, whether its screaming headlines are wielded by the corrupt or the well-intentioned. Rather than improving in any way the depiction of the press, promotion for the film simply claimed that it had done so, one more publicity angle. A pressbook article stated that Curtiz had once thought that newspapers were just as the movies depicted them— "reporters wore gin bottles for boutonnieres, threw everything on the floor, typed with their feet on the desk," etc.—but after visiting three newsrooms he changed his mind. In *Four's a Crowd* "reporters and executives . . . act the way real newspapermen do." It is true that the newsroom is pretty tidy, but the film also says, and basically shows, that "to a newspaper publisher . . . honor, decency, integrity—they don't mean a thing." More bamboozling.[121]

One film strived to depict the local newspaper as a genuine community service, a crucial public trust, as well as a private enterprise. *The Arkansas Traveler* starred Bob Burns, a folksy comedian whom Paramount eagerly billed as the second coming of Will Rogers, a highly desirable comparison amid the drive toward *human* films. He played the Traveler, an itinerant sage who settles in one town long enough to help a widowed mother and her children hang on to the family newspaper, with the help of an army of hoboes. It celebrates the small town, as well as its newspaper, eschewing the slickness and cynicism associated with metropolitan movie newsrooms, along with their bumbling idiots, in favor of the plain common sense and wisdom of the folk.

The film was smartly dedicated to William Allen White, famed pub-lisher of the *Emporia (KS) Gazette* and national spokesman for mid-dle America and small-town values. His name featured extensively in publicity for the film and in commentary on it. Its foreword presented White as a kind of vital relic: "To the small-town man who envies the glamour of the city, he is living assurance that small-town life may still be profitable. . . . To the city man who looks back with longing on a small-town youth, he is a living example of simplicity, kindliness and common sense" (ellipses in original). White proves the virtues of the small town to those who wish they lived some place else and embodies its symbolic value for those content to romanticize it from afar. *The Arkansas Traveler* likewise offers a paean to a passing institution. In it, nothing better represents the tension between the small town's notional endurance and pending irrelevance than the local newspaper.

Ben Allen could have done "big things" in "any big city," but he was devoted to the paper he founded, and his widow, Martha (Fay Bainter), wants to keep his dream alive. She succeeds with the timely help of the Traveler, a copy setter and man of the people, who was an old friend of Ben's. The newspaper is endangered by Matt Collins (Lyle Talbot), who controls the rest of the town with the help of a corrupt mayor. Matt is trying to have a dam built at the peoples' expense, from which he will privately profit, and he wants the paper to serve as a platform to "educate the townspeople" about why they should support the bond measure. The *Record* defends the true interests of the town and op-poses the dam. It turns out, however, that the real reason Matt wants the newspaper has nothing to do with its value as an organ of public opinion. Indeed, it has nothing to do with the paper at all. Rather, Ben Allen had seen the future, and the future was radio. "He believed that sooner or later every newspaper would have to own its own radio sta-tion," and he acquired the government license for a station, as well as the exclusive wire service franchise. Big things are indeed possible in a small town.

Before Matt can take control of these assets, the Traveler sends word to hundreds of his hobo friends, who ride the rails into town to help build the radio tower before the license is forfeit. The day is saved as a result of the first local broadcast, in which Traveler and the mayor's son, Johnnie Daniels (John Beal), expose the dam scheme. Radio is treated as a public rather than a privately consumed medium. Their words carry over many shots of people gathered together around radios—in the town square, in a barbershop, in stores, in cars, even out-side the *Record*'s office, where a speaker brings the voices to the street. The bond for the dam is defeated; Johnnie is elected mayor by write-in; and the *Record* is saved by the medium that obviates it, which not only delivers news but fosters good citizenship and democratic action while reestablishing the town as a dynamic community.

If White wondered about the treatment of radio as both the salvation of and substitute for the newspaper, or the credibility of the hoboes *ex machina,* he considerately kept quiet. He attended a screening of *The Arkansas Traveler,* and Paramount included a statement in the press-book that praised the film for rejecting conventional newsroom and small-town stereotypes. For films that did not, some journalists took a tongue-in-cheek approach. B. R. Crisler of the *New York Times* wrote, "When it comes to libel, never let it be said that American newspapers can't take it as well as dish it out. The two so-called roving reporters who rove through 'Time Out for Murder' . . . aren't just bad; it seems to us that if they aren't legally actionable, it is time to put teeth into the criminal code." These clowns were an opportunity for a jab not a dia-tribe. If they reflected badly on anything, Crisler suggested, it was not on the newspaper business but rather on the mediocrity of the movies.[122]

Not everyone was so jocular. Reviewers had little to say about the treatment of public relations in *Four's a Crowd,* but a few noted its harmful depiction of their business. A reviewer for the *Wall Street Journal* wrote, "Hollywood still refuses to admit that a newspaper office is not some fantastic place where all the laws of economics and human decency as well as those of the United States are violated—that a news-paper cannot deliberately make false accusations on the front page." According to another review, "the newspaper set-up is about the most impossible, implausible journalistic institution I have ever seen. If any newspaper printed the stuff this one does it would have ten million dollars' worth of libel suits on its hands." The "libel" this sort of film indulged in was more metaphorical than actual, a sign of the difference between the fictional liberties of the movies and the responsibilities as-sociated with the press. One could fairly say that newspapers were the one business that the movies treated even worse than its own, in part by treating it so much like its own, as an enterprise given over to the zany disregard of decorum, common sense, and reality.[123]

The demands for fair and favorable treatment conveyed the newspa-pers' sense that the movies mattered. About midway through MPGY, *Variety* took it upon itself to remind the film industry that the press mattered, too. Inaccurate screen portrayals of newsmen and their work "may at first seem trivial," but they actually have "a very important and direct bearing on the relationship . . . between the industry and the press." It brought up the example of the managing editor of a metropolitan daily, who told his reviewer "to criticise severely any picture in which a reporter or any other member of the staff was unfairly depicted, and moreover to keep pounding away" at the film while it was still showing. More important, however, resentment was felt in the sting of newspapers' broader criticisms of the movies as a whole, from double features and the star system to "the sameness of stories and the trend of cycles" that "after a while become tiresome and boring." *Variety* talked to editors in the field. They understood that the film industry has "many complicated problems," and it proposed that "newspapers are more than willing to be the friends of the film business," if the film business proved itself willing to be friends of theirs.[124]

Hundreds of thousands of dollars in paid MPGY ads as evidence of the film industry's faith in newspapers, not to mention the daily expenditures on theater advertising: none of this was friendly enough. If the film industry wanted to get the press off its back, it would have to acknowledge the public relations messages of its own products. *Variety* urged recognition of and respect for the power of the press and for the symbiotic relationship of the media. Individual studios might care little about a few negative comments about particular films, but the cumulative effect might be measured in reportorial and editorial challenges to the basic structure, methods, and products of the industry, in which all of the majors had a stake. This was a particular concern with the antitrust lawsuit. Only three sample newspapers did not run an article about the lawsuit in the days after it was announced. About 25 percent of the articles were short, straightforward announcements of the suit, but most went into the specific charges, focusing on the effects of anticompetitive practices on independents, often at some length, and in Thurman Arnold's own words. One syndicated article was distinctly hostile in tone toward the industry, noting, "the 119-page complaint accused the movie magnates of driving independents out of business, discouraging new capital investments, throttling artistic expression, and denying 88 million weekly theater patrons a free choice of pictures." The costs were borne by exhibitors, artists, and the entire moviegoing public. MPGY was an attempt to counteract many kinds of bad publicity, including the potential fallout from the lawsuit, which had made the industry actual hard news and not just fodder for the gossip columnists.

Whether *Variety*'s crass calculation was accurate or not, the industry had spent $575,000 to build the good will of the nation's newspapers only to endanger it with yet more films that cultivated their hostility. And with the conclusion of MPGY the industry could have used all the press friends it could get.[125]

Conclusion

Motion Pictures' Worst Year

The MPGY campaign got off to an excellent start, amid the blaze of publicity for which the industry was so famous. Reports in both the trade and mainstream press touted its salubrious effect on box-office receipts, beginning with a big Labor Day weekend. The numbers were predictably fuzzy and flexible but communicated an aura of triumph. A 10 to 30 percent increase in box office over the previous year was cited, with improvements as great as 45 percent in some areas. An Associated Press story announced that the film business "was leaping into the black from the red" as "every key city in the United States reported heavy business." In late September, according to the *Los Angeles Examiner,* Howard Dietz predicted as much as a 50 percent upsurge before the end of the year. He estimated that more than thirty-two million quiz booklets had been distributed, and he anticipated more than eight million entries to the contest; in mid-October the figure had risen to ten million. Independent exhibitors continued to pledge financial support, swayed, one imagines, by all the attention the campaign had generated and by their sense that it might really be helping to improve business. Doubters maintained, however, that business almost always improved in September and that it was impossible to separate the effects of the campaign from the usual seasonal recovery.[1]

There was other good news as well. The movie famine appeared to be over. Commentators reported that an unusually good crop of new films heralded the start of the campaign, and this not just from the usual ravers within Hollywood. Having expected September's films "to hit a somewhat common average," W. Ward Marsh of the *Plain Dealer* instead found them "so vastly improved over the same month, 1937, that Hollywood has every right to feel proud of its advanced steps." Jimmie Fidler praised the industry for "snapp[ing] out of its lethargy" and "turning out top-notch entertainment"; even "the average picture has been stepped up in class." Frank Nugent of the *New York Times* pronounced it "motion pictures' greatest September." These were the sorts of endorsements that might well satisfy the organizers.[2]

The MGM, RKO, and Warners data indicate that for these companies, at least, the quiz pictures helped their bottom line, although we cannot know exactly what role the campaign or contest played in their profitability (see table 1). MGM's domestic revenues for films released between July 29 and October 31, 1938, were up almost $5 million from the same period in 1937, and it saw a spectacular return to profitability after the heavy losses of the previous year. Warners' domestic revenues also rose, albeit less dramatically, and its estimated $602,000 profit for the 1937 period increased to $929,000 for the MPGY films. RKO's struggles continued. Its domestic revenues declined by about 16 percent from the 1937 to 1938 period; however, foreign revenues tumbled more than 40 percent. By making fewer films during MPGY and spending less on them, RKO managed to eke out a $6,000 profit with its campaign pictures, despite the decline in revenues. Even this meager figure represented a significant improvement over the substantial losses of the 1937 period. The proportion of domestic revenues to total revenues increased at all three studios, by slightly less than 4 percent at Warners to 5 percent at MGM and 8 percent at RKO, as one might expect if the campaign had a positive impact on moviegoing. But the data are inconclusive. The international markets were disrupted by war and threats of war, including the Munich crisis and Hitler's invasion of the Sudetenland within weeks of the campaign's opening. Regardless, these modest increases were not in line with the kinds of numbers bandied about in the press as evidence of the campaign's miraculous effect on box-office receipts.[3]

One notable feature of the data is the failure of the most expensive films. In an article on Hollywood profitability trends in the domestic market, Michael Pokorny and John Sedgwick have found that the highest revenues tended to be generated by high-cost pictures, but they were also the ones most likely to lose a lot of money. The bigger the risk, the bigger the potential rewards, but for those three months in 1937

TABLE I   PRODUCTIONS, DOMESTIC REVENUES (U.S. AND CANADA),
AND WORLDWIDE PROFITS FOR FILMS RELEASED BY MGM, RKO, AND
WARNER BROS. BETWEEN JULY 29 AND OCTOBER 31, 1937, AND JULY 29
AND OCTOBER 31, 1938

	Productions		Revenues		Profits	
	1937	1938	1937 ($m)	1938 ($m)	1937 ($)	1938 ($)
MGM[1]	12	12	9,444	14,375	–785,000	2,472,000
RKO[2]	15	12	5,425	4,544	–662,000	6,000
WB	18	13	7,964	8,440	602,000	929,000

SOURCES: Data from the Eddie Mannix (MGM), C.J. Trevlin (RKO), and William Schaefer (Warner Bros.) ledgers (see chapter 4, note 1). Warner Bros. profits estimated by John Sedgwick.
NOTE: Only worldwide profit figures are available.
[1] Excludes the independently produced *Block-Heads* (no data).
[2] Includes independently produced releases.

and in 1938, the more epic the losses. In the 1937 period there were two films from MGM that cost more than $2 million to produce—*The Good Earth* and *Conquest*—and one from each studio at more than $1 million: *Broadway Melody of 1938* (MGM), *The Toast of New York* (RKO), and *Varsity Show* (Warners). MGM made $271,000 on *Broadway Melody* but lost a whopping $1,893,000 on the other two (most of it on Garbo's turn as Napoleon's Polish mistress in *Conquest*). *The Toast of New York* lost $530,000, *Varsity Show* $217,000. Among the campaign films, once again four of the five that cost more than $1 million lost money. *Carefree* dropped $68,000 for RKO. (*Room Service*, the studio's second most expensive film, lost $330,000.) MGM made $12,000 on *Sweethearts* (which cost just a shade under $2 million) but lost a total of $1,522,000 on three films that cost between $1.5 and $3 million: *Marie Antoinette*, *The Great Waltz*, and *Too Hot to Handle*. Indeed, MGM's return to profitability during these three months was largely due to the success of a single film, *Boys Town*, which turned a worldwide profit of $2,112,000 on a modest production cost of $772,000. Warners' best performer was *Four Daughters*, which cost only $564,000 to make and resulted in a $576,000 profit for the studio, eight times the combined profit of its two most expensive films, *The Sisters* and *Valley of the Giants*. RKO's most profitable MPGY film was *Mother Carey's Chickens*, which cost a mere $358,000 and made $110,000. The dismal results of the superspecials, the most publicized and closely watched films at any time, and the success of the middle-range films suggest that the campaign might better have been billed as Motion Pictures' Most Moderate Year.[4]

With a name like that the industry might have staved off some of the embarrassment that followed. As MPGY unfolded, there were many reports that public interest in the campaign was underwhelming. As we have seen, some exhibitors who reneged on their pledges cited not only difficulties getting quiz pictures but also the public's indifference as their reason for not paying. Small independents were not the only ones disheartened. As early as mid-October, a memo to theater managers in the Balaban and Katz circuit ended with a feeble pitch for the contest: "*Do Not Be Deceived!* There is more Picture Fan interest in the Movie Quiz Contest than the average Exhibitor will admit. It may not appear on the surface, but there *IS* a strong undercurrent of excitement among the Contestants." In November the trade press reported that attendance was waning and revenues were down. Ever helpful, Fidler noted, "Box office reports from the nation at large indicate that the movie industry is still sick." Before it was over, internal reports on the campaign at the MPPDA raised doubts about "the direct box office values of the recent drive." In a premature November postmortem, David Palfreyman asserted that the campaign had improved the "editorial attitude" of newspapers toward the industry and, more vaguely, that "thoughtful people in the business" believed it had made public opinion "more favorable" as well, but he also acknowledged the legitimacy of exhibitor complaints about the impact of the campaign on "immediate results" in "dollars and cents return . . . [at] the box office." In other words, he thought that the public liked the movies again, but it was not clear that people wanted to go see them.[5]

There was much to criticize, according to Palfreyman: the similarity between the contest and other giveaway schemes; the abstract, ineffectual nature of the advertising; the lack of enthusiasm among many exhibitors; the hasty organization. Much of the blame for the campaign's failure fell on the ill-conceived contest, described by late September as "a great pain in the neck to the master-minds behind it." Among the troubles was the well-publicized revelation that questions for five films in the contest booklet contained errors of fact that rendered them impossible to answer correctly. Any answer would be accepted, which meant that entrants were on their honor to see all thirty pictures. The errors also gave the unfortunate impression that people within the industry could not be bothered to watch their own films.[6]

Exhibitors complained about the "hissing and razzing of trailers" that promoted the contest. In October the state of Missouri declared it an illegal lottery. About two million people entered rather than eight or ten. And in a lesson straight from *The Gladiator,* organizers and exhibitors began to realize "that contests are always fraught with dissatisfaction and that the final results . . . are bound to create squawks." According to *Variety,* Harold Franklin even sent letters to exhibitors urging them "not to overplug the Quiz, since that's the thing that usually irks fans," after so much money and energy had been spent plugging away. Too late the industry wondered if the old-fashioned ballyhoo would undermine its public relations ambitions.[7]

Contest winners were announced nationwide on the night of February 27 from the stages of theaters that had participated in the campaign. This event was described as generating "only mild interest." The idea was to boost business on a Monday by attracting moviegoers who hoped to win a prize; the actual winners were notified in advance to "attend 'their customary theatres'" that night. One newspaper condemned the industry for "deliberately wooing the ill-will of a large share of those 2,000,000 who will go to the theater . . . just to discover they did a lot of work for nothing." The prize money had been divided in such a way that top prizes provided an incentive for entering the contest, while the large number of awards assured a wide distribution of winners across regions and theaters. The localized efforts to publicize the contest made local winners necessary. But in Tucson, for example, where the attention lavished on the campaign and the contest included radio broadcasts, a float in the Labor Day parade, street streamers and banners, and tie-ins at local restaurants and shops, the contest resulted in just six ten-dollar prizewinners, hardly an amount from which dreams were fulfilled. It was possible to win and not even make back what one had spent on seeing the contest pictures.[8]

The grand prize went to Elizabeth Benincasa of San Francisco. As predicted, there were hard feelings. The top prize in Washington, D.C., was $500, but an article on the contest in the *Washington Daily News* featured a photograph of Ambrose McGreevy, a ten-dollar prizewinner. Wagging a finger and looking angry, he "challenged" the winner of the $50,000 prize "to publish her essay and 'let the public decide whether she is entitled to the award.'" A letter writer to campaign headquarters demanded the names of the winners and copies of their essays. "Facts in my possession show this contest was a racket—and the picture business is now and will continue to feel the opinion of the Public." These are only two examples among more than two million entrants, but they show that even winners could feel like losers and that losers could feel as though the contest was rigged. Many others must have felt similarly betrayed by the industry, which had promised so much but delivered so little.[9]

The industry saw the campaign as an unfortunate episode to put behind it. Industry spokesmen did not publicly admit its failure, but any claims made for it were exceptionally modest. In his annual report of March 1939 Will Hays briefly mentioned the previous year's "Campaign for Increased Attendance," praising it as "a splendid example of industry cooperation" that had "received full newspaper and trade press support." He declined to say what kind of support it had received from the public. George Schaefer described "the value of cooperation of all branches of the industry to its mutual interest" as the "most" important lesson of the campaign, and he applauded "the whole-hearted support that the committee received from independent exhibitors, circuits, distributors and producers," evidence to the contrary. Hays also invited members of the film industry to "make cooperation our watchword in 1939" and continue to build "an atmosphere of mutual trust, mutual responsibility and mutual help," through which "the industry can best progress." These analyses of a campaign designed to build public relations emphasized the overstated effects on industry relations. If the self-praise over all this newfound cooperation was designed to generate momentum for a consent decree, it failed in this regard. The Justice Department at least remained convinced that the film industry was a big and serious business.[10]

In the mainstream and trade press the campaign came to be seen as a flop. Whatever MPGY had achieved in "ton[ing] down the hostile blasts" against the film industry was only temporary. Hays's press summaries—a compilation of articles from around the country on various issues of importance to the film industry—were full of negative commentary by the end of the year and beyond. The contest provided one ready target; others were more troubling. The early enthusiasm for the campaign films cooled, and MPGY itself became the framework for unfavorable end-of-year assessments of the state of Hollywood film: "What the moving picture industry failed to do throughout the contest was to make good pictures." Prior to MPGY the film industry had thought of its problems as something that good pictures alone would not cure; however, good pictures had at least to be part of the solution.

The same three-month period of 1937 had brought a number of unremarkable films before the public, but the MPGY films were a forgettable bunch as well, and even its best films do not rank among the great films of the 1930s. The difference was that the industry had gone on record that such pictures as *Suez, Too Hot to Handle, The Cowboy and the Lady, Room Service, Letter of Introduction,* and *The Texans,* not to mention B films such as *Secrets of an Actress, Vacation from Love,* and *Juvenile Court,* were the best it ever had done or could do. As Martin Quigley, the publisher of the *Motion Picture Herald,* which had once warmly embraced the campaign, wrote in his analysis of its failure and the challenges that lay ahead: "Some motion pictures, but not all of them, are the public's best entertainment—a fact which the public understands clearly and is not likely to forget."[11]

By the end of the year several movie reviewers bemoaned the difficulty of selecting the top ten films because there were simply too few contenders. Paul Harrison succinctly commented, "There were not 10 distinguished pictures made in 1938." Some reviewers remarked that 1938 had in reality been the greatest year for the English film industry, which had produced *The Lady Vanishes, The Beachcomber, Pygmalion, To the Victor,* and *The Edge of the World,* among other films. And in September the French film *Grand Illusion* (1937) was released in the United States to acclaim. It was not at all uncommon for several foreign pictures, mostly from Britain, to figure prominently on top-ten lists for the year, a notable distinction, or demerit, depending on where you made films. Sam Shain wrote in *Motion Picture Daily* that the New York film critics "have started something for Hollywood and the trade as a whole to ponder," when so many of them individually picked from four to seven foreign films as the ten best of the year. Howard Barnes, of the *New York Herald Tribune,* remarked that "our screen industry has made its own slogan of 'motion picture's greatest year' ring very hollow." It was "chiefly thanks to the disorganized producing which has gone on in England and France that one is enabled to pick a decent number of films and craftsmen for the special commendation that is customary here and now." His ten-best list featured four British pictures and two French.[12]

Or was it five British pictures? *The Citadel,* voted best picture of the year by both the New York Film Critics Circle and the National Board of Review, was produced by MGM in England with a British cast (headed by Robert Donat) and technicians; its director (King Vidor) and female lead (Rosalind Russell) were both Hollywood talents. *The*

Citadel was based on A. J. Cronin's best-selling novel about an idealistic doctor who recommits to medical research on diseases affecting coal miners, after a lucrative but soulless foray among London's wealthy female hypochondriacs. It was scheduled for release on November 3, a few days after the deadline for MPGY films. Writers often called it a foreign film, as Shain did in his article. Thus Walter Winchell's acid remark that the success of *The Citadel* and *Grand Illusion* with critics "indicat[ed] to Hollywood that movies are your best entertainment even if the colony has nothing to do with them." *The Citadel*'s provenance could be used as a club against studio filmmaking as usual, providing writers evidence either of Hollywood's irrelevance or, almost as dismissively, of its potential.[13]

One reason reviewers favored foreign films was that they have "shown that [they] can still deal with reality." Marsh, who included two on his list, was one of several critics to point an "accusing finger" at Hollywood, after having announced its "right to feel proud" of the new films a few months back. His reluctance had as much to do with the nature of the year as with the nature of the films: "It was not easy to name ten Hollywood pictures fit to be considered among the Best Ten in such an eventful and turbulent year as 1938." The failure of Hollywood was in part its failure to engage with a world that demanded to be represented. It continued, instead, in its "determination to create only that type of film which affords an avenue of 'escape,' and its disastrous inclination to construct false values, tell fake stories founded upon fact, and so fictionize every tale it touches."[14]

Complaints about the triteness and falseness of Hollywood films were, of course, long-standing. But the chorus of disapproval at this moment was louder than ever, and it was different. The industry had more or less invited censure by bringing its problems so visibly to the fore and by floundering so publicly in its attempts to deal with them. The critics of Hollywood were reluctant to let everyone be "your own best" critic, which is to say, they had their own ideas about what the public disaffection with the movies before and after MPGY might mean. The *human* films were an attempt to respond to the call for a certain kind of relevance, and reviewers continued to insist that in the wake of the campaign's failure, "the only way to get customers into the theaters is to give them stories about real people with real problems—stories audiences can understand and appreciate because they are part of themselves; stories with subjects that are contemporary, as fresh and stimulating as the front page of a daily newspaper." Pleas for more Andy Hardys persisted, but they diminished, in part because there wasn't much need to keep telling Hollywood to make cheap and enormously profitable pictures. But there were numerous appeals for films that were significant, that dealt with "real problems" larger than those faced by robust American teenagers, the kind one read about on front pages. These came from newspaper editors as well as movie critics, and not only from the metropolises. Thus, several commentators offered another explanation for the declining attendance that had prompted the campaign and for its failure to rekindle public enthusiasm for the movies. Calling MPGY "one of the noisiest and most infantile of contemporary publicity stunts," the *Bloomington (IL) Argus* challenged the film industry: "A world watching itself slip slowly into a new Dark Age has little patience for the weak attempts at reality that you've tried to pawn off on it. You've steered clear of controversial subjects because you were afraid; and who in the world of today has time for a coward?"[15]

Now that the $250,000 "bank night, in the grand manner," was over, "the industry must realize that it has made no progress toward the solution to its problem." The campaign had been an expensive distraction, which in the end had failed to do anything but focus attention on what really plagued the industry. Having begged so promiscuously for recognition and acclaim, but having found itself unable to prove to anyone's satisfaction, including its own, that it had achieved its goals, the film industry had created a remarkable opportunity for others to hammer home the point that there was more to movies than relaxation and freedom from care, that ideas mattered, and that if the industry did not see that they mattered, it would cease to matter. Thus, the virtue of *The Citadel*, which garnered almost $1 million in profits for MGM:

> [The film] says little enough . . . but it does say something, and the public is obviously so grateful for that something. . . . The truth that underlies the present troubles of the movie-makers, that explains the falling away of the public from the box-office, would seem to be so simple. It is only this: If you say nothing, no one will listen to you long. . . . It is just possible that they [the studio heads] do not know that they are using this medium to say nothing. It may be possible, even, that they have nothing to say. And, if these things are so, they need not worry about the future of pictures, for they will have nothing to do with it.[16]

Critics saw themselves as giving voice to the public's palpable, if inarticulate, longing for significance, the real meaning behind its unwillingness to be bribed back into theaters. At the same time, industry professionals prodded Hollywood from within, and MPGY provided an opportunity to make their case, too. Walter Wanger, Fredric March, Fritz Lang, Dudley Nichols, and others joined with artists and intellectuals outside the industry to form Films for Democracy, a group that proposed "using Hollywood methods" to make movies "designed to combat intolerance and reaction and safeguard American democracy" for a broad audience, according to one editorial in praise of this ambition. At the New York Film Critics Circle Awards, where so many foreign films were lauded, Nichols said that "the public stays away" from the Hollywood "masterpieces," "so they [the movie companies] resort to contests, schemes, advertising in a dizzy whirl that takes them even farther from the truth. The truth is that motion pictures must use the strong materials of life or eventually go into the discard." As with the remarks on *The Citadel,* these words were more warning than threat. Motion Pictures' Greatest Year might herald the beginning of Hollywood's last years.[17]

An essay by the poet Archibald MacLeish argued that no "art which ignored everything comprehended under the term 'social issues' in this time could have vitality—could have the fourth dimension of life." Hollywood films "do not know their own time, do not present their own time, do not belong to their own time, and therefore, quite naturally, have lost the interest of their own time." He had not far to look for evidence of their fantastic disconnect:

> To be invited in the autumn of 1938, with Hitler swallowing the Czechs . . . with France crushing a general strike by force of arms, with England accepting the indecency of Munich . . . with Japan tearing at the gigantic carcass of China, with the Jews suffering unspeakable indignities in Germany . . . to sit through such films as *The Cowboy and the Lady, The Shining Hour, Marie Antoinette, Suez,* and *The Great Waltz* is almost an impertinence. To be asked to sit through no films except these films and others like them is pretty close to insulting.

Audacity becomes abuse with the lack of alternatives, with Hollywood's refusal to veer from the course of distracting entertainment and temper the frivolous with the trenchant and meaningful. Again, the choice presented is not between significant and insignificant films but between any films from Hollywood and none. "The movies, if they are vigorous and alive and truly forms of art, can outlive any pressure group. The movies, if they are cowardly and insincere and boring, cannot live at all."[18]

The usual rebuttal to such arguments was that the movies were an industry as well as an art, their artistry was necessarily constrained by business considerations, and their financial viability depended on entertaining the largest audience possible. The push for motion pictures to "say something" was either to embroil them in controversies that would offend some or doom them to the category of propaganda that would alienate all. The institutional ads had said something quite different—that it was impossible for motion pictures to please everyone. Their aim was "a pretty high-average" of satisfaction. This was in part, of course, so much sales talk, a way to defend against criticism from the people displeased by individual films. But it was also a fundamental truth about the vagaries of moviemaking. Quigley, a vociferous opponent of "propaganda" in the movies, acknowledged in his end-of-year reckoning that "there are different types and kinds of audiences, each with an inclination toward a certain grade or class of film. Occasionally—but only occasionally—there is the picture of universal appeal. . . . Pictures succeed or fail in the market stratum for which they are intended." Although there was no shortage of people claiming to speak on behalf of "the public" as a singularity that demanded films of social significance, just as others spoke for a singularity that repudiated them, one way to think about *significance* was as a market stratum. One choice among many, with its detractors but also its fans, it could function like the gangster film or a Crawford picture or, for that matter, the "better" films based on literary classics in an era when, as film historian Lewis Jacobs wrote in 1939, future "production policy must take into account the fact that the eighty million people who go to movies today are no longer made up of one group or level of intelligence."[19]

The film industry "has become so standardized and commercialized" that "the public, which for years avidly swallowed whatever Hollywood fed it, is now beginning to regurgitate, and is showing its indisposition by staying away from the theaters," according to Clara Beranger, a former screenwriter and founding faculty member of USC's School of Cinematic Arts. Her point was as much a commercial consideration about the need for variety, for giving people different choices, as it was a simple plea for more relevant films. Putting "adult ideas and current problems on the screen" would help to meet the "ever-increasing public demand for a variation from the regular standardized fare." Moreover, the prominent success of lower-budget films proved that huge sums need not be risked in making such pictures, that they could be commercially viable without attracting large audiences. The drive toward significance did not signify an end to the staples of Hollywood filmmaking. Wanger became the most famous of the industry's own critics of "Hollywood escapism" following the release of *Blockade*

(1938), a film about the Spanish Civil War that generated a number of protests, as well as staunch support. Even he "admitted the necessity of 'pure entertainment,' the 'backbone of the industry.' 'For heaven's sake, don't think I believe that all Hollywood films should be in this classification.'" The interest in socially significant films could easily be assimilated into Hollywood's traditional worldview. At the end of *America at the Movies* Margaret Farrand Thorp noted that the industry was inclined to treat the recent "desire for films with content" as another "one of those unaccountable public whims."[20]

For others the latest fancy was not unaccountable at all. The force of the criticism of Hollywood, in the wake of MPGY, was to establish a vital connection between providing good entertainment and giving the audience something to think about. MacLeish's point was not simply that Hollywood films were insulting or dishonest but that they were "boring." The same argument was made in an "Open Letter to Producers" from the *Madison Capital Times,* which called the movie quiz contest "almost a complete failure" as "a means of getting some of your lost patrons back in the theaters." Favorably mentioning a speech by Wanger, the paper wrote, "The public still wants entertainment, but in a world where there are so many problems, the old time movie habit of being off on a plane that had no real connection with everyday life no longer interests the spectators." If the industry sought to revive the moviegoing habit, it would fail if it did not recognize that habits change, that a new world called for new films.[21]

Even portions of the trade press, which tended to be conservative on the subject of movie content, picked up on this point. It was critical of the Films for Democracy plan and its attempt "to pervert the entertainment screen from its avowed purposes of entertainment." Some writers, however, observed that ideas about what constituted entertainment were changing. And they noticed that Hays had noticed. Citing a speech he had given to the kind of organizations—civic, religious, youth—that usually bothered about the movies, *Boxoffice* pondered the czar's new language: "When he uses such phrases as 'part of the world on fire' and 'foes even in our own household' and 'danger of contagion from a distance,' could it not be that he has in mind a re-direction of industry function to embrace a realization of facts and developments in the world at large which this business, purporting to be a kind of a mirror of its times, cannot in all consciousness ignore?" Hays "is aware published opinion in many directions has been creating a clamor about the state of the film institution. It is calling upon Hollywood to stop boring its customers. It is petitioning the producers to cease shadow boxing with the vibrant issues of the day." The article raises an ethical point— what the industry should do during times of peril, when the world is "on fire"—but also a practical, bottom-dollar point, the same one that MacLeish as a spokesman for art made: Hollywood might want to start entertaining its patrons again, to recognize that important issues are "vibrant," which is to say, they are the opposite of "boring."[22]

The Hollywood Reporter put it even more directly. A writer for the *Baltimore Evening Sun* praised the trade paper for saying "that 'expensive as is our product of today and as fine as it is, it's too old-fashioned and not sufficiently exciting to stir an audience away from the radio, newspapers or family arguments around the fireside. . . . The greatest interest in this civilized world today is the tremendous international drama that is being played each hour throughout that world. Current events are packed with thrills. . . . Our pictures are not competing with those events.'" The *Reporter* spoke Hollywood's own language. *Thrills* was a ubiquitous word in movie advertising, a quality to which not only action films but romances and melodramas such as *Four Daughters* aspired. But movies were losing a struggle with the news media to interest and excite the public. Exhibitors resented the impact of radio, as a free showcase for movie stars and stories, on attendance, but the competition for the entertainment dollars of the public extended, as well, to its coverage of electrifying world events, which the film industry had eschewed. As the *Chicago Daily Times* put it in an editorial in September 1938, during the Munich crisis: "Hollywood in its wildest flights of fancy never touched this. Stupendous? It's super colossal drama." Americans purchased more radio sets during the three weeks that the crisis was broadcast than in any previous three-week period. It was self-evident to critics that the "world is so interesting and fascinating that people buy newspapers to read about it and photo magazines to visualize it." Hollywood needed to turn to "subjects that are contemporary, as fresh and stimulating as the front page of a daily newspaper" or a radio broadcast, not to educate or propagandize the audience but rather to entertain a good portion of it.[23]

All of these criticisms were "published opinion," as *Boxoffice* called it, not necessarily public opinion, although MPGY itself was born and took shape out of a conviction that the influence of the one upon the other was great. It was clear that something was awry, that the attempt to rekindle the affection of moviegoers, to build good will toward the movies as a vital institution and a bold, dynamic industry had not succeeded. Instead, attention was more sharply focused than ever on Hollywood's flaws, on its triviality and cowardice, on "emasculating or stultifying concessions to foreign censors, domestic reformers, juveniles and jitterbugs," the sort of spinelessness that made it "the ostrich of the arts." Indeed, in the wake of the campaign, the industry's public relations problems could well be thought to have intensified; at any rate, they certainly were not over.[24]

It is hard to know to what extent industry developments were influenced by these cries for a new kind of "better" entertainment, as opposed to other factors during this turbulent time. The PCA was coming under increasing criticism for its unmandated interference in the political content of films, for example, during the production of Wanger's ultimately rather timid *Blockade*. The 1938 antitrust lawsuit charged that the Code and the domination of exhibition allowed the major companies to exercise effective control over film content, "restricting the production of innovative approaches to drama or narrative" that might challenge their "monopoly power." Richard Maltby argues that the lawsuit made it expedient to allow more controversial content into films, to demonstrate that there really was "freedom of the screen." It has also often been noted that there was a distinct turn to the explicit treatment of democratic themes in 1939, that "Americanism" became the rage as Hitler gained momentum in Europe. Thomas Elsaesser likewise credits the economic threat posed by the lawsuit with the "conscious" cultivation of "an image of public and ideological responsibility" within such films. Another reason given for the trend has been the necessity of compensating domestically for diminishing foreign box offices, as wars' disruptions took their inevitable toll.[25]

In the same annual ritual of self-congratulation that gave MPGY only cursory mention, Hays praised the industry for "a succession of pictures which dramatized present-day social conditions." The difference from the previous year's speech, "Self-Regulation in the Motion Picture Industry," came across in the title: "Enlarging Scope of the Screen." Hays's support for films of "social import" was new and suggestive, as was even the anemic comment that "there is nothing incompatible between the best interests of the box-office and the kind of entertainment that raises the level of audience appreciation" of any issue. A *New York Times* editorial chastised Hays a bit for overstating what the industry had already accomplished but praised his discussion of "an Americanism cycle" and announcement that new films would "stress the struggle for freedom, the heritage of democracy, the triumph of man's spirit over material obstacle." These changes represented "not a haphazard development but one deliberately entered into because of 'the impact of public opinion.'" A few months later Dietz noted the turn to American themes and portraits of "democratic life" and asked: "Who makes these films?" "One can not evade the conception that the public is behind these films," by which he meant that the public is the "author": "the people in Hollywood are ghostwriters for the public." Democratic messages derive from the democratic filmmaking process; the medium has become the message.[26]

The prospect of a new movie diet met with approval on the grounds of entertainment value, too. Loosening the "restrictions on controversial matters" should "bring some meaty, exciting stuff to the screen." Nugent, writing in the *Nation,* described the new cycle: "Hollywood has begun to wave the flag. It has discovered America, discovered democracy. . . . If perhaps you stopped going to the movies about the time they started the Motion Pictures' Greatest Year campaign, as so many of you did, you may not have noticed." He mentioned such films as *Confessions of a Nazi Spy* (1939), *Let Freedom Ring* (1939), and *The Great Dictator* (1940), the production of A-level westerns and two biographies of Lincoln, and the revival of "Personal History" (which became *Foreign Correspondent* [1940]), among other projects. "What we have, in sum, is an astonishing picture of Hollywood expressing a point of view, seemingly in defiance of its frequently stated policy that the primary, and often the sole, purpose of the motion picture is to entertain." Nugent thought that the industry might have "awakened to the public's interest in democracy," but he seemed more willing to attribute the change to the randomness with which "cycle follows cycle for no apparent reason," including "the homespun cycle" of 1938.[27]

This is not, of course, to say that the studios threw caution to the wind or that the PCA withdrew all objections to films on the grounds of their political ideas. It tried to discourage Warner Bros. from making *Confessions of a Nazi Spy,* the first explicitly anti-Nazi film, and challenged other such projects. Flag-waving celebrations of America and its democratic traditions were not politically controversial in the way that, say, direct attacks on Germany were. And yet they were controversial as *entertainment.* What such films signified was a breaking down, however partial and uneven, of conventional thinking about the "invariable distinction" between entertainment and what was so loosely called *propaganda* in the 1930s. In addition to the pressures associated with the antitrust lawsuit, political content—*significance*—seemed attractive to an industry whose business, after all, was the attempt to anticipate and gratify public whims, unaccountable or not, to temper the same as usual with the new for now. The industry was concerned about foreign revenues, but it worried over the domestic situation as well. That is, Americanism in the movies may have been not only about replacing international moviegoers with new American ones but also part of the ongoing effort to bring the old domestic audiences back to theaters on a more frequent basis, to accomplish what MPGY had not.[28]

The "homespun" and the human, the interest in people like us, expressed itself in American settings and characters for the vast majority of MPGY films, several of which also fostered the development of Americanism as a theme, in particular through the $2,112,000 lesson of *Boys Town* that a movie can preach democratic values for ninety minutes and still please a lot of people. A few films promoted Americanism even more explicitly, including *Gateway,* a programmer about eager immigrants at Ellis Island, and *Sons of the Legion,* a B picture that professed hostility to discriminations between "high or low, rich [or] poor . . . race or creed" in the formation of a junior version of the American Legion. *Sons of the Legion* lectured against "the rising tide of un-Americanism" and those who are "sowing the seeds of destruction, destruction of American principles and ideals." The precise content of the threat is unstated; the film focuses on positive values: "justice, free-dom, loyalty, and democracy." Whatever the reactionary implications of the self-appointed definers and defenders of the American way, the thrust of the film is not on routing the enemy but on helping to reform Butch (Donald O'Connor), a poor tough who seems destined for a life of crime. "Unashamed flag-waving" meets the juvenile delinquency cycle. This film enabled Paramount to demonstrate its patriotism and pursue a ready-made market on the cheap (it premiered at the convention of American Legionnaires in Los Angeles), but it would take more thoughtful and ambitious pictures than either *Sons of the Legion* or *Gateway* to demonstrate a broader commitment to Americanism as a force for entertainment.[29]

It is impossible to know how two million contest entrants responded to these and other MPGY films, but extant essays, from the winners of the top twenty-four prizes ($1,000 and above), allow us to consider what a handful of moviegoers thought about them, as well as which responses were most highly valued. A panel of five judges—Bruce Barton (congressman and advertising guru); Helen Reid (a vice president at the

New York Herald Tribune); James E. West (chief Scout executive of the Boy Scouts of America); Helen Wills Moody (tennis player); and Henrik Willem van Loon (historian and children's writer)—chose the winners from a tiny fraction of the submissions. Fourteen films from among the ninety-four quiz pictures were named as favorites: *Alexander's Ragtime Band, Boys Town, Dark Rapture, Four Daughters, Gateway, The Great Waltz, Marie Antoinette, Men with Wings, Mother Carey's Chickens, Spawn of the North, Stablemates, That Certain Age, Valley of the Giants,* and *You Can't Take It with You.* MGM led, with four films selected by the top winners. Fox, Paramount, Warners, and Universal each had two films on the list, Columbia and RKO one apiece. Monogram was, unsurprisingly, shut out. No one selected a film from United Artists either. The UA omission did not indicate a rejection of the kind of big-budget pictures that this anomalous company specialized in. Six superspecials were the favorites of nine winners; however, the majority of films were more moderately priced features. Spectacle appealed to fans of action films *Men with Wings,* which dealt with the history of aviation, and *Spawn of the North,* about conflicts among salmon fishermen in Alaska, and other top-budget pictures. But homier comedy-dramas carried the day. Taking a page, perhaps, from the way the films were promoted and reviewed, five of the essays used the word *human* in praise of their favorites. The only three films named by more than one winner all weighed heavily on the *human* side. *Four Daughters* was the favorite of three essayists, *You Can't Take It with You* four, and *Boys Town* was chosen by six entrants, one-quarter of the top prize winners.

Among the winning essays were tributes to some of Hollywood's pet themes. Benincasa chose *Four Daughters* as her favorite film:

> For ninety minutes I lived a lifetime—
> I had four daughters, lived four lives,
> from tragedy to happiness—lived every emotion to the rich full
>   completeness
> that life can give them—Lived I, who
> have lived not at all in my private life.

Her essay went beyond mere escapism. It celebrated the film not simply for representing the range of human experiences but for providing a fulfilling substitute for them. Real people, real problems on the screen: these could, as critics of mass culture often lamented, feel more real than one's own life.[30]

Several winners acknowledged the movies' ability to transport them to a more interesting or pleasurable place and time, following a theme of such institutional ads as "Four Walls That Hold a World" as well as the sample essay in the contest booklet, which offered a clue to what organizers were looking for in this response to *Snow White*: it "was so sincere and beautiful and so full of humor and tenderness. . . . It made me feel like a child again instead of a grown-up with all grown-ups' troubles." Frances Hotalen ($1,000) reminisced about the "happy hour" spent with *Valley of the Giants,* a Technicolor film set in the redwood forests of Northern California: "Have you lived all your life in a mining town where the air hangs heavy with coal dust and all the things are dead or stunted?" Henry Roemer ($1,000) wrote about *Dark Rapture,* a documentary by Armand Denis and the only independent production to be named. This most un-Hollywood film achieved familiar Hollywood goals: "Out of my humdrum existence I was whisked into Belgium Congo. . . . Since the movies' inception I've journed [sic] far and wide—in a comfortable theatre seat." Conrad James ($5,000) also welcomed the opportunity to transcend limitations and travel "in a movie seat" with *Men with Wings.* "I forgot the theatre . . . the crutches. . . . I was free . . . skimming the clouds . . . a man with wings!" *The Great Waltz* took E. R. Morrison ($1,000) and his wife back "to 'the gay nineties,'" allowing them to escape from the present through a welcome reminder of the people they once were: "It erased the years!—Like witchery, the Strauss magic took us back . . . to the most romantic and glorious period of our lives!—to our happy sweetheart days!—We came to see a movie: we left with Youth!" Deanna Durbin had the same effect on Betty Finch ($2,000), whose response likewise blended escapism and identification: "Out in the rush of the city, my schooldays are a memory. Here—in the darkness of the theatre, I am again—'That Certain Age.'"[31]

People prized films that made them feel good. Mary Hilton ($10,000), who preferred *Stablemates,* "love[d] horses." She found the film "as exciting as the race's last lap" and cherished its "human blend of loyalty, friendship, laughs, throat-lumps better known as Life." Movies that spoke to "life" were as popular as those that offered a respite from it. *Four Daughters* was singled out by the other winners for its achievements in this regard. Rae Charhan Phillips ($1,000) noted the superiority of the film over literature as a medium for true-to-life representations: "The lovable characters of Fannie Hurst's heart-warming and human story were even more convincing when enlivened by the superb cast of the motion picture." Helen Kyle Bernard ($1,000) praised it for the "quiet, tender unfolding of a simple story, simply told, [that] touched upon life itself. Here were no blatant dramatics or forced climaxes, but real people, in whom we believed. Only true sincerity could have created 'Four Daughters.'" Jack Warner would have been pleased.[32]

The language used for the essays on *Gateway, You Can't Take It with You,* and especially *Boys Town* suggested an interest in movies that did more than provide an evening's distraction. *Gateway* reminded Raymond K. Visconti ($2,000) of the past too—not the pleasures of youth but rather the "agony" of waiting at Ellis Island, which "proved to be the way to freedom for me as . . . for countless thousands." *You Can't Take It with You* entertained the winners, while it also "taught" Birdie Jackson ($1,000) "an exhilarating truth, that fighting and worrying don't get us what we really want—human good-will—which is both priceless and free." "I laughed, but I also thought." J. Howell Talley ($10,000) admired "its rare quality of depth with a surface of laughter." Helen Beane Faxon ($1,000) thought the film promised to "develop character" by "stimulat[ing] right thinking and the desire to do good." For Will Wayne ($5,000), *You Can't Take It with You* "makes the world look brighter; leaves a pleasant after-taste; mingles laughter and tears in splendid proportion; presents live and lovable characters." He was touched by its "fine home-spun philosophy, free from moralization." Feeling was not antagonistic to thinking for the essayists. The movies' capacity to move viewers corresponded to their capacity to enlighten them.[33]

The message of *Boys Town* was also an important component of the pleasure it delivered. Father Flanagan's unselfish actions on behalf of boys, "regardless of race, color or creed," renewed $25,000, second-prize winner, Laura Carpenter's "faith in God in a World torn with strife over religious and racial hatred." Instead of forgetting about "grown-ups' troubles," two writers were reminded of difficult childhoods. Vera Horgan ($5,000) knew "first hand, the influence of environment over circumstance" as a ward in "the Episcopal Orphanage. . . . Life may begin for many where the picture ends." The film was not just human but in "the service of humanity." Dan C. Haley ($5,000) wrote:

> "There, but for the grace of God, walk I." "Boys Town" paints a picture of the boy I might have been.
> It left tears on my cheek, but a smile in my heart, for it left hope—hope for a future for handicapped youth.
> "Boys Town" points a way.

The essay of Lucinda von Kamecke ($2,000) simply rehearsed the message of the film: "We see here faith at work. Faith of a man in God and in a potential goodness in all boys. That good food, cleanliness, work and play, love and understanding are all essentials to character building, and that it is better to save the boy than to salvage the man." Like *The Citadel, You Can't Take It with You* and *Boys Town* may not have said much, but they said a little something. And if these essays reflect in part what the writers thought the industry wanted to hear, it is notable that they emphasized lessons learned as well as fantasies fulfilled.[34]

Campaign officials expressed the intention to analyze the essays as "a widespread expression of public taste," but it appears that nothing was ever done with them, evidence of the industry's inertia following the campaign and its fickleness regarding public relations. Howard Dietz was adamant about the importance of an ongoing public relations effort and argued that the work of MPGY had just begun. "We must continually present the press with the story of motion pictures in the best light." He sought to build an organization with a paid staff to serve as a permanent "clearing house" of information. Its mission would be "the proper handling" of press relations, for the good of the whole industry, and to gather data that would at last approach the problem of public opinion of the movies from a "scientific" basis. "I am recommending primarily, research, house to house canvasses, polls, continuous exhibitor and patron interviews. . . . A real effort to find out the subjects the public is interested in. What they think about motion pictures. Why they go and why they don't go." In other words, he advocated less guessing, more information, and no more expensive and noisy stopgaps. Dietz's recommendation was discussed and reported in the trade and mainstream press, but it went nowhere. The need for sustained public relations research for the industry as a whole continued to be debated off and on into the 1940s. An industry-wide program began to look like a near certainty in 1942, as Hollywood continued to search for its "lost film fans" early in that year. Gallup himself angled for the job, but this plan, too, was abandoned. The wartime upturn in box office was already getting under way, and that, apparently, was all the public relations the industry needed. World War II, at least, helped to confer a seriousness of purpose on Hollywood and restored, albeit temporarily, the moviegoing habit.[35]

It may have been hard to enlist support for a long-term program following a short-term failure, even one that could be blamed on hasty execution. In a sense MPGY accomplished the opposite of what it had set out to do. It publicized the real scope of the industry's troubles far more effectively than Goldwyn or beleaguered exhibitors had ever done. The film industry had stopped simply proclaiming its virtues and set out to test them. By fiat it had declared a middling year its best ever, but neither the press nor the public had finally been persuaded. Instead, MPGY demonstrated the industry's difficulties in producing acclaimed films and its inability to promote patrons back into theaters. The industry still struggled in 1939. The average ticket price dropped 13 percent from the previous year, although the national economy was in recovery. Weekly attendance rose by six million, after declining by more than three million in 1938, but gross revenues continued their slide: from $676 million (1937) to $663 million (1938) and finally $659 million (1939). The good news was the films. There is general consensus among film scholars that 1939 really was Hollywood's greatest year. Thus the irony that the year of *Gone with the Wind, Mr. Smith Goes to Washington, Wuthering Heights, The Wizard of Oz,* and John Ford's American trilogy, among other outstanding pictures, was far more modestly celebrated as the fiftieth anniversary of the movies. If the industry had only waited, MPGY might have been seen as evidence of its keen intuitions about quality, of its ability to distinguish between the truly "colossal" and the merely promotional uses of that term, of a certain integrity and a kind of genius. Instead, the proposed anniversary celebration was characterized by a restraint designed to distinguish it from the unfortunate excesses of MPGY. The *Los Angeles Times* described it as "a quiet campaign with no contests or other spectacular exploitation stunts." The MPPDA, still smarting from the recent debacle, instructed exhibitors not to proclaim the films of the upcoming season "as the best, the greatest or the most colossal parade of hits in history," for fear of antagonizing a skeptical public. The right vocabulary, it turned out, was unavailable during the right year.[36]

Newspapers in the Sample, by State

One daily newspaper per state and the District of Columbia was selected at random. All newspapers, even on microfilm, are not equally accessible, and I often had to try several before finding one available through interlibrary loan. Thus, this is not, strictly speaking, a random sample. Newspapers from small cities are disproportionately unrepresented because fewer have been reproduced and are available. Still, the sample provides information about campaign coverage in local dailies in cities with between one theater and more than one hundred in all regions of the country.

Alabama	*Huntsville Times*
Arizona	*Nogales Herald*
Arkansas	*Arkansas Gazette* (Little Rock)
California	*Humboldt Standard* (Eureka)
Colorado	*Boulder Daily Camera*
Connecticut	*Stamford Advocate*
Delaware	*Wilmington Morning News*
Florida	*Ft. Lauderdale Daily News and Evening Sentinel*
Georgia	*Rome News-Tribune*
Idaho	*Idaho Falls Post-Register*
Illinois	*Alton Evening Telegraph*
Indiana	*Elkhart Truth*

Iowa	*Waterloo Daily Courier*
Kansas	*Hays Daily News*
Kentucky	*Ashland Daily Independent*
Louisiana	*Baton Rouge Morning Advocate*
Maine	*Waterville Morning Sentinel*
Maryland	*Frederick Daily News*
Massachusetts	*Quincy Patriot Ledger*
Michigan	*Detroit Free Press*
Minnesota	*Austin Daily Herald*
Mississippi	*Biloxi Daily Herald*
Missouri	*Kansas City Star*
Montana	*Daily Missoulian*
Nebraska	*Fremont Daily Tribune*
Nevada	*Reno Evening Gazette*
New Hampshire	*Concord Daily Monitor and New Hampshire Patriot*
New Jersey	*New Brunswick Daily Home News*
New Mexico	*Santa Fe New Mexican*
New York	*Rochester Democrat and Chronicle*
North Carolina	*Raleigh News and Observer*
North Dakota	*Bismarck Tribune*
Ohio	*Xenia Evening Gazette*
Oklahoma	*Tulsa Daily World*
Oregon	*Oregon Statesman* (Salem)
Pennsylvania	*Canonsburg Daily Notes*
Rhode Island	*Providence Journal*
South Carolina	*Charleston News and Courier*
South Dakota	*Sioux Falls Daily Argus-Leader*
Tennessee	*Chattanooga Daily Times*
Texas	*San Antonio Express*
Utah	*Salt Lake Tribune*
Vermont	*Burlington Free Press and Times*
Virginia	*Bristol Herald Courier*

Washington	*Bellingham Herald*
Washington, D.C.	*Washington Post*
West Virginia	*Raleigh Register*
Wisconsin	*Wisconsin State Journal* (Madison)
Wyoming	*Casper Tribune-Herald*

Motion Pictures Included in the Motion Pictures' Greatest Year Movie Quiz Contest, by Studio

Names of independent producers are given parenthetically where relevant.

COLUMBIA

Crime Takes a Holiday (Larry Darmour)

Girls' School

The Gladiator (David L. Loew)

I Am the Law

Juvenile Court

The Lady Objects

Thoroughbred (never produced)

You Can't Take It with You

MGM

Block-Heads (Hal Roach)

Boys Town

The Chaser

The Crowd Roars

The Great Waltz

Listen, Darling

Marie Antoinette

Rich Man, Poor Girl

Stablemates

Sweethearts

Three Loves Has Nancy

Too Hot to Handle

Vacation from Love

Young Dr. Kildare

MONOGRAM

Barefoot Boy

Mr. Wong, Detective

Under the Big Top

Wanted by the Police

PARAMOUNT

The Arkansas Traveler

Bulldog Drummond in Africa

Campus Confessions

Give Me a Sailor

In Old Mexico (Harry Sherman)

King of Alcatraz

Men with Wings

The Mysterious Rider (Harry Sherman)

Professor Beware (Harold Lloyd)

Sing You Sinners

Sons of the Legion

Spawn of the North

The Texans

Touchdown, Army!

RKO

The Affairs of Annabel

Breaking the Ice (Sol Lesser)

Carefree

Fugitives for a Night

I'm from the City

The Mad Miss Manton

Mother Carey's Chickens

Mr. Doodle Kicks Off

Painted Desert

The Renegade Ranger (in contest booklet as "Ranger Code")

Room Service

Smashing the Rackets

TWENTIETH CENTURY–FOX

Alexander's Ragtime Band

Gateway

Hold That Co-ed

Keep Smiling

Little Miss Broadway

Meet the Girls

My Lucky Star

Mysterious Mr. Moto

Safety in Numbers

Speed to Burn

Straight, Place and Show

Submarine Patrol

Suez

Time Out for Murder

UNITED ARTISTS

Algiers (Walter Wanger)

The Cowboy and the Lady (Samuel Goldwyn)

Drums (Alexander Korda)

There Goes My Heart (Hal Roach)

The Young in Heart (David O. Selznick)

UNIVERSAL

Dark Rapture (Armand Denis)

Freshman Year

The Last Express

Letter of Introduction

The Missing Guest

Personal Secretary (in contest booklet as "The Comet")

The Road to Reno

Swing That Cheer

That Certain Age

Youth Takes a Fling

WARNER BROS. (INCLUDES FIRST-NATIONAL)

The Amazing Dr. Clitterhouse

Boy Meets Girl

Broadway Musketeers

Brother Rat

Four Daughters

Four's a Crowd

Garden of the Moon

Girls on Probation

Mr. Chump

Racket Busters

Secrets of an Actress

The Sisters

Valley of the Giants

Notes

WHC   Will H. Hays Collection, L560, Manuscripts and Rare Books Division, Indiana State Library

WLK   Frank C. Walker Papers, University of Notre Dame Archives, South Bend, Indiana

Journals and Newspapers

CPD   *Cleveland Plain Dealer*

DFP   *Detroit Free Press*

HR   *Hollywood Reporter*

MPD   *Motion Picture Daily*

MPH   *Motion Picture Herald*

NYHT   *New York Herald Tribune*

NYT   *New York Times*

RDC   *Rochester Democrat and Chronicle*

SRW   *Screen & Radio Weekly*

WAA   *Washington Afro-American*

WDC   *Waterloo (IA) Daily Courier*

WP   *Washington Post*

XEG   *Xenia (OH) Evening Gazette*

YV   *Youngstown Vindicator*

INTRODUCTION

1. Irving Hoffman, "Tales of Hoffman," *HR*, April 15, 1938, 3; "Double Exposure," *Variety*, May 18, 1938, 3; W. R. Wilkerson, "Wake Up," *HR*, July 7, 1938, 2; and Oscar A. Doob, "It's a State of Mind Says Loew's Advertising Head," *MPH*, July 16, 1938, 87. The recession, also called the "new" or "second" Depression, was severe. The stock market fell again by more than a third, and by the end of the winter of 1937–38 unemployment was back up from eight to ten million, or 19 percent of the workforce. See David Kennedy, *Freedom from Fear: The American People in Depression and War, 1929–1945* (New York: Oxford University Press, 1999), 350. Richard Maltby calls Hollywood's eternal state of crisis one of its "most persistent myths" in *Harmless Entertainment: Hollywood and the Ideology of Consensus* (Metuchen, NJ: Scarecrow, 1983), 42.

2. On audience research see Garth Jowett, "Giving Them What They Want: Movie Audience Research before 1950," in *Current Research in Film: Audiences, Economics, and Law*, ed. Bruce A. Austin, vol. 1 (Norwood, NJ: Ablex, 1985), 19–35; Susan Ohmer, "The Science of Pleasure: George Gallup and Audience Research in Hollywood," in *Identifying Hollywood's Audiences:*

Cultural Identity and the Movies, ed. Melvyn Stokes and Richard Maltby (London: BFI, 1999), 61–80; and Ohmer, *George Gallup in Hollywood* (New York: Columbia University Press, 2006), esp. chaps. 1 and 6 through 10.

3. Charles Maland mentions MPGY in "1939: Movies and American Culture in the *Annus Mirabilis,*" in *American Cinema of the 1930s: Themes and Variations,* ed. Ina Rae Hark (New Brunswick, NJ: Rutgers University Press, 2007), 227. Studies of censorship and self-regulation and their impact on classical Hollywood films and filmmaking are legion. Significant books include Leonard J. Leff and Jerold Simmons, *The Dame in the Kimono: Hollywood, Censorship, and the Production Code from the 1920s to the 1960s* (New York: Grove Weidenfeld, 1990); Leah Jacobs, *The Wages of Sin: Censorship and the Fallen Woman Cycle, 1928–1942* (Madison: University of Wisconsin Press, 1991); Gregory D. Black, *Hollywood Censored: Morality Codes, Catholics, and the Movies* (Cambridge: Cambridge University Press, 1994); *Movie Censorship and American Culture,* ed. Francis G. Couvares (Washington: Smithsonian Institution Press, 1996); Frank Walsh, *Sin and Censorship: The Catholic Church and the Motion Picture Industry* (New Haven, CT: Yale University Press, 1996); Ruth Vasey, *The World according to Hollywood, 1918–1939* (Madison: University of Wisconsin Press, 1997); and *Controlling Hollywood: Censorship and Regulation in the Studio Era,* ed. Matthew Bernstein (New Brunswick, NJ: Rutgers University Press, 1999).

4. Edgar Dale, "Motion Picture Industry and Public Relations," *Public Opinion Quarterly* 3 (April 1939): 252; Howard T. Lewis, *The Motion Picture Industry* (New York: D. Van Nostrand, 1933), 389; Margaret Farrand Thorp, *America at the Movies* (New Haven, CT: Yale University Press, 1939), 1; Hays, cited in Richard Maltby, "The Production Code and the Hays Office," in Tino Balio, *Grand Design: Hollywood as a Modern Business Enterprise* (Berkeley: University of California Press, 1993), 52; and "Better Pictures," August 10, 1936, WHC, reel 16. Maltby's essay is crucial to understanding the trade considerations that drove the industry to develop and enforce self-regulation. On the effort to improve films by making students more educated consumers of them see Anne Morey, *Hollywood Outsiders: The Adaptation of the Film Industry, 1913–1934* (Minneapolis: University of Minnesota Press, 2003), chap. 5; and Eric Smoodin, *Regarding Frank Capra: Audience, Celebrity, and American Film Studies* (Durham, NC: Duke University Press, 2004), chap. 3. On the desire to build new audiences, as well as remake the public, see Maltby, "Sticks, Hicks and Flaps: Classical Hollywood's Generic Conception of Its Audiences," in Stokes and Maltby, *Identifying Hollywood's Audiences,* 23–41.

5. See Ohmer, *George Gallup in Hollywood.* In reception studies the text is considered to be in a continuous process of transformation, with every viewer creating something new based on his or her desires and needs. See, for example, Henry Jenkins, *Textual Poachers: Television Fans and Participatory Culture* (New York: Routledge, 1992); and Janet Staiger, *Media Reception Studies* (New York: New York University Press, 2005).

6. See "Umbrella," *Time,* Sept. 5, 1938 (www.time.com/time/archive). The trade press reported that Gaumont-British was invited to join MPGY, too, and

that after originally declining, it and Republic sought to participate. They were refused on the grounds that contest booklets were already in production. See "Detailed Work Assigned for Big Ad Drive," *MPD*, August 2, 1938, 1, 4; and "Republic Request to Enter Drive Denied," *MPD*, August 24, 1938, 1, 4.

7. Douglas Gomery, *Shared Pleasures: A History of Movie Presentation in the United States* (Madison: University of Wisconsin Press, 1992), 38; Michael Pokorny and John Sedgwick, "Profitability Trends in Hollywood, 1929 to 1999: Somebody Must Know Something," *Economic History Review* 63, no. 1 (2010): 58. In addition to Balio's *Grand Design* see Gomery, *The Hollywood Studio System* (New York: St. Martin's, 1986). Sometimes the oligopoly is conceptualized as the five "majors"—the companies that owned substantial theater chains—and the three "minor majors." The government action targeted all eight companies, and unless otherwise specified I use the term *majors* to refer to them all. United Artists was an anomaly even among its smaller cohort. It was essentially a distribution company for independent producers who made quality films, and it did not engage in block booking. See Balio, *United Artists: The Company Built by the Stars* (Madison: University of Wisconsin Press, 1976).

8. Leo Rosten, *Hollywood: The Movie Colony, the Movie Makers* (New York: Harcourt, Brace, 1941), 4; Heywood Broun, "Howard Dietz on the State of the Art, as Recorded by Broun" (1938); repr. in *MPH*, Sept. 24, 1938, 30; Hortense Powdermaker, *Hollywood, the Dream Factory* (New York: Grosset & Dunlap, 1950), 284; and Chester B. Bahn, "The Industry . . . and a Good Press," *Film Daily*, Oct. 14, 1938, 1. On the importance of hunches and instincts see Lewis, *The Motion Picture Industry*, 83–84; Thorp, *America at the Movies*, 16–18; and Rosten, *Hollywood*, 48–49.

9. Bahn, "The Industry . . . and a Good Press." As Maltby notes in "Sticks, Hicks and Flaps," despite the industry's rhetorical commitment to a "mass audience," producers, distributors, and exhibitors knew about and actively courted "different 'taste publics'" (26). In *Hollywood Outsiders* Morey describes the development of "a culture of moviegoing that was, at least ostensibly, participatory rather than passive" (1) between the 1910s and the early 1930s. Her case studies—juvenile series fiction about Hollywood, a screenwriting correspondence school, religious groups who interfered in production, and educators who sought to improve the taste and judgment of young viewers—reveal a commitment to the power of the public or, rather, of select and refashioned portions of it, as consumers, and the various means by which this power was promoted and shaped by organizations to further their own agendas.

10. "The Public Is Not Damned," *Fortune*, March 1939, 83; "Twentieth Century–Fox," *Fortune*, Dec. 1935, 138; and Roland Marchand, *Creating the Corporate Soul: The Rise of Public Relations and Corporate Imagery in American Big Business* (Berkeley: University of California Press, 1998). On the intangibility of film see also Wilkerson, "Tradeviews," *HR*, August 18, 1938, 2; and Roy Chartier, "The Year in Pictures," *Variety*, Jan. 4, 1939, 9, 48.

11. All campaign films are from 1938; the years for these films only will not be cited parenthetically within the text.

12. Richard Maltby and Melvyn Stokes, introduction to *Going to the Movies: Hollywood and the Social Experience of Cinema*, ed. Maltby, Stokes, and

Robert C. Allen (Exeter: University of Exeter Press, 2007), 2. See also "In Focus: Film History, or a Baedeker Guide to the Historical Turn," ed. Sumiko Higashi, in *Cinema Journal* 44 (Fall 2004): 94–142.

1. ANNUS HORRIBILIS

1. See Jane Feuer, *The Hollywood Musical*, 2nd ed. (Bloomington: Indiana University Press, 1993), 54–57. Unless otherwise noted, information about the production and reception of *The Goldwyn Follies* comes from A. Scott Berg, *Goldwyn, a Biography* (1989; repr. New York: Riverhead Books, 1998), 298–305.

2. Review of *The Goldwyn Follies*, *MPH*, Jan. 29, 1938, 48; Joe F. Wright, Cedar Theatre, Cedartown, GA, *MPH*, May 14, 1938, 62; Charles L. Fisk, Fisk Theatre, Butler, MO, *MPH*, May 28, 1938, 86; and Harland Rankin, Plaza Theatre, Tilbury, ON, Canada, *MPH*, June 25, 1938, 80.

3. *The Goldwyn Follies* supplement, *HR*, Feb. 8, 1938, 7; review of *The Goldwyn Follies*, *HR*, Jan. 26, 1938, 3.

4. Ruth Waterbury, "Close Ups and Long Shots," *Photoplay*, Feb. 1938, 13–14; Waterbury, "Close Ups and Long Shots," *Photoplay*, April 1938, 14.

5. On the decline in revenues and attendance in 1937–38, and plans for retrenchment, see "Pix a Bit Disappointed," *Variety*, Sept. 29, 1937, 3, 21; "Pix Production Budgets Must Be Pruned to Keep Pace with the B.O.," *Variety*, Nov. 24, 1937, 1, 2; "Paramount's $5,000,000 Prod. Cut," *Variety*, Dec. 1, 1937, 3; Roy Chartier, "The Grosses," *Variety*, Jan. 5, 1938, 5; "B.O. Continues Its Slide; Off 18 to 20% Generally," *HR*, Feb. 17, 1938, 1, 2; "December B.O. Worst in 18 Months," *Variety*, March 2, 1938, 2; "January, 1938, Rise in Amus. Taxes Reflects Sharp Tilt in B.O. over Dec.," *Variety*, March 23, 1938, 2; "Theatre Closings Loom," *HR*, March 28, 1938, 1; and "Boxoffice Grosses Off 20 P.C. from 1937 Level," *HR*, May 17, 1938, 2.

6. Zanuck, cited in John C. Flinn, "Zanuck Analyzes Film," *Variety*, May 18, 1938, 3; Goldwyn, cited in "Goldwyn Issues a Warning for the Movie Capital," editorial, *WDC*, April 26, 1938, 4; and "'Clean House,' Goldwyn Warning to Hollywood," *Los Angeles Herald and Express*, April 25, 1938, A-8. Goldwyn hated double features, which he blamed for the B movies that damaged the reputation of the industry as a whole and his own prestige pictures when they shared a screen. His concerns eventually prompted a 1940 Gallup poll on double features. See Ohmer, *George Gallup in Hollywood*, 101–9.

7. Ad, Independent Theatre Owners Association, *HR*, May 3, 1938, 5; Louella O. Parsons, "Showmen's Three-Strike Call on Joan, Garbo, Etc., Knocks Filmdom for Loop," *WDC*, May 5, 1938, 6. See also "Ed Sullivan in Hollywood," *DFP*, May 7, 1938, 9; "In Hollywood with Hedda Hopper," *WP*, May 10, 1938, 8; and Paul Harrison, "Film Moguls Not Displeased by Exhibitors' Harsh Blast," *New Brunswick Daily Home News*, May 15, 1938, 9. I sampled newspapers dated from April 26 to April 29, 1938, for references to Goldwyn's remarks and from May 4 to May 7 for the "box-office poison" story (the fifth article in the *Xenia Gazette* actually appeared on May 9). It is worth mentioning that the "box-office poison" controversy may have

stimulated additional interest in Goldwyn's criticisms; I found commentary on them in three more newspapers, including a column by Sullivan in the *Detroit Free Press*, during the May dates.

8. Rosten, *Hollywood*, 40; "Million Dollar Pep Drive On," *HR*, July 28, 1938, 10; "Double Exposure," *Variety*, May 18, 1938, 3; and Terry Ramsaye, "Sales Heat," *MPH*, May 14, 1938, 7.

9. Wilkerson, "A Call to Arms," *HR*, June 15, 1938, 1; Wilkerson, "Shut Up, Hollywood!" *HR*, June 18, 1938, 1, 2; "H.M. Warner Blasts Producers," *HR*, June 20, 1938, 1, 3; ad, Warner Bros., *MPH*, June 25, 1938, 19–26; and "Trade Stuff Reacts Badly When Public Hears of It through Dailies," *Variety*, July 6, 1938, 3. See also Ramsaye, "Lady Hollywood," *MPH*, June 25, 1938, 7, 8; "Warner Charges Film 'Hoarding,'" *MPH*, June 25, 1938, 36; and Parsons, "Warners against Hoarding Big Films till Fall and Reissuing Old Movies," *WDC*, June 22, 1938, 12. I examined newspapers published between June 20 and June 23, 1938, for coverage of Warner's remarks.

10. See Jimmie Fidler, "Joan Blondell to Make Film Exit; More Time for Baby, She Pleads," *Salt Lake Tribune*, August 25, 1938, 14.

11. "Want 'Sympathetic' Crix," *Variety*, Dec. 15, 1937, 7; Ramsaye, "Delusions of Grandeur," *MPH*, Feb. 4, 1939, 8; Wilkerson, "Tradeviews," *HR*, March 14, 1938, 1; and Flinn, "Zanuck Analyzes Film," 3.

12. Wilkerson, "Produce," *HR*, June 27, 1938, 2; "Fear B.O. Film Shortage," *Variety*, May 4, 1938, 1; and "Jack Warner Decries the 'Wild Guessing' among Film Producers," *Variety*, April 13, 1938, 2.

13. Maltby and Stokes, introduction to *Going to the Movies*, 2; Wilkerson, "Produce," 2; Gilbert Seldes, *The Movies Come from America* (London: B.T. Batsford, 1937), 10, 6, 13; and Wilkerson, "Produce," 2. "For the majority" of participants in Annette Kuhn's ethnohistory of moviegoing in Britain in the 1930s, "going to the pictures is remembered as being less about films and stars than about daily and weekly routines, neighbourhood comings and goings and organising spare time" (*Dreaming of Fred and Ginger: Cinema and Cultural Memory* [New York: New York University Press, 2002], 100). See also Kathryn H. Fuller-Seeley and George Potamianos, "Introduction: Researching and Writing the History of Local Moviegoing," in *Hollywood in the Neighborhood: Historical Case Studies of Local Moviegoing*, ed. Fuller-Seeley (Berkeley: University of California Press, 2008), 3–19, as well as the collection's essays.

14. Frank S. Nugent, "What's Wrong with the Movies?" *NYT*, Nov. 20, 1938 (ProQuest); Seldes, *The Movies Come from America*, 107.

15. "Hollywood Hot for Action Pictures," *HR*, April 27, 1938, 6; Seldes, *The Movies Come from America*, 107; "Big Pix to Buck Hot Weather," *HR*, June 6, 1938, 2; Bosley Crowther, "In the Opinion of Mr. Schenck," *NYT*, Sept. 11, 1938 (ProQuest); and Wilkerson, "Produce." See also "Trouble Is: B's Are D's," *Variety*, Feb. 23, 1938, 3.

16. "Tales of Hoffman," *HR*, April 15, 1938, 3; "Double Exposure," 3; Flinn, "Pix Slipping in Stix," *Variety*, July 20, 1938, 4; Wilkerson, "Produce," 2; and Wilkerson, "Wake Up," *HR*, July 7, 1938, 2.

17. For a criticism of polls conducted on various aspects of movies see "Pix Audience Polls a Gag," *Variety*, Sept. 28, 1938, 17.

18. "Double Exposure," 3; "Tales of Hoffman," *HR*, April 15, 1938, 3; and "Tales of Hoffman," *HR*, April 16, 1938, 3.

2. EXHIBITORS, THE MOVIE QUIZ CONTEST, AND A DIVIDED INDUSTRY

1. "Pep Business Drive Launched," *HR*, July 19, 1938, 1, 4; "Industry Pep Drive Gets Half Million for Exploitation," *HR*, July 20, 1938, 1, 4; and "Outline of Discussion by G.J. Schaefer," July 27, 1938, HFC, folder 8. See also "Dietz Heads Unit for Trade Drive," *MPD*, July 18, 1938, 1, 3; "Entire Industry Rallies to Put Over Ad Campaign," *MPD*, July 28, 1938, 1, 6; and "Million Dollar Pep Drive On," 1, 10.

2. Ad, "The Call to Arms!" *MPD*, July 27, 1938, 5.

3. "Movies Will Open Good-Will Drive," *NYT*, July 28, 1938 (ProQuest). The article quotes Paul Gulick, campaign coordinator and former director of publicity for Universal.

4. "Hollywood Primes the Pump," *NYT*, July 31, 1938 (ProQuest); "New York Pledges to Campaign Fund at $25,000 Mark," *MPD*, August 19, 1938, 5. See "Notes on Meeting of Special Committee on a National Motion Picture Publicity Campaign," n.d., MPPDAA; and "U.S. Brings Suit Charging Monopoly in the Industry," *MPD*, July 21, 1938, 1, 6. The planning document ends by noting that the committee would meet again on July 18, just before the announcement.

5. "Entire Industry Rallies to Put Over Ad Campaign," 6. "See Indie Frankensteins" included Griffith and Lightman on a list of circuits large enough "to assume monopoly powers" in the event of theater divorcement in the antitrust lawsuit (*Variety*, August 3, 1938, 3).

6. See Organizational Chart, n.d., HFC, folder 2. Scully was dropped from the general committee, apparently for health reasons. H.M. Richey, an independent exhibitor associated with another large circuit, Co-operative Theatres of Michigan, was later added to the committee. On the contributors at the Astor meeting see "Over $825,000 Is Pledged; $175,000 Sought for Drive," *MPD*, July 28, 1938, 1, 6; and "Detailed Work Assigned for Big Ad Drive," *MPD*, August 2, 1938, 1, 4. The number of theaters is given in a memo from David Palfreyman to Will Hays, Nov. 25, 1938, 2, MPPDAA.

7. Palfreyman to Hays, memo, Nov. 25, 1938, 1.

8. "Entire Industry Rallies to Put Over Ad Campaign," 1; "$250,000.00 Movie Quiz Contest" booklet (1938), unpaginated.

9. Ad, Fox West Coast Theatres, *Los Angeles Times*, Sept. 1, 1938, II 14 (ellipses in original, my emphasis).

10. John C. Flinn, "Mix 'em Up and Keep Away from Standardization, Schenck Formula," *Variety*, Feb. 23, 1938, 2; "'Giveaways' Blasted," *HR*, Jan. 17, 1938, 40; and "Exhibitors Not 'Selling' Pix," *Variety*, Feb. 16, 1938, 3.

11. "Outline of Discussion by G.J. Schaefer"; "Theatres' Drive Budget 2 Million," *MPD*, August 22, 1938, 1; "Campaign to Boost Movies Is Underway," *Ashland (KY) Independent*, Sept. 1, 1938, 3.

12. "Over $825,000 Is Pledged; $175,000 Sought for Drive," 1; Cohen, cited in "New York Pledges to Campaign Fund at $25,000 Mark," 5.

13. Michael Conant, *Antitrust in the Motion Picture Industry* (Berkeley: University of California Press, 1960), 68. See "Movie Quiz Contest Big Boost for Second Runs," *HR*, August 8, 1938, 2; and "Outline of Campaign," n.d., unpaginated, WLK, box 102, folder 10.

14. "New York Pledges to Campaign Fund at $25,000 Mark," 5; "ITOA Fears Pep Drive," *HR*, August 25, 1938, 1; "Second Run Houses Won't Aid Movie Quiz Contest," *HR*, August 30, 1938, 2; and "N.J. Allied Opposed Sharing in Ad Drive," *MPD*, August 17, 1938, 15. Suspicions that MPGY "was rushed through and timed to force exhibitors to accept the distributors' terms on new season's product to get in on the contest" is also mentioned in the memo from Palfreyman to Hays, Nov. 25, 1938, 2.

15. "Independents File Chicago Trust Action," *MPD*, Sept. 20, 1938, 2. See also "Chicago Pushes 'Quiz,'" *MPD*, Sept. 1, 1938, 13.

16. Frank Walker served as general counsel and a vice president of Comerford Theatres, a circuit of about one hundred houses. There is no neat list of the independent theaters that joined MPGY. The most complete information about who paid can only be gleaned from heavily annotated lists of exhibitors who received refunds after the campaign ended, having spent less than it raised. In cases where an individual or company owned multiple theaters, it can be tricky to figure out which theaters were involved; exhibitors did not always subscribe all their theaters, and sometimes only the name of the entity that received the refund check is given. There are partial lists of pledges as the campaign went on and copies of thousands of individual pledges and bills that were sent to exhibitors. By combining these sources, I was able to figure out who pledged and paid for which independent theaters in Cleveland. All information about theater size and the ownership of chains with four or more theaters comes from the *Film Daily Yearbook of Motion Pictures*, ed. Jack Alicoate (New York: Film Daily, 1939), unless otherwise noted.

17. W. Ward Marsh, "Film Industry Starts Its New Year Today with a Million-Dollar Contest," *CPD*, Sept. 1, 1938, 8; "Sharp Wits and Sharp Pencils," editorial, *CPD*, Sept. 2, 1938, 8. All ads cited are from *CPD* unless otherwise noted.

18. Marsh, "Circle's Feature," *CPD*, Sept. 2, 1938, 16; Nelson B. Bell, "Film Revivals Enlist the Interest of National Observers of Cinema," *WP*, June 20, 1938, 9. In *America at the Movies* Thorp notes 245 reissues of old pictures in 1938 (170).

19. The Warners neighborhood theaters did not play films directly from the other major theaters, even the studio's own pictures. This sort of division of territory, whereby Loew's and RKO theaters had a lock on screenings of top films after the first showing in Cleveland, with Warner Bros. enjoying reciprocal privileges in other cities, was an issue in the lawsuit.

20. On the promise of thirty quiz pictures see John Danz to Independent Theatre Owners, Oct. 4, 1938, HFC, folder 6; and letters from Harold Franklin to exhibitors in WLK, box 106, folder 12.

21. See "Refund List, 1940–1942," n.d., WLK, box 109, folder 15. MPGY records raise questions about the accuracy of some of the *Yearbook*'s information. For example, there are sometimes discrepancies regarding size of theaters. The *Yearbook* seats the Eclair at 450, but it was subscribed for five hundred, a difference of five dollars in the campaign pledge, and thus a number it was hardly likely to have inflated.

22. See "List of Unpaid Pledges," Nov. 10, 1938, WLK, box 103, folder 12; and P. Gustovie pledge card, August 19, 1938, WLK, box 106, folder 13.

23. See "List of Unpaid Pledges"; and "Refund List," folder 15.

24. See "Refund List," folder 16. According to the *Yearbook*, Charleston also had the Lincoln, which served the black community and did not advertise in the *News and Courier*.

25. See Indiana-Illinois Theatres pledge card, July 27, 1938, WLK, box 103, folder 16. See theater ads, *Elkhart (IN) Truth*, Sept. 1, 1938, 8; and Oct. 1, 1938, 3.

26. Ads, Nogales Theater, *Nogales (AZ) Herald*, Sept. 1, 1938, 8; Oct. 5, 1938, 8; and Oct. 8, 1938, 8.

27. See theater ads in the *Arizona Star*, Sept. 1 through Dec. 31, 1938.

28. See "Pledges Received from Following," Sept. 14, 1938, WLK, box 103, folder 15; and "Refund List," folder 15.

29. "Outline of Campaign."

30. "Tucson Theatres Prepare for Opening of Greater Show Season Today," *Arizona Star*, Sept. 1, 1938, 4; "Legit Contests Oust Film Theatre 'Bank Night,'" *HR*, Nov. 15, 1938, 5.

31. Ad, America, Rialto, and Rex theaters, *Casper (WY) Tribune-Herald*, Sept. 1, 1938, 9; ad, Strand Theatre, *Hays (KS) Daily News*, Dec. 28, 1938, 2.

32. See William Cronin to Schaefer, memo, Sept. 8, 1938, WLK, box 102, folder 22; "Progress Report of MPGY Campaign as of September 15, 1938," WLK, box 103, folder 8; "Report 16: Summary of Receipts and Disbursements, from July 25, 1938, to Nov. 11, 1938," n.d., WLK, box 102, folder 17; "List of Unpaid Pledges"; "Refund List," folders 14–16; and "Motion Pictures' Greatest Year: Statement of Receipts and Disbursements and Supporting Statements for the Period from July 25, 1938, to May 15, 1939," n.d., WLK, box 102, folder 31. Concerns about exhibitor follow-through on pledges caused organizers to spend almost $100,000 less on institutional advertising than the budget called for. See "Motion Pictures' Greatest Year: Statement of Receipts and Disbursements"; and Schaefer to E. J. Churchill, August 26, 1938, WLK, box 102, folder 22.

33. Franklin to Schaefer, memo, Sept. 8, 1938, WLK, box 102, folder 22; N. J. Brossoit to Walker, Sept. 10, 1938, WLK, box 106, folder 10.

34. H. C. McNulty to MPGY, Oct. 28, 1938, WLK, box 106, folder 12; "What the Exhibitor Must Do," *MPD*, August 15, 1938, 6; A. Adolph to Walker, Oct. 31, 1938, WLK, box 106, folder 10; and "Squawks on Delayed Clearances Resulting in Extending Film Quiz beyond Dec. 31 for Indies' Benefit," *Variety*, Sept. 28, 1938, 7.

35. G. E. Widger to MPGY, Sept. 17, 1938, WLK, box 106, folder 10.

36. A.L. Cowart and F.S. Shingler to Walker, Sept. 28, 1938, WLK, box 106, folder 10; C.V. Schofield to Walker, note, n.d., WLK, box 106, folder 12; Adolph to Walker; and W.E. Anderson to Franklin, Nov. 14, 1938, WLK, box 106, folder 10.

37. On the proposal for self-regulation see, for example, "Trade Reforms on Program to Make History," *MPD*, Dec. 2, 1938, 1, 5.

38. Schaefer to Cronin, Sept. 12, 1938, WLK, box 102, folder 22; "Statement of Mr. George J. Schaefer against Extension of Movie Quiz," Oct. 26, 1938, WLK, box 102, folder 19. See "Squawks on Delayed Clearances." On the promise of refunds see the letters from Franklin to exhibitors (see note 20 above).

39. Moe Rosenberg to MPGY, Oct. 31, 1938, WLK, box 106, folder 10; R.J. Cooper to Albert Battisti, n.d., WLK, box 106, folder 12; C.M. Olsen to MPGY, Nov. 28, 1938, WLK, box 106, folder 10; William Cooke to MPGY, Nov. 1, 1938, WLK, box 106, folder 10; and H.O. Ekern to MPGY, Dec. 23, 1938, WLK, box 102, folder 23.

40. Max Lefkowich to MPGY, Jan. 16, 1939, WLK, box 105, folder 15; M.B. Horwitz to Walker, August 24, 1938, WLK, box 105, folder 15; and William Danz to Franklin, Nov. 10, 1938, WLK, box 106, folder 6. See Battisti to Franklin, memo, Nov. 14, 1938, WLK, box 103, folder 27; "List of Pledges from Exhibitors," n.d., WLK, box 103, folder 14; and M.A. Lightman pledge card, July 27, 1938, WLK, box 103, folder 16.

Horwitz's Globe advertised in neither the *Plain Dealer* nor the *Press* but did so occasionally in the *Cleveland Gazette,* an African American weekly. The Haltnorth, another Horwitz theater, also catered to an African American clientele, but it received lots of quiz pictures.

3. THE CAMPAIGN AND THE PRESS

1. Wilkerson, "Shut Up, Hollywood!" *HR,* June 18, 1938, 1; Wilkerson, "Tradeviews," *HR,* August 18, 1938, 2; and "Notes on Meeting of Special Committee on a National Motion Picture Publicity Campaign." See "Confidential Budget," n.d., WLK, box 102, folder 17; and "Favorite Recreations," *Fortune,* Jan. 1938, 88. On the growing dominance of radio in the 1930s see Bruce Lenthall, *Radio's America: The Great Depression and the Rise of Modern Mass Culture* (Chicago: University of Chicago Press, 2007). According to Lenthall household ownership of radios increased from 40 percent in 1930 to 86 percent in 1940 (56). The decision not to sponsor advertising for the campaign on radio caused no little friction. The head of Public Relations for the National Association of Broadcasters noted the constant free plugs for Hollywood stars and films on radio programs and suggested that radio would not be so generous with unpaid publicity in the future. See "Radio Warns of Reprisal on Ad Drive," *MPD,* August 31, 1938, 1, 8. The media were too interdependent at this point for the protests to gain much traction, and MPGY garnered free radio publicity on syndicated shows and local programs. See Richard B. Jewell, "Hollywood and Radio: Competition and Partnership in the 1930s," *Historical Journal of Film, Radio and Television* 4, no. 2 (1984): 125–41; and

Michele Hilmes, *Hollywood and Broadcasting: From Radio to Cable* (Urbana: University of Illinois Press, 1990), chap. 3. On the press-radio "wars" over the delivery of news see Gwenyth L. Jackaway, *Media at War: Radio's Challenge to the Newspapers, 1924–1939* (Westport, CT: Praeger, 1995).

2. "Report to George J. Schaefer from the Advertising Committee," n.d., MPPDAA, 5; Ramsaye, "By These Advertisements Industry Tells the World," *MPH*, Sept. 3, 1938, 16, 17.

3. All eleven of the ads ran in New York City, and they can be found in the following newspapers: "The Average Movie-Goer Speaks His Mind," *New York World-Telegram*, August 31, 1938, 25; "Two Hundred Million People Can't Be Wrong!" *New York World-Telegram*, Sept. 7, 1938, 29; "It Could Only Happen in the Movies," *New York Daily News*, Sept. 1, 1938, 47; "Joe Doakes," *New York Daily News*, Sept. 8, 1938, 55; "The Unseen Hand," *NYHT*, Sept. 2, 1938, 11; "One Tornado and Three Hopi Indians," *NYHT*, Sept. 9, 1938, 17; "A Message to You," *New York Sun*, August 31, 1938, 29; "Four Walls That Hold a World!" *New York Sun*, Sept. 8, 1938, 33; "You Are Your Own Best Movie Critic," *New York Mirror*, Sept. 6, 1938, 25; "What Is Your 'Stake' in Motion Pictures?" *New York Journal American*, Sept. 9, 1938, 19; and "276," *New York Post*, Sept. 2, 1938, 15. Because the language of the ads is so repetitive, I do not provide citations for quotations from ads below except in circumstances so noted. I say the ads ran in *virtually* every daily English-language newspaper because there were a few anomalies. The *Wall Street Journal* ran only one ad and the *Chicago Journal of Commerce* none. They were business dailies with few theater ads, which may explain the discrepancy with other papers but not the differential treatment between them.

4. "The movies provide one of the few ways in which the need for participation in a group ritual can be met in a society where social relations are impersonal and indirect" (Leon Reisman, "Cinema Technique and Mass Culture," *American Quarterly* 1 [Winter 1949]: 317).

5. On assumptions about gender and audience see Leo A. Handel, *Hollywood Looks at Its Audience: A Report of Film Audience Research* (Urbana: University of Illinois Press, 1950), 99–100; and Ohmer, *George Gallup in Hollywood*, 133–34.

6. Stuart Ewen, *PR! A Social History of Spin* (New York: Basic, 1996), 190; Sarah E. Igo, *The Averaged American: Surveys, Citizens, and the Making of a Mass Public* (Cambridge, MA: Harvard University Press, 2007), 19. Marchand writes in *Creating the Corporate Soul* that the figures and "idiom of average citizens" (213) became "prominent . . . as elements of the corporation's image" (214) in the late 1930s.
The white middle-class Average Movie-Goer also, implicitly, makes a case against the ideal spectator he might be thought to embody, and whose creation has long been described as one of the signature effects of the classical Hollywood cinema. Miriam Hansen, for example, has argued that the early experience of moviegoing enabled the formation of "an alternative public sphere" for marginalized social groups, such as white working-class ethnics and women, possibilities that were shut down in the classical Hollywood period, as films and the theater experience became more uniform, and viewers were positioned as spectators, an effect of

the "film as product" (*Babel and Babylon: Spectatorship in American Silent Film* [Cambridge, MA: Harvard University Press, 1991], 43, 23). The insistence on an arc from activity to passivity, from audience to spectator, has been subject to critique on the grounds that there is never a single mode of "cinematic address," "exhibition," or "reception" (Janet Staiger, "Writing the History of American Film Reception," in *Hollywood Spectatorship: Changing Perceptions of Cinema Audiences,* ed. Melvyn Stokes and Richard Maltby [London: BFI, 2001], 19) and that local exhibition practices did not simply become standardized to match a more uniform narrative style. Richard Butsch points out, with reference to Hansen, that neighborhood and working-class theaters in particular continued to serve as "public spaces for social interaction" where individual and community bonds were recognized and celebrated (*The Citizen Audience: Crowds, Publics, and Individuals* [New York: Routledge, 2008], 47). On the narrative and stylistic codes that provided much of the groundwork for theories of the discursive spectator see David Bordwell, Janet Staiger, and Kristin Thompson, *The Classical Hollywood Cinema: Film Style and Mode of Production to 1960* (New York: Columbia University Press, 1985).

7. Edward L. Bernays, *Biography of an Idea: Memoirs of Public Relations Counsel* (New York: Simon & Schuster, 1965), 287.

8. See ads, *New Yorker Staats-Zeitung und Herold*, Sept. 1, 1938, 5; *Il Progresso Italo-Americano*, Sept. 1, 1938, 5; and *Jewish Daily Forward*, Sept. 1, 1938, 7.

9. Ad, "Un Habitué de Cinéma Dit ce Qu'il Pense," *La Presse Montréal*, August 31, 1938, 11; Igo, *The Averaged American*, 84. Lewis Jacobs gave one description of the early cinema's project of acculturation: "the movies gave the newcomers, particularly, a respect for American law and order, an understanding of civic organization, pride in citizenship and in the American commonwealth" (*The Rise of the American Film: A Critical History* [New York: Harcourt, Brace, 1939], 12). Calling the acculturation thesis "one of American mass culture's most powerful myths of its own origins," Hansen offers her account of the theater as an oppositional public sphere by way of challenge to it, as does Judith Mayne, who emphasizes the "fantasies of resistance" that movies offered immigrants to "the new culture of consumerism" (see Miriam Hansen, "Early Cinema: Whose Public Sphere?" in *Early Cinema: Space, Frame, Narrative,* ed. Thomas Elsaesser [London: BFI, 1990], 228; and Judith Mayne, "Immigrants and Spectators," *Wide Angle* 5, no. 2 [1982]: 38).

10. Anna Everett, *Returning the Gaze: A Genealogy of Black Film Criticism, 1909–1949* (Durham, NC: Duke University Press, 2001), 193.

11. See "The Average Movie-Goer Speaks His Mind," *WAA*, Sept. 10, 1938, 5; "Joe Worker," *WAA*, Oct. 8, 1938, 5; and "A Message to You" *WAA*, Nov. 5, 1938, 10.

12. "Movie Fans to Get $250,000," *WAA*, Sept. 10, 1938, 5.

13. Louis Lautier, "$250,000 Movie Contest Shows Lack of Sepias," *WAA*, Oct. 15, 1938, 11.

14. Selig, cited in Lautier, "Film Industry to Make Sepia Appeal Pictures," *WAA*, Nov. 5, 1938, 10.

15. Campaign Committee to Howard Dietz, Oscar Doob, H. B. Franklin, Paul Gulick, and James Danahy, memo, Sept. 6, 1938, HFC, folder 6; Sullivan,

"Looking at Hollywood," *Chicago Tribune*, Sept. 8, 1938, 17 (second ellipses in original); and "Ed Sullivan's Movie Quiz," *Omaha Morning World Herald*, Sept. 18, 1938, 6-C.

16. "Ed Sullivan in Hollywood," *DFP*, Oct. 31, 1938, 11.

17. Fidler, "Gossip Picked Up around Hollywood," *Salt Lake Tribune*, August 20, 1938, 18; Fidler, "Norma Shearer Sells Her M-G-M Stock; Wants to Stand on Own Merits," *Salt Lake Tribune*, Sept. 10, 1938, 21. For more on Fidler, his influence, and his contract with Warners see James Reid, "The Phenomenon Named Fidler," *Motion Picture*, August 1938, 30–31, 62; and Grover Jones, "Knights of the Keyhole," *Colliers*, April 16, 1938, 25–28.

18. Parsons, "Selznick Stroke of Good Showmanship Co-stars Carole Lombard, Bill Powell," *WDC*, August 8, 1938, 5; "Walter Winchell on Broadway," *WDC*, August 10, 1938, 4; "Paul Harrison in Hollywood," *Fremont (NE) Daily Tribune*, August 9, 1938, 3; and "In Hollywood with Hedda Hopper," *WP*, Oct. 25, 1938, 8.

19. Robbin Coons, "Columnist Offers Suggestions for Movie Campaign," *Sioux Falls Daily Argus-Leader*, Sept. 13, 1938, 7.

20. "Pittsburgh Daily Co-operates by Killing a U.P. H'wood Story Panning Quiz," *Variety*, Sept. 14, 1938, 6. On Skolsky and the *Detroit Free Press* see "Films and the Press," *Variety*, August 21, 1935, 14. Other papers sometimes published the Associated Press columns of Coons and Hubbard Keavy without a byline.

21. "Report to George J. Schaefer from the Advertising Committee," 4; Oscar Doob, Harry Goldberg, and John Dowd, "Bulletin from Theatre Committee . . . Motion Pictures' Greatest Year!" n.d., HFC, folder 6; and Comerford Theatres Manual, n.d., 5, HFC, folder 6. The "Bulletin" and "Manual" predate the start of MPGY. Some newspapers also published ads of their own in support of it.

22. "Campaign to Boost Movies Is Underway," *Ashland (KY) Independent*, Sept. 1, 1938, 3; "Motion Picture Campaign Under Way in Nation," *Daily Missoulian*, Sept. 2, 1938, 11. See also "Celebration Motion Picture Industry's Greatest Year Begins," *Biloxi Daily Herald*, Sept. 1, 1938, 9; "Movie Quiz Contest Features Celebration of Greatest Year," *Waterville (ME) Morning Sentinel*, Sept. 1, 1938, 8; and "Motion Picture Campaign and Quiz Contest Being Launched," *XEG*, Sept. 1, 1938, 12.

23. "Bristol Theatres in Prize Contest," *Bristol (VA) Herald Courier*, Sept. 3, 1938, 10; "Bellingham Joins Film Campaign," *Bellingham (WA) Herald*, Sept. 1, 1938, 1, 16.

24. Will Baltin, "$250,000 in Prizes Tempt Many Local Movie Fans to Join National Film Contest," *New Brunswick Daily Home News*, Sept. 4, 1938, 6; ad, Grand, Princess, Wood River, and Wildey theaters, *Alton (IL) Evening Telegraph*, Sept. 8, 1938, 19. Marchand notes "a 'contest rampage'" in *Advertising the American Dream: Making Way for Modernity, 1920–1940* (Berkeley: University of California Press, 1986), 305.

25. "Movie-Day Proclaimed," *Providence Journal*, Sept. 11, 1938, 4; Doob, Goldberg, and Dowd, "Bulletin." The HFC includes numerous proclamations signed by mayors and governors.

26. H. B. Franklin to all regional chairmen, circuit heads, exhibitors, managers, and publicity directors, memo, Oct. 15, 1938, MPPDAA; Chester B. Bahn, "The Industry . . . and a Good Press," *Film Daily*, Oct. 14, 1938, 1; and "Report to George J. Schaefer from the Advertising Committee," 4. The undated report is presented as the transcript of an oral report delivered to the advertising committee on Oct. 11.

27. Editorials, *Atlanta Journal*, Sept. 3, 1938; *Dallas Dispatch-Journal*, Oct. 1, 1938; *Jackson (MI) Citizen Patriot*, Sept. 6, 1938; *Massillon Independent*, Sept. 6, 1938; *Hollywood Citizen-News*, Sept. 1, 1938; and "Theatres Join in Movie Quiz with $250,000 Prizes," *WDC*, Sept. 1, 1938, 8. All editorials are from "Excerpts from Editorials," n.d., unpaginated, WLK, box 102, folder 17. Unless a page number is given, further references to editorials are also from "Excerpts." Editorials are identified by title if one was provided.

28. Editorials, *Illinois State Journal*, Oct. 1, 1938; "Appeal of the Movies," *Indianapolis Star*, n.d.; *New Rochelle (NY) Standard-Star*, Sept. 2, 1938; *Telegraph-Journal*, Sept. 10, 1938; *Boston Evening Transcript*, Sept. 1, 1938.

29. Editorials, *New Rochelle Standard-Star; Stockton Record*, Sept. 23, 1938; and *Lawton Constitution*, Sept. 1, 1938. On the early promotion of theaters as a community service see George Potamianos, "Building Movie Audiences in Placerville, California, 1908–1915," in Fuller-Seeley, *Hollywood in the Neighborhood*, 75–90.

30. Editorials, *Jackson Citizen Patriot*, Sept. 6, 1938; *Galveston Tribune*, Oct. 11, 1938; *Charleston (WV) Gazette*, Sept. 19, 1938; "Motion Pictures Lead the Way," *Davenport (WA) Times*, Oct. 15, 1938; *Massillon Independent*; and "Films Benefit Business," *Homestead Messenger*, Sept. 2, 1938.

31. Editorials, "Films Benefit Business"; *Greensburg (PA) Review*, Sept. 6, 1938.

32. Bahn, "The Industry . . . and a Good Press"; editorials, *New Rochelle Standard-Star; Buffalo Courier-Express*, Sept. 16, 1938; "A Continuing Campaign," *Bowling Green Times Journal*, Sept. 2, 1938; *Oakland Post Enquirer*, Sept. 8, 1938; "The Editor Says," *New York Journal and American*, Sept. 9, 1938; *Clovis (NM) News-Journal*, Sept. 2, 1938; and *Cincinnati Enquirer*, Sept. 19, 1938.

33. Editorials, *New Rochelle Standard-Star; Kansas City (MO) Journal*, Oct. 13, 1938; *Burlington Free Press and Times*, Oct. 10, 1938; "The Boss of Motion Pictures," *Wilkes-Barre (PA) Record*, Sept. 27, 1938; "Picture Industry Shows Sense," *Cairo Citizen and Bulletin*, Sept. 17, 1938; and *Boston Traveler*, Sept. 13, 1938.

34. Editorials, *Sioux Falls Daily Argus-Leader*, Sept. 2, 1938; "The Boss of Motion Pictures"; "The Motion Picture Industry," *Cadillac Evening News*, Sept. 29, 1938; *Indianapolis News*, n.d.; and Schaefer, cited in "Million Dollar Pep Drive On," *HR*, July 28, 1938, 10.

35. Editorials, "The Entertainment Year," *Austin (MN) Daily Herald*, Sept. 10, 1938, 2; "A Grown-Up Industry," *Frederick Daily News*, Oct. 8, 1938, 4; "Movie Revival," *Kansas City Star*, Sept. 3, 1938, D; and "Movies Growing Up," *Burlington Free Press and Times*, Oct. 10, 1938, 4. See also "Attending the Movies," *Sioux Falls Daily Argus-Leader*, Sept. 2, 1938, 6. On the

importance of the film industry to the economy see also the editorials "The First Movie," *Reno Gazette,* Oct. 21, 1938, 4; and *Humboldt (CA) Standard,* Sept. 8, 1938, 2. On the importance of newspapers to the delivery of advertising messages see the editorials "Million for Advertising," *RDC,* Sept. 2, 1938, 16; "Movies Select Newspapers," *Alton (IL) Evening Telegraph,* Sept. 14, 1938, 4; and *Humboldt Standard.* In the sample there were a few other favorable editorials on motion pictures that did not mention MPGY specifically; see, for example, the editorial on *Alexander's Ragtime Band* in the *Oregon Statesman* (Sept. 4, 1938, 4), which praised the high standards of the new movie season.

36. Editorial, "Clew to Recovery," *Hays Daily News,* Oct. 14, 1938, 2.

37. Editorials, *Charleston (WV) Gazette;* "Hollywood Teaches and Builds America," *New York Daily Mirror,* Sept. 8, 1938; and *Cleveland News,* n.d.

4. "THE FINEST ARRAY OF PRODUCTIONS"

1. In producing more pictures of moderate cost, Warners reverted to a production strategy that had served it well during the mid-1930s. See John Sedgwick and Michael Pokorny, "The Risk Environment of Film Making: Warner Bros. in the Inter-War Years," *Explorations in Economic History* 35 (April 1998): 196–220. Data on production costs, foreign and domestic revenues, and profits are available for MGM in the Eddie Mannix ledger (MHL) and for RKO in the C. J. Trevlin ledger (now unavailable). Data concerning production costs and revenues at Warner Bros. is from the William Schaefer ledger (WBA). John Sedgwick provided me with a tidy spreadsheet of the data and estimated the profits of some Warners films, which are not included in its ledgers, based on the relationship between profits, costs, and rentals found in the MGM and RKO ledgers. See the appendix to Pokorny and Sedgwick, "Profitability Trends in Hollywood, 1929 to 1999," for the equations on which these calculations are based.

2. I could not find information about the specific terms of Monogram's participation.

3. See "Patrons Dictate Plots for 94 New Release Pictures," *Reno Evening Gazette,* August 27, 1938, 11.

4. Ibid. See also Barnes, "On the Screen," *NYHT,* July 21, 1938, *The Amazing Dr. Clitterhouse* PCAF; Nugent, "The Screen," *NYT,* July 21, 1938, *Clitterhouse* reviews, WBA. Bob Lord, the associate producer of *The Amazing Dr. Clitterhouse,* preferred to cast Charles Boyer (in "The Amazing Dr. Reynard"), Ronald Colman, or Melvyn Douglas, thinking that Robinson's "physical type and past history in pictures" did not suggest the necessary "*contrast* between a handsome, suave, aristocratic physician and the low, cheap thieves with whom he becomes associated" (Lord to Hal Wallis, memo, Nov. 2, 1937, *Clitterhouse* Story Folder, WBA).

5. "Growth of Series Is Seen as Solution to 'B' Problem," *HR,* Nov. 5, 1938, 4; "Series Prod'n on Downgrade," *HR,* Dec. 28, 1938, 1.

6. "Films Return to Subtler Style," *DFP,* August 29, 1938, 11.

7. Katherine Albert, "Charm? No! No! You Must Have Glamour," *Photoplay,* Sept. 1931, 38; Mary Biddle, "Beauty Advice," *Modern Screen,* Sept.

1932, 83; and Kirtley Baskette, "Is It Garbo or Hepburn?" *Photoplay*, March 1934, 29. On Hollywood glamour in the 1930s see Stephen Gundle, *Glamour: A History* (Oxford: Oxford University Press, 2008), 172–98; Annette Tapert, *The Power of Glamour: The Women Who Defined the Magic of Stardom* (New York: Crown, 1980); and Sarah Berry, *Screen Style: Fashion and Femininity in 1930s Hollywood* (Minneapolis: University of Minnesota Press, 2000).

8. Biddle, "Beauty Advice," 83; Albert, "Charm?" 101; Jessie Henderson, "Glamour Is the Bunk!" *Screen Book*, Sept. 1938, 43; and Myrna Loy, "This Glamour Business," *SRW*, ca. 1930s, Myrna Loy clipping file, MHL. The Loy article mentions the forthcoming film, *To Mary, with Love*, which came out in mid-1936.

9. Howard Barnes, "Lost Allure!" *Photoplay*, Oct. 1938, 24; Elizabeth Wilson, "Are the Stars Really Doomed?" *Screenland*, Sept. 1938, 26. See also Kirtley Baskette, "Where Is Hollywood's Glamour?" *Photoplay*, June 1935, 42–43, 106–8; and "Glamour under Fire," *Business Week*, May 14, 1938, 18, 20. On the democratization of glamour in the 1930s see Berry, *Screen Style*, xii–xiv. For Gundle, glamour in or out of Hollywood has intrinsically democratic associations as the product of modern and bourgeois society, rooted in consumerism's promises for self-transformation.

10. Balio, *Grand Design*, 144; Paul McDonald, *The Star System: Hollywood's Production of Popular Identities* (London: Wallflower, 2000), 11.

11. Tapert, *The Power of Glamour*, 12. See R. J. Obringer to Arthur Preston, Oct. 16, 1937, Kay Francis Legal File, folder 1, WBA. During the 1936–37 season, Francis's pictures ranked sixth, eighth, and tenth in terms of cost, with a range of $513,000 to $552,000 per picture; the following year they ranked twenty-second, twenty-eighth, and thirty-first, with a range of $197,000 to $485,000. One Warners employee described "a campaign of harassment and humiliation" against her (Stuart Jerome, *The Crazy, Wonderful Years When We Ran Warner Bros.* [Secaucus, NJ: Lyle Stuart, 1983], 38).

12. "Ed Sullivan in Hollywood," *DFP*, May 7, 1938, 9; "Hays Will Try to Calm Irate Film Exhibitors," *Chicago Tribune*, May 6, 1938 (ProQuest); MGM studio publicist, cited in Jane Ellen Wayne, *Crawford's Men* (New York: Prentice Hall, 1988), 11; and Wilson, "Are the Stars Really Doomed?" 78. *Life* magazine called Crawford the "Shopgirl's Dream" in an article that named her the "First Queen of the Movies" (cited in Wayne, *Crawford's Men*, 12). See also Harrison, "Film Moguls Not Displeased by Exhibitors' Harsh Blast," *New Brunswick Daily Home News*, May 15, 1938, 9; and Gladys Hall, "What Stars Are Slipping—and Why?" *Screenland*, May 1938, 18–19, 87–89.

13. Hall, "What Stars Are Slipping," 18; Landon Laird, "New Films, New Stars in the Making in the Same Old Hollywood," *Kansas City Star*, Sept. 11, 1938, 2C. On Crawford's star persona see Charlotte Cornelia Herzog and Jane Marie Gaines, "'Puffed Sleeves before Tea-Time': Joan Crawford, Adrian and Women Audiences," in *Stardom: Industry of Desire*, ed. Christine Gledhill (London: Routledge, 1991), 74–91.

14. Waterbury, "Close Ups and Long Shots," *Photoplay*, August 1938, 4; Hall, "What Stars Are Slipping," 87. See also "Crawford at Work with New Contract," *XEG*, May 7, 1938, 1; and "The Biggest Money Making Stars of

1937," *MPH*, Dec. 18, 1938, 13, 16. In fact, only *The Bride Wore Red* failed to make money among Crawford's previous five films before the controversy. Even *The Gorgeous Hussy* (1937) turned a profit. This fact does not undermine the exhibitors' claims; it simply suggests her films were not doing as well at many subsequent-run theaters. Alexander Walker sees in MGM's new contract for Crawford evidence only that revenues were declining overall, not that her "reputation" was "slipping" (*Joan Crawford: The Ultimate Star* [London: Weidenfeld and Nicolson, 1983], 118). This was not true for long. Of her following five films only one, *Strange Cargo* (1940), earned money.

15. Richard Schickel, *Common Fame: The Culture of Celebrity* (London: Pavilion, 1985), 73; Richard Dyer, *Stars*, 2nd ed. (1979; repr. London: BFI, 1999), 35; and Dora Albert, "The Truth about Box-Office 'Poison,'" *Movie Mirror*, August 1938, 76. See also Alexander Walker, *Stardom: The Hollywood Phenomenon* (London: Michael Joseph, 1970), 195–208; and Edgar Morin, *The Stars: An Account of the Star-System in Motion Pictures*, trans. Richard Howard (New York: Grove, 1960), 16–20. On stars as homebodies see, for example, Martha James, "Hollywood Housewives," *SRW*, Sept. 25, 1938, 10; and Fred MacMurray, "Hollywood Is Just a Place to Work," *DFP*, Sept. 30, 1938, 10.

16. Wilson, "Are the Stars Really Doomed?" 79; Joseph Epstein, *Fred Astaire* (New Haven, CT: Yale University Press, 2008), 58. In story conferences for the film that became *My Lucky Star*, Zanuck was adamant that Henie's "wholesomeness and cleanliness" be protected ("They Met in College" Conference with Mr. Zanuck, April 14, 1938, Twentieth Century–Fox Collection, USC).

17. "Myrna Loy Had Sex but Movies Guessed It Wrong," *Life*, Oct. 11, 1937, Loy clipping file, MHL; Dixie Wilson, "The Revealing True Story of Myrna Loy," *Photoplay*, July 1938, 80; Cyril Vandour, "Why Men Like Myrna Loy," *Motion Picture*, Feb. 1938, 37; and "Mother Myrna!" *Milwaukee Journal*, Sept. 10, 1938, Loy clipping file. Maria DiBattista notes Loy's "transforming influence" on Gable, which makes him "gentler than he generally feels he can afford to be" in *Test Pilot* and *Too Hot to Handle* (*Fast-Talking Dames* [New Haven, CT: Yale University Press, 2001], 144, 145).

18. Quotes are from variations of the "Natural Girl" articles that appeared under different titles, often under the byline of Marian Young: "'Natural Girl' Takes Spotlight as Glamour Type Does Fadeout," *YV*, Sept. 2, 1938, 17; "Healthy, Robust Color of the 'Natural Girl' Outmodes Exotic Pallor of Her Glamour Sister," *YV*, Sept. 3, 1938, 9; "'Natural Girl' and Her Clothes Are Always Unaffected; She's Never an Overdressed, Glamorous Clothes-Horse," *YV*, Sept. 5, 1938, 11; "'Natural Girl' Succeeds Old-Fashioned Glamor Girl," *San Antonio Express*, Sept. 7, 1938, 7; "'Natural Girl' Is Queen Now!" *Pittsburgh Press*, Sept. 12, 1938, 18; "Natural Girls Prefer to Win Admiration," *Pittsburgh Press*, Sept. 15, 1938, 16; "Natural Girl Is New Vogue," *Idaho Falls Post-Register*, Sept. 16, 1938, 6; and "Natural Girl," *New Brunswick Daily Home News*, Sept. 25, 1938, 9. See also Biddle, "Beauty Advice," 83.

19. Baskette, "Where Is Hollywood's Glamour?" 42; Gundle, *Glamour*, 189.

20. Young, "Natural Girl Is New Vogue"; "Glamour-Lack Wins Girl Big Role!" *Men with Wings* pressbook, 37, Paramount Pictures Press Sheets, MHL;

Alicia Hart, "Active Sport Interest One of Best Cosmetics," *Fremont (NE) Daily Tribune*, April 26, 1938, 5; Arleen Whelan photograph with caption, *Fremont Daily Tribune*, Sept. 9, 1938, 7; and "Just Act Natural, Lady," *Arkansas Gazette Sunday Magazine*, Oct. 2, 1938, 10. On the pursuit of new talent in the wake of the "box-office poison" ad see Coons, "Screen Life in Hollywood," *Raleigh (WV) Register*, June 22, 1938, 4; "Trend away from Star System in Hollywood," *Humboldt (CA) Standard*, June 23, 1938, 11; and "New Stars Get Break Because of Economy Trend," *Oregon Statesman*, May, 12, 1938, 6.

21. Sara Hamilton, "Hedy Wine," *Photoplay*, Oct. 1938, 23.

22. "Million Outlay to Boost the Gross $20,000,000 Is Drive Goal," *MPH*, July 30, 1938, 30.

23. "Patrons Dictate Plots for 94 New Release Pictures," 11; Frederick Othman, "Film Joneses Famed but Not Individually," *Miami Herald*, Dec. 6, 1938, 2-B.

24. Horn and Morgan, Inc., Star Theater, Hay Springs, NE, *MPH*, July 17, 1938, 83; Gladys E. McArdle, Owl Theater, Lebanon, KS, *MPH*, August 14, 1938, 108.

25. Sidney Kaufman, "Motion Picture Material," *Theatre Arts*, Nov. 1938, 816; "Movies Growing Up," *Burlington (VT) Free Press and Times*, Oct. 10, 1938, 4; Edward Carberry, "Comedy a Triumph of Homely Realism," *Cincinnati Post*, August 13, 1938, *Love Finds Andy Hardy* Production Files, MGMC; ad, *Love Finds Andy Hardy*, Loew's Midland Theatre, *Kansas City Star*, July 21, 1938, 13; "Judge Hardy's Family Back in New Happenings," Exhibitor's Service Sheet, *Love Finds Andy Hardy*, n.d., 1, MGMC; and review, *Love Finds Andy Hardy*, *HR*, July 11, 1938, 3.

26. See Robert B. Ray, *The Avant-Garde Finds Andy Hardy* (Cambridge, MA: Harvard University Press, 1995), 146–48, for a splendid riff on Betsy and Garland in *Love Finds Andy Hardy*. Betsy's song invokes her difficulties with "grammar" and "glamour," both of which have rules that she cannot discover. Ray suggests that Garland herself remains perpetually suspended between "two words/worlds," and this space "in between" is crucial to understanding the star: "This ambiguity, this alternation, forms the basis of Garland's attraction, her unexpected power to *cast a spell*" (148). This is another way of saying that Garland's peculiar kind of glamour lay in her inability fully to inhabit it.

27. "Industry Takes Cue from Public," *HR*, Sept. 3, 1938, 4; ad, "The World Is Ours," Sparks Theater, *Reno Evening Gazette*, Nov. 24, 1938, 2. On the Hardy cast see "Stage Set for Start of Industry's Million-Dollar Box Office Drive," *MPH*, August 27, 1938, 15–16.

28. See "Wall Street Approves of Family Cycle of Films Because of Budgets," *Variety*, Sept. 28, 1938, 2.

29. Ad, *Young Dr. Kildare*, Ritz Theatre, *Tulsa Daily World*, Dec. 17, 1938, 13; ad, *Young Dr. Kildare*, Loew's Theatre, *Wilmington (DE) News*, Dec. 22, 1938, 25.

30. Wilkerson, "Tradeviews," *HR*, August 25, 1938, 1; Waterbury, "Close Ups and Long Shots," *Photoplay*, July 1938, 10; "Main Street Rediscovered," editorial, *YV*, Sept. 17, 1938, 4; and "Public Relations—First in the Order of Business," *Business Week*, Jan. 23, 1937, 32.

31. Wilkerson, "Tradeviews," *HR*, August 25, 1938; "Tales of Hoffman," *HR*, April 16, 1938, 3; and Charles Mulcahy, "Trends in Entertainment Forecast a Renaissance of American Family Drama," *YV*, July 10, 1938, C-9.

32. See Rick Altman, *Film/Genre* (London: BFI, 1999), chap. 4.

33. Sheilah Graham, "She's a Frank Starlet," *Kansas City Star*, Sept. 8, 1938, 9.

34. Clarke Wales, review of *Youth Takes a Fling*, *SRW*, Oct. 2, 1938, 5; review of *Youth Takes a Fling*, *MPD*, Oct. 3, 1938, PCAF; Kaspar Monahan, "The Show Shops," *Pittsburgh Press*, Oct. 17, 1938, 12; and ad, *Youth Takes a Fling*, New Opera House, *New Brunswick Daily Home News*, Dec. 15, 1938, 12 (ellipses in original). On Leeds's marriage plans see Graham, "She's a Frank Starlet."

35. Michael Wood, *America in the Movies* (1975; repr. New York: Columbia University Press, 1989), 8.

36. James Harvey, *Romantic Comedy in Hollywood, from Lubitsch to Sturges* (1987; repr. New York: Da Capo, 1998), 108.

37. On the egalitarian and democratic tendency of these films see DiBattista, *Fast-Talking Dames;* and Thomas Schatz, *Hollywood Genres* (New York: Random House, 1981), 150–65. David Shumway takes issue with the argument that screwball comedy is "fundamentally about the overcoming of class differences," finding this narrative the exception rather than the rule (*Modern Love: Romance, Intimacy, and the Marriage Crisis* [New York: New York University Press, 2003], 96).

38. Martin Rubin, *Showstoppers: Busby Berkeley and the Tradition of Spectacle* (New York: Columbia University Press, 1993), 36; William R. Weaver, review of *Carefree*, *MPH*, Sept. 3, 1938, PCAF. Rick Altman notes that "more than in any other genre, the musical calls on actors to play themselves," an element that helps it to facilitate "a merging of the real and the ideal" (*The American Film Musical* [Bloomington: Indiana University Press, 1987], 80). With Astaire's turn as a psychoanalyst the convergence of actor and role is less available in *Carefree* than in the previous Astaire-Rogers films. *Carefree* has been called the "twilight movie" of the series (Arlene Croce, *The Fred Astaire and Ginger Rogers Book* [New York: E.P. Dutton, 1972], 140). They costarred in only two more films over the next ten years.

39. Analysis of dancing and film technique in *Carefree* is in Croce, *The Fred Astaire and Ginger Rogers Book*, 146–50; and John Mueller, *Astaire Dancing: The Musical Films* (New York: Knopf, 1985), 139–47.

40. See the preview notes for *Carefree*, August 3, 1938, Mark Sandrich Papers, folder 12, MHL. Astaire's *Damsel in Distress* (1937) lost $65,000. Rogers's films *Stage Door* (1937) and *Vivacious Lady* (1938) earned a combined $156,000, but *Having Wonderful Time* (1938) lost $267,000.

41. On Roach and his "goal of being a respected feature producer" see Richard Lewis Ward, *A History of the Hal Roach Studios* (Carbondale: Southern Illinois University Press, 2005), 97.

42. Unfortunately, there is no information on gross earnings or profits for *There Goes My Heart*. Ward writes that the film was a disappointment at the box office and cites a letter from Tom Walker, Roach's New York representative,

to the effect that UA was having difficulty selling *all* of its films of the 1938–39 season and mentioned three other MPGY titles. See Ward, *A History of the Hal Roach Studios*, 105. An undated pamphlet promotes the business *There Goes My Heart* did at three theaters in small cities and towns. See "Is Your Theatre Like . . . ?" pamphlet, n.d., United Artists Corporate Records, Paul Lazarus Sr., Sales Correspondence, box 2, folder 2, Wisconsin Center for Film and Theater Research, Wisconsin Historical Society. An accompanying note explains it as "an effort to help keep the independent and small theatres interested" in the film, which suggests that it was having trouble outside first-run markets (Lynn Farnol to Harry Gold, note, n.d.).

43. Review of *Three Loves Has Nancy*, *Film Daily*, Sept. 6, 1938, PCAF. See Albert, "Charm?"

44. B.R. Crisler, review of *The Cowboy and the Lady*, NYT, Nov. 25, 1938, PCAF.

45. Review of *The Cowboy and the Lady*, HR, Nov. 8, 1938, PCAF.

46. *Sing You Sinners* pressbook, inside cover, Paramount Pictures Press Sheets, MHL; review of *Sing You Sinners*, MPD, August 9, 1938, PCAF; and J.P., "On the Screen," NYHT, August 18, 1938, *Sing You Sinners* PCAF.

47. Geoffrey T. Hellman, "Thinker in Hollywood" (1940); repr. in *Frank Capra: The Man and His Films*, ed. Richard Glatzer and John Raeburn (Ann Arbor: University of Michigan Press, 1975), 9; Frank Capra, *The Name above the Title: An Autobiography* (New York: Macmillan, 1971), 247; Robert Sklar, "The Imagination of Stability: The Depression Films of Frank Capra," in Glatzer and Raeburn, *Frank Capra*, 122; Leonard Quart, "Frank Capra and the Popular Front," in *American Media and Mass Culture, Left Perspectives*, ed. Donald Lazere (Berkeley: University of California Press, 1987), 178; and Richard Maltby, "*It Happened One Night*: The Recreation of the Patriarch," in *Frank Capra: Authorship and the Studio System*, ed. Sklar and Vito Zagarrio (Philadelphia: Temple University Press, 1998), 156.

48. Ardis Smith, "*You Can't Take It with You* Is Now Movie with Message," *Buffalo News*, Sept. 30, 1938, Scrapbook, FCC. All reviews are from Capra's Scrapbook unless otherwise noted.

49. Groverman Blake, "This Show Business," *Cincinnati Times-Star*, n.d.; Harvey, *Romantic Comedy in Hollywood*, 141.

50. Capra, *The Name above the Title*, 186.

51. See letters to Capra, *Can't Take It* Correspondence folders, FCC. In *Slow Fade to Black: The Negro in American Film, 1900–1942* (Oxford: Oxford University Press, 1977), Thomas Cripps briefly refers to the "bland maid" as a "thoughtless racist bit" (305). The group shots were discussed by William Paul in "No Escaping the Depression: Reality, Fantasy and the Aesthetics of Escapism in Frank Capra's *You Can't Take It with You*," Society for Cinema and Media Studies Conference, Los Angeles, March 2010.

52. Capra, *The Name above the Title*, front matter.

53. Eddie Cohen, "Screen in Review," *Miami News*, n.d.; Marsh, "Readers Discuss Hann's Play," CPD, Oct. 13, 1938; Nugent, "The Screen," NYT, Sept. 2, 1938; Arthur Pollock, "'Can't Take It with You' Filmed," *Christian Science Monitor*, Sept. 6, 1938; Smith, "*You Can't Take It with You* Is Now Movie

with Message"; Capra, *The Name above the Title*, 185; H.T.K., "Voice from the Pit," *New Orleans Item*, Oct. 7, 1938; "We Meet a Noisy Family," *Hollywood Spectator*, *Can't Take It* Publicity folder, FCC; Harry Mines, excerpt, *LA Daily News*, "Preview Quotes on 'You Can't Take It with You,'" August 24, 1938, *Can't Take It* Publicity folder, FCC; and John Condon to Capra, Sept. 23, 1938, *Can't Take It* Correspondence folder, FCC.

54. Untitled review, *The Fight*, Oct. 1938; Marsh, "Readers Discuss Hann's Play."

55. James Dugan, "Movies," *New Masses*, Sept. 13, 1938; Howard Rushmore, "Prize-Winning Play on Screen at Music Hall," *New York Daily Worker*, Sept. 3, 1938; and Dugan, "Movies."

56. "Fame's Paradox: The Story of Frank Capra," *Can't Take It* Souvenir Brochure, n.d., unpaginated, *Can't Take It* Publicity folder; Capra to the Screen Editor, *NYT*, April 2, 1939 (ProQuest); "Coons Picks 'You Can't Take It with You' as Best Moving Picture Offering of Month," *Haverville (MA) Gazette*, August 31, 1938; and Joseph McBride, *Frank Capra: The Catastrophe of Success* (New York: Simon & Schuster, 1992), 380. McBride observes that Capra never had the kind of autonomy he claimed at Columbia, that Harry Cohn still had final authority over his films. Thomas Schatz makes a compelling case that Capra's phenomenal success at Columbia, and difficulties later as an independent producer-director, suggests that he was, in fact, "a consummate studio auteur," whose talents were best suited to its production process ("Anatomy of a House Director: Capra, Cohn, and Columbia in the 1930s," in Sklar and Zagarrio, *Frank Capra*, 34). Total gross receipts and profits for *You Can't Take It with You* are not known, but it cost $1,644,000 and earned $2,138,000 just in the United States and Canada. See "Grosses on Capra Pictures," n.d., *Can't Take It* Film Projects folder; and Production Cost Report, No. 16, n.d., *Can't Take It* Production Budget folder, FCC.

57. Hal Wallis to Henry Blanke, memo, May 6, 1938, *Four Daughters* Story—Memos and Correspondence files, folder 3, WBA.

58. On Garfield's career and his place at Warners see Robert Sklar, *City Boys: Cagney, Bogart, Garfield* (Princeton, NJ: Princeton University Press, 1992).

59. "'Four Daughters' Acclaimed by Paramount Theater Fans," *Salt Lake Tribune*, Oct. 23, 1938, E11; "Well Balanced Film Program for Theaters Next Week," *Reno Evening Gazette*, Nov. 19, 1938, 7; Lou Mishkin, review of *Four Daughters*, *New York Morning Telegraph*, August 20, 1938, *Four Daughters* clipping folder, WBA; and PCA review of *Four Daughters*, July 6, 1938, PCAF. All further reviews for *Four Daughters* without a page number are from the *Four Daughters* clipping folder, WBA.

60. Mishkin, review; Corbin Patrick, review of *Four Daughters*, *Indianapolis Star*, Sept. 24, 1938; Nelson B. Bell, "About the Showshops," *WP*, Oct. 24, 1938, 14; John Rosenfield Jr., review of *Four Daughters*, *Dallas Morning News*, Sept. 18, 1938; and Mishkin, review. Abraham Polonsky offered a concise and powerful assessment of Garfield's career: "The Group trained him, the movies made him, the Blacklist killed him" (introduction to *The Films of John Garfield*, by Howard Gelman [Secaucus, NJ: Citadel Press, 1975], 8). Gelman

discusses the influence on Garfield of the Group Theatre and the Method (14–15, 17, 19, 185–87).

61. Calvin McPherson, review of *Four Daughters*, *St. Louis Post-Dispatch*, Sept. 25, 1938; Gelman, *The Films of John Garfield*, 50.

62. "Fans Acclaim '4 Daughters' at Paramount," *Salt Lake Tribune*, Oct. 19, 1938, 17; Chester B. Bahn, review of *Four Daughters*, *Film Daily*, August 11, 1938; Herbert L. Monk, review of *Four Daughters*, *St. Louis Daily Globe and Democrat*, Sept. 24, 1938; Merle Potter, review of *Four Daughters*, *Minneapolis Journal*, Oct. 16, 1938; Coons, "AP Feature Service," New York, August 19, 1938; Gladys McCardle, review of *Four Daughters*, *MPD*, August 10, 1938; Bell, "About the Showshops," *WP*, Sept. 24, 1938, 10; Jack Grant, "Picture Reports," n.d.; Monk, review; Patrick, review; and Gilbert Kanour, review of *Four Daughters*, *Baltimore Evening Sun*, Sept. 9, 1938.

63. Ad, "I Have Seen *Four Daughters*," *WP*, Sept. 23, 1938, 4.

64. Doris Arden, review of *Four Daughters*, *Chicago Times*, Oct. 7, 1938.

65. Untitled advertising campaign pamphlet, *Four Daughters*, n.d., 1A, 6A, 9A, 3A, WBA. See "Warners Classify 'Daughters' Ads," *MPH*, Sept. 10, 1938, 103.

66. Untitled advertising campaign pamphlet, 10A (all ellipses in original).

67. Ad, *Four Daughters*, Paramount Theatre, *Biloxi Daily Herald*, Oct. 29, 1938, 5; ad, *Four Daughters*, Elco Theater, *Elkhart (IN) Truth*, Nov. 12, 1938, 3.

68. Untitled advertising campaign pamphlet, 4A; McCardle, review of *Four Daughters*.

69. George L. David, "Strong, Human Drama Unfolded in 'Boys Town' at Loew's," *RDC*, Sept. 17, 1938, 12; ad, *Boys Town*, Loew's Theatre, *RDC*, Sept. 16, 1938, 18; Parsons, "Father Flanagan Wins Hollywood through 'Boys Town,'" *WDC*, Sept. 11, 1938, 16; and Harrison Carroll, review of *Boys Town*, *Los Angeles Herald and Express*, Sept. 15, 1938, B-6. The trailer for the film begins with the words "Boys Town is real" and later claims that it "holds a mirror to life."

70. Henry James Forman, *Our Movie Made Children* (New York: Macmillan, 1933), 34, 141, 232, 213. Forman's summary appeared first in articles in *McCall's*. It was "an antimovie polemic" found to lack "scientific objectivity," but it became the public face of the Payne Fund Studies (Garth S. Jowett, Ian C. Jarvie, and Kathryn H. Fuller, *Children and the Movies: Media Influence and the Payne Fund Controversy* [Cambridge: Cambridge University Press, 1996], 6, 107). Forman's intervention furnished one reason for their lack of influence, as the researchers distanced themselves from his interpretation of their findings.

71. The enthusiasm of religious and women's groups is evident from the encapsulated commentary on *Boys Town* in the *Motion Picture Review Digest*, which included reviews from their publications.

72. James Fisher, *Spencer Tracy: A Bio-bibliography* (Westport, CT: Greenwood Press, 1994), 16.

73. Wales, "Mickey Rooney: All Actor," *SRW*, Sept. 25, 1938, 12; Harold Heffernan, "Rooney Grin Is Burlesque-Bred," *Chicago Daily News*, Sept. 17, 1938, 20.

74. Earl J. Morris, "American Whites, Negroes Being Shoved into Background in Movies by Jewish Film Owners," *Pittsburgh Courier*, August 27, 1938, 20. On the assimilationist tendency of blackface in the movies see Michael Rogin, *Blackface, White Noise: Jewish Immigrants in the Hollywood Melting Pot* (Berkeley: University of California Press, 1998).

75. P.T. Hartung, review of *Boys Town*, *Commonweal*, Sept. 23, 1938, 561; Jesse Zunser, review of *Boys Town*, *Cue*, Sept. 17, 1938, 10.

76. Reviews of *Boys Town*: *Variety*, Sept. 7, 1938, 12; John Mosher, *New Yorker*, Sept. 10, 1938, 79; General Federation of Women's Clubs, West Coast, cited in *Motion Picture Review Digest*, Dec. 26, 1938, 9; *Motion Picture Review*, Oct. 1938, 3; Barnes, "On the Screen," *NYHT*, Sept. 9, 1938, 16; Carroll, *Los Angeles Herald and Express*; and Parsons, "Father Flanagan Wins Hollywood through 'Boys Town.'"

77. Review of *Boys Town*, *Time*, Sept. 12, 1938 (online archive); review of *Boys Town*, *Boxoffice*, Sept. 10, 1938, 21; "'Boys Town' Is Praised by Hollywood Paper," *Boulder Daily Camera*, Oct. 8, 1938, 8. See also "Boys Town a Publicity Flop," *DFP*, Oct. 26, 1938, 17.

78. Balio, *Grand Design*, 198; Mark A. Vieira, *Irving Thalberg: Boy Wonder to Producer Prince* (Berkeley: University of California Press, 2009), 384; and letter from Michael Boscia to the editor, *MPH*, Dec. 17, 1938, 56.

79. Wales, "Where Are the Stars?" *SRW*, Oct. 23, 1938, 6; Hubbard Keavy, "Shearer Is Given 'Scarlett' Film Role," *Sioux Falls Daily Argus-Leader*, June 24, 1938, 1; Parsons, "Public Picks Clark Gable," *YV*, June 24, 1938, 24; Parsons, "Shearer, as 'Wind' Star, Would Reform Scarlett in Last of Book," *WDC*, July 8, 1938, 14; and "In Hollywood with Hedda Hopper," *WP*, August 6, 1938, 8.

80. George F. Custen, *Bio/Pics: How Hollywood Constructed Public History* (New Brunswick, NJ: Rutgers University Press, 1992), 13.

81. Stefan Zweig, *Marie Antoinette: The Portrait of an Average Woman*, trans. Eden and Cedar Paul (New York: Viking, 1933), xiii, xi–xii, xiv.

82. Ad, *Marie Antoinette*, Capitol Theater, *Arkansas Gazette*, Sept. 5, 1938, 2; conference notes, R.E. [Robert] Sherwood, Dialogue Continuity, *Marie Antoinette*, Feb. 9, 1934, 123b, 57, 8, Turner/MGM Script Collection, MHL. The document contains notes from Thalberg, Sidney Franklin (who was originally slated to direct), and Albert Levin.

83. Jane Gaines argues that the point of Christina's heterosexual romance is to "*make . . . her want things*" and so "deliver the viewer to consumption in the interests of higher American ideals" ("The Queen Christina Tie-Ups: Convergence of Show Window and Screen," *Quarterly Review of Film and Video* 11, no. 1 [1989]: 50, 52).

84. George Richelavi to Hunt Stromberg, memo, Jan. 21, 1938, HSC, folder 3; [name illegible] to Nicholas Schenck, May 4, 1938, HSC, folder 3. See conference notes, Sherwood, "Dialogue Continuity," 104.

85. Sam B. Girgus, "1938: Movies and Whistling in the Dark," in Hark, *American Cinema of the 1930s*, 213.

86. Alan Byre, a representative of Metrofilms Paris, wrote to Stromberg, cautioning the producer not to represent the French people as too "brutal and

blood-thirsty." He noted Alain Renoir's treatment of the public in *La Marseillaise* (1938), which "all Paris is flocking to see. . . . He shows the masses as most orderly and considerate" (Feb. 15, 1938, HSC, folder 3).

87. Vieira, *Irving Thalberg*, 392–93; "Antoinette Was Would-Be Movie Queen of Her Day," *Marie Antoinette* Campaign Book, n.d., 12, MGMC.

88. Mrs. Walter Ferguson, "Moral from a Movie," *Pittsburgh Press*, August 25, 1938, 10; "A Queen Comes Back," *Photoplay*, July 1938, 22; review of *Marie Antoinette, MPD*, July 11, 1938, PCAF; Garret D. Byrnes, review of *Marie Antoinette, Providence Journal*, Sept. 2, 1938, 13; Barnes, "On the Screen," *NYHT*, August 17, 1938, PCAF; "Opening Today at Salt Lake Theaters," *Salt Lake Tribune*, Sept. 1, 1938, 20; and "The Theater," *Ashland (KY) Independent*, Sept. 25, 1938, 2. See also Wales, "A $2,500,000 Dream Comes True," *SRW*, July 17, 1938, 6–7.

89. Ad, *Marie Antoinette*, Capitol Theater, *Arkansas Gazette*, Sept. 4, 1938, III 4; ad, *Marie Antoinette*, Loew's Theatre, *Wilmington (DE) News*, Oct. 7, 1938, 39; "*Marie Antoinette* Is a Great Picture!" *Marie Antoinette* Exploitation Book, n.d., unpaginated, MGMC; ad, *Marie Antoinette*, Loew's Theatre, *Wilmington (DE) News;* and Norma Shearer, "'Antoinette' Gets New Date, Starts on Warner Screen Friday," *YV*, Sept. 6, 1938, 7.

90. See Frank Whitbeck to Stromberg, "Comparative Figures," memo, July 29, 1938, HSC, folder 4; *Marie Antoinette* Campaign Book, 3; and ad, *Marie Antoinette*, Loew's Theatre, *Wilmington (DE) News*.

91. Stromberg to unknown, telegram, Sept. 1, 1938, HSC, folder 4; Flin., review of *Marie Antoinette*, unidentified source, July 13, 1938, PCAF; Vivian Sobchack, "'Surge and Splendor': A Phenomenology of the Hollywood Historical Epic," *Representations* 29 (Winter 1990): 31; ad, *Marie Antoinette, WP*, Sept. 7, 1938, 8; and "In Hollywood with Hedda Hopper," *WP*, August 29, 1938, 12. See also "Lobby Comments on Marie Antoinette," July 22, 1938, HSC, folder 4.

92. Dorothy Day, "Norma Shearer Brings Court Intrigue to Life," *Chicago Herald and Examiner*, August 28, 1938, IV 5; Will Baltin, "The Rialto Reporter," *New Brunswick Daily Home News*, May 8, 1938, 4.

93. Review of *The Great Waltz*, *Variety*, Nov. 2, 1938, PCAF. See Ralph G. Giordano, *Social Dancing in America: A History and Reference*, vol. 1 (Westport, CT: Greenwood Press, 2007), 101–2.

94. George F. Custen, "I Hear Music and . . . Darryl and Irving Write History with *Alexander's Ragtime Band*," in *Authorship and Film*, ed. David A. Gerstner and Janet Staiger (New York: Routledge, 2003), 86.

95. Ad, "Why Make Fine Pictures?" *Arizona Star*, Nov. 16, 1938, 11; ad, *The Great Waltz*, Orpheum Theater, *Wisconsin State Journal*, Nov. 11, 1938, 3; Leon C. Bolduc, Majestic Theatre, Conway, NH, *MPH*, Nov. 5, 1938, 42–43; and "Loew's, Inc." (1939); repr. in *The American Film Industry*, ed. Tino Balio (Madison: University of Wisconsin Press, 1976), 335. On MGM's efforts to rebuild its reputation for quality in the early 1940s see Jerome Christensen, "Studio Identity and Studio Art: MGM, *Mrs. Miniver*, and Planning the Postwar Era," *ELH* 67, no. 1 (2000): 257–92.

96. On the studios' circumvention of the MPPDA's ban on gangster films see Jonathan Munby, *Public Enemies, Public Heroes: Screening the Gangster from "Little Caesar" to "Touch of Evil"* (Chicago: University of Chicago Press, 1999), 110–14. On Dewey's appeals for public cooperation see Richard Norton Smith, *Thomas E. Dewey and His Times* (New York: Simon & Schuster, 1982), 159–60.

97. Review of *Crime Takes a Holiday*, *HR*, April 29, 1938, PCAF; ad, *Racket Busters*, State Theater, *Chattanooga Daily Times*, Sept. 24, 1938, 11 (ellipses in original); ad, *Racket Busters*, Palace Theatre, *Stamford (CT) Advocate*, August 17, 1938, 5; "Racket Film Called Lesson for Everyone," *Milwaukee Sentinel*, August 6, 1938, *Racket Busters* clipping folder, WBA; ad, *I Am the Law*, *Elkhart (IN) Truth*, Oct. 27, 1938, 8; and James S. Pooler, "Movie Studios Owe a Huge Debt of Gratitude to District Attorney Dewey," *DFP*, Sept. 15, 1938, 8.

98. "Racket in Film Labor Charged at Los Angeles," *Lewiston (ID) Morning Tribune*, Sept. 8, 1938, 1, 3. See Memo re: "Giant Killer," March 10, 1938, *I Am the Law* PCAF; and Finley McDermid, "Comparison of *Racket Busters* final script and Synopsis of 'It's Your Fault,'" May 13, 1940, *Racket Busters* Story File, WBA. The Bioff story was printed in several of the newspapers sampled for this book. The quote about the "company union rackets" is from Jeff Kibre, head of the reformist wing of the International Alliance of Theatrical Stage Employees and Motion Picture Machine Operators (IATSE). Bioff was associated with the Frank Nitti crime syndicate of Chicago. He and Schenck went to jail along with George Browne, the actual president of IATSE, on charges relating to the payoff. On the history of labor racketeering in Hollywood in the 1930s see Mike Nielsen and Gene Mailes, *Hollywood's Other Blacklist: Union Struggles in the Studio System* (London: BFI, 1995), 15–70. Eugene Rosow notes the parallels between the gangster genre and what he calls "the movie racket" in *Born to Lose: The Gangster Film in America* (New York: Oxford University Press, 1978), chap. 8.

Warners' *Marked Woman* (1937), the precursor of the MPGY racket films, is the one film in the cycle to have attracted some critical attention. It was inspired by Dewey's prosecution of Charles "Lucky" Luciano and starred Bette Davis as a "hostess" (PCA for prostitute) and Humphrey Bogart as the ambitious prosecutor. It was notable for its sympathetic treatment of the women and an outstanding ending, which challenges the power of the law to help those who made its enforcement possible and who most need its protection, in sharp contrast with the celebratory tone of the MPGY films.

99. "'I Am the Law' Rings Bell," *HR*, August 18, 1938, PCAF.

100. Joseph I. Breen to Harry Cohn, April 5, 1938, *I Am the Law* PCAF; Breen to Cohn, April 18, 1938, *I Am the Law* PCAF. In March of 1938 Hays directed that the PCA distinguish between the "administrative" function of the PCA (Code enforcement) and its "advisory" function on matters pertaining to industry welfare, and that they be handled in separate letters to studios (Vasey, *The World according to Hollywood*, 222). Potential problems were to be pointed out, according to Vasey, but specific changes not requested. The change

in policy reflected the concern that overly broad applications of the Code would fuel government antitrust activity. Breen's lack of enthusiasm for the change, which Vasey notes, is evident in the pressure he exerted on Cohn.

101. "'Boy Meets Girl' Daft and Droll, Smartly Ironic," *New York Daily Tribune*, Jan. 20, 1938, *Boy Meets Girl* Story File—Memos and Correspondence, WBA. On the purchase price see Budget, *Boy Meets Girl*, Feb. 2, 1938, WBA.

102. Menjou wanted $50,000. Warners cast Bellamy at $11,250. See Maxwell Arnow to Wallis, memo, Jan. 24, 1938, *Boy Meets Girl* Story File—Memos and Correspondence, and Budget.

103. Wallis to [Lloyd] Bacon, memo, March 13, 1938, *Boy Meets Girl* Story File—Memos and Correspondence. "Hollywood's goal was a certain type of stylistic practice, *not* the display of the hand of a worker" (Bordwell, Staiger, and Thompson, *The Classical Hollywood Cinema*, 110). See also Mary Ann Doane, "Ideology and the Practice of Sound Editing and Mixing," in *Film Sound: Theory and Practice*, ed. Elisabeth Weis and John Belton (New York: Columbia University Press, 1985), 54–62.

104. James T. Farrell, "The Language of Hollywood," in *The League of Frightened Philistines and Other Papers* (New York: Vanguard, 1945), 175; Rosten, *Hollywood*, 308.

105. "Interesting FACTS about 'Boy Meets Girl,'" *Boy Meets Girl* pressbook, n.d., 4, WBA; "Fans Do Right by Marie Wilson," *Boy Meets Girl* pressbook, 3.

106. Review of *Boy Meets Girl*, *Hollywood Motion Picture Review*, July 28, 1938, *Boy Meets Girl* clipping folder, WBA; Joe Blair, "Small Towns Registering Kicks on 'Boy Meets Girl' Film," *Hollywood Motion Picture Review*, Oct. 1, 1938, *Boy Meets Girl* clipping folder; and Harrison, "In Hollywood," Nov. 27, 1938, *Boy Meets Girl* clipping folder.

107. Morris Friedberg to Warner Bros. Studio, telegram, *Boy Meets Girl* Picture File, WBA.

108. Kenneth McCaleb, "'Boy Meets Girl'—and Hollywood Enjoys a Laugh at Itself," *New York Sunday Mirror Magazine*, August 24, 1938, 19, *Boy Meets Girl* clipping folder; review of *The Affairs of Annabel*, HR, July 8, 1938, PCAF. Mae D. Huettig noted the self-aggrandizing and inconsistent claims of importance and determined that the film industry ranked only forty-fifth among all American industries. See *Economic Control of the Motion Picture Industry: A Study in Industrial Organization* (Philadelphia: University of Pennsylvania Press, 1944), 56–57.

109. Review of *The Affairs of Annabel*, MPH, July 16, 1938, PCAF; Bahn, "The Industry . . . and a Good Press"; review of *The Affairs of Annabel*, HR; review of *The Affairs of Annabel*, MPH; and Harrison, "In Hollywood," Nov. 27, 1938, *Boy Meets Girl* clipping folder.

110. Notes from Conference with Mr. Zanuck, *Little Miss Broadway*, Dec. 18, 1937, Twentieth Century–Fox Collection, USC. For exhibitor comments on Temple's diminishing appeal and the failure of *Little Miss Broadway* see "What the Motion Picture Did for Me," MPH, Oct., Nov., and Dec. 1938 issues. In

Twentieth Century's Fox: Darryl F. Zanuck and the Culture of Hollywood (New York: Basic Books, 1997), George F. Custen notes Zanuck's uncertainty over "what to do with an in-between star" (220) after *Rebecca of Sunnybrook Farm*. Temple left the studio in 1940.

111. See trade press reviews, *The Gladiator* PCAF.

112. Breen to Goldwyn, August 24, 1938, *Boy Meets Girl* PCAF; Breen to Leo Spitz, May 3, 1938, *The Affairs of Annabel* PCAF; Breen to J.R. McDonough, June 7, 1938, *Fugitives for a Night* PCAF; and Breen to L.B. Mayer, April 28, 1938, *Too Hot to Handle* PCAF.

113. Review of *Keep Smiling*, unidentified clipping, n.d., PCAF; review of *Keep Smiling, Variety*, August 17, 1938, PCAF; review of *Fugitives for a Night, Variety*, August 28, 1938, PCAF; and John Hamrick to Hays, Sept. 13, 1938, WHC, reel 21.

114. Final Script, *Safety in Numbers*, Sept. 9, 1938, 67, Twentieth Century–Fox Collection, USC.

115. Gorden M. Goodfellow to Breen, Sept. 26, 1938, *There Goes My Heart* PCAF; John W. Jarvis to Warner Bros., Nov. 22, 1938, *Brother Rat* Picture File, WBA.

116. Marion Tuttle Marzolf, *Civilizing Voices: American Press Criticism, 1880–1950* (New York: Longman, 1991), 139; James Stahlman (president of the American Newspaper Publishers Association), cited in "Newspapers' Ad Power Ranked 1st," *Pittsburgh Sun-Telegraph*, April 28, 1938, 2; and *Mutual Film Corp. v. Industrial Commission of Ohio* (1915). Marzolf notes that later research showed only around 60 percent of newspapers were hostile to Roosevelt. On the problems of the newspaper business in the Depression see Leonard Ray Teel, *The Public Press, 1900–1945: The History of American Journalism* (Westport, CT: Praeger, 2006); and Jackaway, *Media at War*. Newspaper articles and editorials during MPGY lamented a recent spate of newspaper closings, including the "historic" *News-Bee* of Toledo, a Scripps-Howard paper (Oswald Garrison Villard, "Newspapers of Nation Are Hit," *Lewiston (ID) Morning Tribune*, Sept. 11, 1938, 8). See also "Many Good Newspapers Have Given Up Ghost," editorial, *Boulder Daily Camera*, Oct. 7, 1938, 2; and "Another Newspaper Folds Up," editorial, *DFP*, August 29, 1938, 6.

117. "Movies Promise Knox to Depict Newsmen Fairly," *Chicago Daily News*, April 28, 1938, 7; "Future Films Will Show Real Newsmen," *Los Angeles Herald and Express*, April 28, 1938, A15. These unfavorable images, as Alex Barris notes, were often the invention of former newspapermen, who were among the most successful and prolific screenwriters. See *Stop the Presses! The Newspaperman in American Films* (Cranbury, NJ: A.S. Barnes, 1976).

118. "Future Films Will Show Real Newsmen"; editorial, *Daily Missoulian*, May 8, 1938, 8; and "No Prize Paintings," editorial, *Austin (MN) Daily Herald*, Dec. 5, 1938, 4. See also "Cautions Smaller Newspapers," *Burlington Free Press and Times*, April 27, 1938, 1, 13. On the MPPDA's response to theater advertising see "Hays Claims Studios Aware of Problems," *RDC*, April 25, 1938, 17. Two weeks later the paper published a follow-up article announcing that Loew's would not allow advertising films in its theaters. See "Loew's

Theaters Bar Screen Advertising," *RDC*, May 4, 1938, 10. Bell urged the public, as well as the press, to complain. See "Advertising, It Is Unanimous, Has No Place upon the Screen," *WP*, April 29, 1938, 16.

119. The audience poll is described in Francis Heacock, publicity draft, n.d.; and "So Long Ago Seems 1904–8 as Seen in 'The Sisters,'" *Sunday Mirror Magazine* (city unidentified), Oct. 16, 1938, *The Sisters* clipping folder, WBA.

120. Review of *Four's a Crowd*, *MPH*, August 16, 1938, PCAF; Harold W. Cohen, "The New Films," *Pittsburgh Post-Gazette*, Sept. 3, 1938, 9; and *Four's a Crowd* pressbook, n.d., 3, WBA.

121. "City Room the McCoy in New Comedy," *Four's a Crowd* pressbook, 16.

122. Crisler, review of *Time Out for Murder*, *NYT*, Oct. 7, 1938, WHC, reel 21, 479. See statement by William Allen White, *The Arkansas Traveler* pressbook, 3, Paramount Pictures Press Sheets, MHL.

123. M.F.L., review of *Four's a Crowd*, *Wall Street Journal*, August 12, 1938, *Four's a Crowd* clipping folder, WBA; Sidney B. Whipple, review of *Four's a Crowd*, *New York World Telegram*, n.d., *Four's a Crowd* clipping folder.

124. "Press' Pet Peeves," *Variety*, Oct. 19, 1938, WHC, reel 21, 489–90.

125. "Uncle Sam after Movies Producers," *Tulsa Daily World*, July 21, 1938, 2.

CONCLUSION

1. "Movies' Drive Gets Pleasing Results," *RDC*, Sept. 15, 1938, 14; "Advertising Aids Movies' Drive," *Los Angeles Examiner*, Sept. 26, 1938, 24; and "Dietz Figures 30% Business Increase Due to Film Drive," *MPD*, Sept. 27, 1938, 1, 4. On reports of the campaign's success see also "Receipts Up 10 Per Cent as New Season Starts," *MPH*, Sept. 17, 1938, 12–14; "Estimates of Business Gain in Campaign Rise to 30 Per Cent," *MPH*, Oct. 1, 1938, 25–26; "Paramount's Theatres Find Drive Helping," *MPD*, Sept. 16, 1938, 1, 3; "Recovery in Picture Grosses Held 'Gratifying,'" *Variety*, Sept. 28, 1938, 5; and "Movie Drive Booms Trade at Theaters," *Pittsburgh Press*, Oct. 10, 1938, 8. On the response of exhibitors see "More Pledges in for Greatest Year Drive," *MPD*, Oct. 18, 1938, 5; and David Palfreyman to Will Hays, memo, Nov. 10, 1938, 1, MPPDAA.

2. Marsh, "One Moment, Please!" *CPD*, Oct. 9, 1938, 13-B; Fidler, "Norma Shearer Sells Her M-G-M Stock; Wants to Stand on Own Merits," *Salt Lake Tribune*, Sept. 10, 1938, 21; and Nugent, "Notes on a Bright September," *NYT*, Oct. 2, 1938 (ProQuest).

3. On the inability to measure the effects of MPGY on box offices see Palfreyman to Hays, memo, Nov. 25, 1938, 1, MPPDAA.

4. See Pokorny and Sedgwick, "Profitability Trends in Hollywood, 1929 to 1999," 61–62.

5. Maurice Rubens to All Managers, memo, Great States Division, Balaban and Katz, Oct. 12, 1938, HFC, folder 6; Fidler, "Studios Fighting to Whittle Star Salaries Down to Saner Level," *Salt Lake Tribune*, Dec. 2, 1938, 10; Gabe

Yorke, "Should a Jubilee Year Be Celebrated?" n.d., MPPDAA, 1; and Palfreyman to Hays, memo, Nov. 10, 1938, 1. See also "Films' 50th Anniversary Next Yr.," *Variety,* Oct. 19, 1938, 5, 19; "No Life in National Boxoffice," *HR,* Nov. 23, 1938, 1, 7; "Admission Levies Drop $612,346 in Four-Month Period," *MPD,* Nov. 25, 1938, 10; "46 Weeks B.O. Off 22% Average," *HR,* Nov. 30, 1938, 1, 7; and Roy Chartier, "The Grosses," *Variety,* Jan. 4, 1939, 29, 52.

6. Heffernan, "Movie Quiz Brings Grief to Showmen," *Chattanooga Daily Times,* Sept. 25, 1938, 25.

7. Franklin to All Regional Chairmen, Circuit Heads, Exhibitors, Managers and Publicity Directors, memo, Oct. 29, 1938, 3, MPPDAA; "Films' 50th Anniversary Next Yr.," 5.

8. "Quiz Winners Announced Creates Mild Enthusiasm," *MPD,* Feb. 28, 1938, 1; "$50,000 Film Prize Is Won by Woman," *NYT,* Feb. 28, 1939 (ProQuest); and Arthur Spaeth, "Deliberately Wooing Ill-Will," *Cleveland News,* Feb. 8, 1939, WHC, reel 22, 99. Tucson prizewinners are listed in "$10 Prizes," n.d., WLK, box 102, folder 16. Plans for the campaign in Tucson are discussed in "Tucson Campaign 'Motion Pictures' Greatest Year,'" n.d., HFC, folder 6.

9. "A Windfall and a Challenge," *Washington Daily News,* Feb. 28, 1939, n.d., from scrapbook, La Falce Collection, Motion Picture Reading Room, Library of Congress, box G-054; R. Ogle to MPGY, May 25, 1939, WLK, box 102, folder 31.

10. Will Hays, "Enlarging Scope of the Screen," March 27, 1939, WHC, reel 22; Schaefer, cited in Al Steen, "The 1938 Industry Drive," in *The 1938 Film Daily Year Book of Motion Pictures,* ed. Jack Alicoate (New York: Film Daily, 1939), 73; and Hays, "Cooperation," in *The 1938 Film Daily Year Book,* 35.

11. Yorke, "Should a Jubilee Year Be Celebrated?" 1; William Boehnel, "Picture Quality," *New York World Telegram,* Jan. 7, 1939, WHC, reel 22, 14; and Martin Quigley, "What the Industry Faces in 1939," *MPH,* Dec. 17, 1938, 8. Quigley's article also appeared in *MPD,* Dec. 16, 1938, 3. On trade press criticism see "46 Weeks B.O. Off 22% Average"; "Sinking Movie Quiz Attacked as Unfair by Canadian Indies," *HR,* Dec. 19, 1938, 3; and "The Film Drive—Remember?" *Variety,* Dec. 28, 1938, 3.

12. Harrison, "Hollywood Highlights," *Rome (GA) News-Tribune,* Dec. 27, 1938, 4; Sam Shain, "Insiders' Outlook," *MPD,* Jan. 4, 1939, 2; and Barnes, "A Sorry Period," *NYHT,* Jan. 1, 1939, WHC, reel 22, 18.

13. "Walter Winchell," *Miami Herald,* Dec. 30, 1938, 3-B.

14. Barnes, "Reality on the Screen," *NYHT,* Jan. 15, 1939, WHC, reel 22, 35; Marsh, "High Time Hollywood Blows America's Horn," *CPD,* Jan. 8, 1939, WHC, reel 22, 38; and Marsh, "Loves Hollywood, But . . ." *CPD,* Jan. 22, 1939, WHC, reel 22, 70.

15. Boehnel, "Picture Quality"; "Advertising Campaign," editorial, *Bloomington (IL) Argus,* Jan. 10, 1939, WHC, reel 22, 80.

16. "No Progress toward Solution," editorial, *Lincoln (NE) State Journal,* March 2, 1939, WHC, reel 22, 121; Ben Ray Redman, "Thou Shalt Not Offend," *Saturday Review of Literature,* Dec. 31, 1938, WHC, reel 22, 38 (first two ellipses in original).

17. Barnes, "Films for Democracy," *NYHT*, Dec. 4, 1938, WHC, reel 21, 556; "Films for Democracy," editorial, *Atlanta Journal*, Nov. 26, 1938, WHC, reel 21, 547; and Nichols, cited in Barnes, "Reality on the Screen."

18. Archibald MacLeish, "Propaganda vs. Hollywood," *Stage*, Jan. 1939, WHC, reel 21, 16 (ellipses in original).

19. Quigley, "What the Industry Faces in 1939," 9; Jacobs, *The Rise of the American Film*, 432.

20. Clara Beranger, "For a New Deal," *New York Liberty*, Jan. 21, 1939, WHC, reel 21, 39; Wanger, cited in Matthew Bernstein, *Walter Wanger: Hollywood Independent* (Berkeley: University of California Press, 1994), 129, 140; and Thorp, *America at the Movies*, 301.

21. "Open Letter to Producers," *Madison Capital Times*, March 4, 1939, WHC, reel 22, 121.

22. Quigley, "Again—The Propagandists," *MPD*, Nov. 16, 1938, 1; Maurice Kann, "Mr. Hays Reads a Signpost," *Boxoffice*, Jan. 23, 1939, WHC, reel 22, 69.

23. Gilbert Kanour, "The Trade Press Speaks," *Baltimore Evening Sun*, Jan. 4, 1939, WHC, reel 22, 14; "Super Colossal," editorial, *Chicago Daily Times*, Sept. 14, 1938, 35; and Kaspar Monahan, "The Show Shops," *Pittsburgh Press*, Nov. 27, 1938, Society sec., 8. On the urgency of radio news at this time see Susan J. Douglas, *Listening In: Radio and the American Imagination, from Amos 'n' Andy and Edward R. Murrow to Wolfman Jack and Howard Stern* (New York: Times Books, 1999), 161–66. It was his coverage of the Munich crisis for CBS that turned H. V. Kaltenborn into a radio "star," who played himself in *Mr. Smith Goes to Washington* (1939).

24. J.P. McEvoy, "The Back of Me Hand to You," *Saturday Evening Post*, Dec. 24, 1938, 48; Barnes, "The Ostrich of the Arts," *NYHT*, Oct. 23, 1938, WHC, reel 21, 485. Marsh also uses the "ostrich" metaphor in "High Time Hollywood Blows America's Horn."

25. Maltby, "The Production Code and the Hays Office," in Balio, *Grand Design*, 68–70; Thorp, *America at the Movies*, 297; and Thomas Elsaesser, "Film History as Social History: The Dieterle/Warner Brothers Bio-pic," *Wide Angle* 8, no. 2 (1986): 28.

26. Hays, "Enlarging Scope of the Screen," 1, 2, 1; "Causes Worth Fighting For," editorial, *NYT*, March 29, 1939, WHC, reel 22, 160; and Dietz, cited in "Americanism, and Not Competition, Bars Films from Foreign Screen," *Variety*, Sept. 6, 1939, 8.

27. Virginia Wright, "Meaty Stuff," *Los Angeles Evening News*, Jan. 16, 1939, WHC, reel 22, 70; Nugent, "Hollywood Waves the Flag," *Nation*, April 8, 1939, 398, 399, 400, 398.

28. Leo Braudy, "Entertainment or Propaganda?" in *Warners' War: Politics, Pop Culture & Propaganda in Wartime Hollywood*," ed. Martin Kaplan and Johanna Blakley (Los Angeles: USC Annenberg Norman Lear Center, 2004), 27. On anti-Nazi films and the PCA see Steven J. Ross, "*Confessions of a Nazi Spy*: Warner Bros., Anti-fascism and the Politicization of Hollywood," in Kaplan and Blakley, *Warners' War*, 49–59.

29. Review of *Sons of the Legion*, *Variety*, Oct. 5, 1938, PCAF.

30. See contest essay by Elizabeth Benincasa, n.d., WLK, box 102, folder 9. Correspondence between Barton, his staff, and Franklin indicates that judges were sent one thousand essays. Barton did not read even these himself. See correspondence, Bruce Barton Papers, Motion Pictures' Greatest Year (Contest) folder, Wisconsin Historical Society.

31. Quiz booklet, 1938, unpaginated. See contest essays by Frances Hotalen, Henry Roemer, Conrad James (ellipses in original), E.R. Morrison, and Betty Finch, n.d., WLK, box 102, folder 9.

32. See contest essays by Mary Hilton, Rae Charhan Phillips, and Helen Kyle Bernard, n.d., WLK, box 102, folder 9.

33. See contest essays by Raymond K. Visconti, Birdie Jackson, J. Howell Talley, Helen Beane Faxon, and Will Wayne, n.d., WLK, box 102, folder 9.

34. See contest essays by Laura Carpenter, Vera Horgan, Dan C. Haley, and Lucinda von Kamecke, n.d., WLK, box 102, folder 9.

35. "Industry Analyzing 'Quiz' Replies to Conserve Their Future Value," *MPH*, Nov. 5, 1938, 17; "Report to George J. Schaefer from the Advertising Committee," n.d., MPPDAA, 8, 9; and "Where Are Lost Film Fans?" *Variety*, April 15, 1942, 5. On Gallup's efforts to secure the contract see The One Hundred Men and Women of Audience Research Institute to David O. Selznick, telegram, May 10, 1942; and Gallup to Selznick, telegram, May 12, 1942, David O. Selznick Collection, box 3562, Harry Ransom Humanities Research Center, University of Texas, Austin. On the plans for a public relations program see "Where Are Lost Film Fans?"; and "Public Relations Committee and UMPI Both Favor Market Analysis Idea," *Variety*, May 13, 1942, 12.

36. John L. Scott, "Studios Plan Dignified 50th Year Celebration," *Los Angeles Times*, July 23, 1939, C2; "Fiftieth Anniversary Manual," n.d., unpaginated, MPPDAA. On revenues, attendance, and ticket prices see Lary May and Stephen Lassonde, "Making the American Way: Moderne Theatres, Audiences, and the Film Industry, 1929–1945," *Prospects* 12 (1987): 110. Because company information was notoriously unreliable, the authors determined gross receipts using government analysis of consumption expenditures based on taxes collected. They divided film receipts by the average ticket price (according to *MPH*) to determine weekly attendance. The average ticket price rose 4.2 cents, to 28.9 cents, in 1937 and another 1.6 cents in 1938. One wonders what role the increases, after four years of steady prices, played in the box-office and attendance decline that the industry was so eager to blame on everything else.

Index

TEXT:
10/13 Sabon

DISPLAY:
Sabon (Open Type)

COMPOSITOR:
BookComp, Inc.

PRINTER AND BINDER:
IBT Global